German
Review Grammar

J. ALAN PFEFFER
University of Buffalo

D. C. Heath and Company, Boston

MAP BY PALACIOS

Library of Congress Catalog Card Number 61–12682

Preface

The *German Review Grammar* is intended for students who have completed a first course in German emphasizing either the audio-lingual or a more conventional approach to the study of the language. Hence, its twenty-four graded chapters include, on the one hand, a concise presentation of the rules governing living German speech in direct relation to the principles of present-day English syntax. On the other, they present a series of up-to-date verbal segments of the adult German scene, together with a wide range of oral and written exercises wrought from their linguistic fabric.

Specifically, each chapter consists of three parts. Of these, the first or introductory section analyzes and illustrates one or more aspects of the complex of grammatical usage. The second section animates these principles by means of a number of integrated, mnemonic devices. These include: (a) reading selections, titled **Basic Patterns,** which highlight the elements of the lesson; (b) a set of **Questions** based on the readings, as a guide to oral discussion; (c) a group of **Idiomatic Expressions** from the Basic Patterns, singled out for emphasis and drill; (d) a sequence of diverse **Exercises,** which underscore and review the points treated in the chapter and in the units preceding it; and (e) a **Composition** in unadulterated English, designed for reproduction into idiomatic German. The third or supplementary part of the chapter offers various additional materials which emphasize the spoken language and range from the prose rendition of a familiar poem to the unjumbling of anecdotes, the matching of proverbs, and the dramatization of topics from everyday life.

Indices of paradigms and other grammatical details augment the various chapters, which are made fully accessible by complete German-English and English-German vocabularies.

Through its successive stages the *German Review Grammar* benefited considerably from the learning and encouragement of a number of friends and colleagues, including Professors Albert Scholz, of Syracuse University; Ralph Brundrett, Jr., of Western Reserve University; Henry Hollenstine, now director of the T. V. Workshop of the Zürich Opera; Carl Weitlanner, of D'Youville College; George Kreye, of the University of Kansas; and Miss Gertrude Gunther, of Hempstead High School, L.I. Thanks are due also to Mrs. Ilse A. Loeser, of D. C. Heath and Company, for the meticulous care with which she saw the manuscript through the press, and especially to Dr. Vincenzo Cioffari, Modern Language Editor, for the vision and discernment he displayed at every turn. To Bertha M. Pfeffer, wife, critic, and companion, the author owes more than a dedication can convey.

Kind permission was granted to reproduce the following selections: Bertold Brecht, "Wenn die Haifische Menschen wären" from *Kalendergeschichten*, Gebrüder Weiss Verlag, Berlin-Schöneberg, 1959; Hans M. Loew, "Ungenutzte Chance" from *Stimmen der Zeit*, Buch-Kunst-Zeitungsdruckerei Albrecht Dürer, Wien, 1953; Heinrich Spoerl, "Zeit ohne Zeit" from *Der lachende Lesering*, Verlag Bertelsmann, G.m.b.H., Gütersloh, 1959. Some of the remaining "Lesestücke" are adaptations from the public domain.

J. Alan Pfeffer

Munich, Germany
January 20, 1961

Contents

List of Photographs

Grateful acknowledgment is made to the following sources for their kind permission to reproduce the photographs in the *German Review Grammar.*

Cover photo Alsfeld in Hessen by Dr. Harald Busch (Leitz Werke)

German Review Grammar

NORDSEE

OSTSEE

Kiel

Lübeck

Stettin

Hamburg

Bremen

ELBE

ODER

Hannover

WESER

Berlin

Potsdam
Magdeburg

Essen Dortmund

HARZ

Leipzig

Düsseldorf

Kassel

Weimar

Dresden

Köln

Jena

Chemnitz

Aachen

RHEIN

THÜRINGER WALD

Bonn

TAUNUS

Frankfurt

Koblenz

ERZGEBIRGE

MOSEL

MAIN

Trier

Mainz

Bayreuth

Worms

Heidelberg

Nürnberg

BÖHMER WALD

FICHTELGEBIRGE

SAAR

NECKAR

DONAU

ISAR

Stuttgart

Augsburg

INN

SCHWARZWALD

SCHWÄBISCHE ALB

Ulm

München

Freiburg

ALPEN

GERMANY
(East and West)

Maßstab

0   50   100 KM.

CHAPTER ONE

The Principles of Case

1.1 Articles, adjectives, nouns, and pronouns are inflected or declined and have four forms each in the singular and the plural. These forms are referred to as cases. They are the nominative, genitive, dative, and accusative and are used to show relationship to other words in the sentence.

1.2 As in English, the nominative case in German is

(a) the case of the subject:	Mein Freund ist hier.
	My friend is here.
(b) the case of the predicate noun or pronoun after **sein, werden, bleiben, heißen:**	Er ist mein Freund.
	He is my friend.
	Er blieb mein Freund.
	He remained my friend.
(c) the case of the appositive to a noun or a pronoun in the nominative case:	Herr Braun, der Schneider, ist hier.
	Mr. Braun, the tailor, is here.
(d) the case of a noun of address: [1]	Gehen Sie schon, Herr Braun?
	Mr. Braun, are you leaving already?

---

[1] Note that the (appositive) antecedent need not be in the nominative case.

Ich sehe Sie, Herr Braun.	I see you, Mr. Braun.
Ich gehe mit Ihnen, Herr Braun.	I am going with you, Mr. Braun.

1.3   As in English, the <u>genitive</u> or possessive case in German is the case denoting ownership or relationship.

Meines Freundes Buch ist hier.	My friend's book is here.
Das Buch meines Freundes ist hier.	The book of my friend is here.
Er ist der Sohn des Lehrers.	He is the son of the teacher.

The literal equivalent of *The book of my friend is here,* **Das Buch von meinem Freund ist hier,** is colloquial, bordering on substandard usage, although some constructions with **von** are widely accepted, as

> Die Hauptstadt von Frankreich ist Paris.
> The capital of France is Paris.
>
> Er ist ein Freund von mir.
> He is a friend of mine.

1.4   The objective case in English is the case of (1) the direct or (2) the indirect object. The direct object is the noun or pronoun acted upon by the verb. The indirect object is the noun or pronoun which is the indirect recipient of the action of the verb or the recipient of the direct object.

1.5   The direct object in German is in the <u>accusative</u> case. In English it is the objective case which is <u>not governed</u> by the preposition *to*, present or implied.

Er schreibt einen Brief.	He writes a letter.
Er sieht ihn.	He sees him.

1.6   The indirect object in German is in the <u>dative</u> case. In English it is the objective case which is <u>governed</u> by the preposition *to*, present or implied.

Sie gab ihm das Buch.	She gave him the book (*or* She gave the book to him).

Distinctly German are constructions as **Ich nahm ihm das Buch** (**weg**), *I took the book from him.*

1.7   In German the genitive, dative, and accusative cases are also required with prepositions and adverbial constructions as well as with special verbs and expressions (Chapters VI, VII, VIII).

4

BASIC PATTERNS

Der Name Braun klingt deutsch, aber Herr Braun
ist ein echter Amerikaner. Er ist Amerikaner deutscher
Herkunft und ist in einer Vorstadt von New York zu
Hause. Von Beruf ist Herr Braun Lehrer. Als solcher
hat er viele Freunde. Die meisten von ihnen wohnen 5
in New York oder in der Umgebung. Doch sein bester
Freund lebt in Deutschland.

Dieser heißt Müller, Anton Müller. Er ist Studienrat
und wohnt auf dem Lande, in der Nähe von Bonn. Ihn
besucht Herr Braun daher im Sommer bei jeder Gelegen- 10
heit gern, denn er liebt die Ruhe, die frische Luft und
überhaupt die Natur.

Herr Braun plaudert auch gern mit Herrn Müller.
Herr Müller spricht dann viel von Berlin, denn es ist
seine Vaterstadt und die alte Heimat der Familie Braun. 15
Der Urgroßvater des Herrn Braun war dort nämlich
lange Jahre als Sekretär auf dem Finanzamt tätig. Die
Freunde plaudern dann oft bis spät in die Nacht hinein.

Herr Braun bleibt immer einen Monat bei seinem
Freunde. An sonnigen Wochenenden wandert er mit 20
Herrn Müller durch Feld und Wald und genießt die herr-
liche Landschaft. . Manchmal radeln die Freunde auch
in das benachbarte Städtchen.

Nach vier Wochen packt Herr Braun wieder seine
Koffer. Er dankt dem Freund für die Gastfreundschaft 25
und lädt ihn zu sich nach Amerika ein. Am Bahnhof gibt
Herr Müller dem Freund nochmals die Hand und sagt:
,,Gute Reise. Auf Wiedersehen.'' Herr Braun steigt
schnell in ein Abteil zweiter Klasse ein und fährt mit dem
Schnellzug nach Hamburg. In Hamburg besteigt Herr 30
Braun das Schiff und reist wieder nach Amerika zurück.

Questions

1. Was ist Herr Braun von Beruf? 2. Wo wohnt er? 3. Wie
heißt sein Freund in Deutschland? 4. Wer wohnt bei Bonn? 5. Wen
besucht Herr Braun auf dem Lande? 6. Wie oft besucht er ihn? 7. Was

liebt er dort? 8. Wovon spricht Herr Müller gern? 9. Wie lange bleibt
Herr Braun in Deutschland? 10. Wer fährt Herrn Braun zum Bahnhof?
11. Wohin reist Herr Braun mit dem Zuge? 12. Wo besteigt Herr Braun
das Schiff?

Idiomatic Expressions

heißen	to be called
von Beruf	by profession (or trade)
in der Nähe von (dat.)	in the vicinity of
auf dem Lande	in the country(side)
aufs Land	to the country(side)
sprechen von (dat.)	to talk about
lange Jahre	for many years
einen Monat	for a month
bis spät in die Nacht hinein	far into the night
die Hand geben (or reichen)	to shake hands
nach Hause	home(ward)
mit dem Zuge	by train
auf Wiedersehen	good-by, au revoir

EXERCISES

A. Use each of the above expressions in a German sentence.

B. (1) In the following exercise supply the missing forms
of the articles (der, die, das or ein, eine, ein) and possessives (mein,
dein, sein, etc.). (2) Wherever possible, replace the article with
a form of kein.

1. Herr Braun ist ein echter Amerikaner. 2. D-er
Amerikaner wohnt in eine Vorstadt. 3. Er hat nur eine
Freund in Deutschland. 4. S-ein Freund in Deutschland wohnt
auf d-em Lande. 5. Er wohnt in d-er Nähe von Bonn. 6. Herr
Braun liebt d-ie Ruhe. 7. Er besucht seinen Freund gern.
8. Herr Braun gibt d-em Freund d-ie Hand. 9. Herr Müller
fährt d-en Freund zum Bahnhof. 10. Mit d-em Zug fährt
d-er Amerikaner nach Hamburg. 11. In Hamburg besteigt er
ein Schiff. 12. D-as Schiff fährt nach Amerika.

C. Complete the following sentences in German.

1. Der Freund des Herrn Müller heißt . . . . 2. Herr Müller
ist Deutscher, aber sein Freund ist . . . . 3. Herr Braun wohnt

nicht auf dem Lande, sondern .... 4. Herr Müller bleibt im Sommer .... 5. Herr Braun plaudert gern mit .... 6. Der Urgroßvater des Herrn Braun war als Sekretär .... 7. Die Freunde wandern .... 8. Sie radeln gelegentlich ins .... 9. Nach vier Wochen packt .... 10. Er lädt den Freund zu .... 11. Herr Braun reicht .... 12. Von Hamburg fährt ....

D. (1) Use each of the words in the left-hand column or its derivative in the right-hand column in a German sentence. (2) Rewrite these sentences to illustrate the use of the four cases in German. EXAMPLE: Der Lehrer lehrt Deutsch. Der Lehrer lehrt den Schüler. Der Lehrer des Schülers ist Deutscher. Der Lehrer dankt dem Schüler. Er gibt dem Lehrer ein Buch.

der Lehrer	lehren
das Jahr	das Jahrhundert
deutsch	der Deutsche
alt	das Alter
das Amt	amtlich
tätig	tun
radeln	der Radler
benachbart	der Nachbar
sprechen	die Sprache

Composition [2]

1. Mr. Braun and Mr. Müller are friends. 2. Mr. Braun is [an] American and lives in a suburb of New York, but his friend is [a] German and lives in the country near Bonn. 3. Both Mr. Braun and Mr. Müller are teachers. 4. Mr. Braun likes the quiet in the country and he likes to visit his friend in Germany. 5. He visits him almost every year. 6. Then he always stays a month in Europe. 7. On weekends the friends roam through the fields and the woods. 8. Sometimes they ride‿their‿bicycles to the neighboring town. 9. During the week they chat far into the night and enjoy the fresh air. 10. After four weeks Mr. Braun packs his bags again. 11. Mr. Müller drives him to the station. 12. Here the friends say good-by [to] one‿another. 13. Mr. Braun invites his German friend to visit him in New York and leaves by

[2] In the *Composition*, the words in parentheses ( ) are to be translated into German; those in square brackets [ ] are to be omitted in the German and those connected with ligatures ‿ are to be rendered as one in translation.

train for Hamburg. 14. From Hamburg he sails (on) the next day by boat for New York.

Variations

A. Write out in German the answers to the questions based on the first stanza of Goethe's poem, "Heidenröslein," reproduced below. **B.** With the aid of these answers rewrite the stanza in simple German prose.

> Sah ein Knab' ein Röslein stehn,
> Röslein auf der Heiden.
> War so jung und morgenschön,
> Lief er schnell, es nah' zu sehn,
> Sah's mit vielen Freuden.
> Röslein, Röslein, Röslein rot,
> Röslein auf der Heiden.

1. Wer sah ein Röslein? 2. Was sah der Knabe? 3. Was tat das Röslein? 4. Wo stand das Röslein? 5. Wie viele Röslein sah der Knabe? 6. Was war jung? 7. Wer lief schnell? 8. Warum lief der Knabe? 9. Wer hatte viel Freude? 10. Welches Röslein war rot?

Conversation — Kennenlernen

Schlosser:	Guten Morgen, Herr Müller!
Müller:	Wie geht's, Herr Schlosser? Darf ich (Ihnen) Herrn Braun aus Amerika vorstellen?
Schlosser:	(Reicht Herrn Braun die Hand.) Es freut mich sehr, Sie kennenzulernen.
Braun:	(Drückt Herrn Schlosser die Hand.) Sehr angenehm, Herr Schlosser!
Schlosser:	Sind Sie schon lange in Deutschland?
Braun:	Diesmal sind's fast vier Wochen.
Schlosser:	Sie sprechen aber ein ausgezeichnetes Deutsch!
Müller:	Ja, Herr Braun lehrt doch Deutsch in Amerika.
Schlosser:	Nun, den Amerikaner hört man ihm kaum an.
Braun:	(Das ist) Sehr freundlich von Ihnen.
Müller:	(Hat Eile. Empfiehlt sich.) Bitte, grüßen Sie zu Hause.
Schlosser:	Schönen Dank.
Alle:	Auf Wiedersehen.

CHAPTER TWO

The Principles of Tense

2.1 As in English, the verb in German has six basic tenses. The diagram and the notes which follow indicate the similarities and differences in their use.

I show I am showing I do show	Present [1]	**ich zeige**
I showed I was showing I did show	Past	**ich zeigte**
I have shown I have been showing	Perfect [2]	**ich habe gezeigt**
I had shown I had been showing	Past Perfect	**ich hatte gezeigt**
I shall show I shall be showing	Future	**ich werde zeigen**
I shall have shown	Future Perfect	**ich werde gezeigt haben**

(a) *THE PRESENT TENSE*

2.2 Beyond the parallels outlined above, the present tense may be used to express the future in German, usually with the addition of **schon** and some word or phrase expressing time.

> Er kommt allein.   He is coming by himself.
> Das erledige ich (schon) selbst.   I'll take care of that myself.
> Sie haben (schon) morgen eine Antwort.
> You will have an answer by tomorrow.

2.3 Accompanied by a time expression, such as **seit** or **schon seit,** the present tense in German is also used to indicate a past action which is still in progress.

> Er lehrt schon seit drei Jahren.
> He has been teaching for three years.

[1] Note that German does not have separate, equivalent forms for the (a) declarative, (b) progressive, and (c) emphatic forms in English. [2] Cf. **2.5.**

9

(b) *THE PAST TENSE*

2.4 In addition to denoting an act in the past, as in English, the past tense (or preterite or imperfect) in German is used with **schon** to denote a past perfect, as

> Er war schon lange hier, als ich ankam.
> He had been here for some time, when I arrived.

(c) *THE (PRESENT) PERFECT TENSE*

2.5 The present perfect in English is accurately used to describe continuing action begun in the past. In German, a continuing action begun in the past is expressed by the present tense. In conversation, the present perfect is frequently used in German instead of the past, especially in South Germany, Austria, and Switzerland.

> Er ist seit einer Woche da. He has been here for a week.
> Hat er es gesagt? Did he say it?

(d) *THE PAST PERFECT TENSE*

2.6 The past perfect tense is used in English and in German to describe an action completed before another action in the past.

> Sie schrieb mir, nachdem ich She wrote me, after I had writ-
>   ihr geschrieben hatte. ten to her.
> Hatte er es gesagt? Had he said it?

(e) *THE FUTURE TENSE*

2.7 The future tense in German generally corresponds to the future tense in English. However, the future tense in German is not used so commonly as in English. In German it is sometimes used to express present probability, usually with the addition of **wohl** or **schon.**

> Wann werden Sie ihn sehen? When will you see him?
> Das wird wohl wahr sein. That is probably true.

(f) *THE FUTURE PERFECT TENSE*

2.8 The future perfect tense in German generally corresponds to the future perfect tense in English. It is sometimes used to express past probability, usually with the addition of **wohl** or **schon.**

> Bis sechs wird er wieder fort- By six he will have gone again.
>   gegangen sein.
> Er wird es wohl getan haben. He has probably done it.

Das alte und das neue Deutschland.
Oben: Die alte Universitätsstadt Heidelberg
Unten: Der neue Berliner Flughafen

11

BASIC PATTERNS

Herr Braun war Montag abend abgereist. Am
Dienstag klingelte der Briefträger recht früh und gab
Frau Müller ein Brieftelegramm. — In Deutschland
besorgt nämlich die Post alle Telegramme. Gewöhnliche
5 Telegramme werden, sofort wenn sie eingegangen sind,
durch Sonderboten ausgetragen. Brieftelegramme nimmt
der Briefträger mit.

„Ein Telegramm! Aber von wem?" fragte Frau
Müller erstaunt und reichte es ihrem Mann. Dieser
10 öffnete es und las: „Auf der Durchreise nach Münster.
Ankomme 3.39. Erhard." „Erhard? Der Erhard Grün?
Oh wie schön," rief Frau Müller. Erhard Grün war ein
Geschäftsreisender, und Herr und Frau Müller hatten
ihn und seine Frau vor drei Jahren in Frankfurt kennen-
15 gelernt.

Herr und Frau Müller waren daher schon um halb
vier am Bahnhof. Doch der Zug hatte Verspätung, und
Erhard kam erst nach vier an. Herr und Frau Müller
begrüßten ihn herzlich. „Na, wie geht's Ihnen, Erhard,"
20 fragte Herr Müller. „Was machen Sie denn? Wie geht
es Ihrer Frau und Ihren Kindern?" „Danke, danke,"
sagte Erhard. „Meiner Familie geht es gut. Mein Sohn
studiert Medizin, und meine Tochter ist schon fast ein
Jahr verheiratet. Ich mache gerade eine Geschäftsreise
25 und komme von Marburg. Heute abend fahre ich nach
Düsseldorf. Wie geht es euch? Wann kommt ihr wieder
nach Frankfurt? Meine Frau wird sich freuen, wenn ich
ihr sage, ich war bei euch zu Besuch."

Da Erhard Grün seine Reise schon um halb acht
30 fortsetzen wollte, beschlossen die Müllers, mit ihrem
Gast im Städtchen zu Abend zu essen. Bei einem Glas
Bier erkundigte sich, Herr Müller nachher über die
Geschäftsverhältnisse in Frankfurt, und Frau Müller
wollte wissen, wo das junge Ehepaar wohne, wie es ihm
35 gehe, und womit sich der Schwiegersohn beschäftige.

12

Um sieben Uhr war Erhard wieder am Bahnhof. Diesmal war der Zug pünktlich und setzte sich genau um halb acht in der Richtung Münster in Bewegung.

Questions

1. Wann war Herr Braun abgereist? 2. Was geschah am Dienstag recht früh? 3. Was brachte der Briefträger? 4. Von wem war das Telegramm? 5. Was stand in dem Telegramm? 6. Wer war Erhard Grün? 7. Wie viele Kinder hatte Erhard? 8. Was studierte sein Sohn? 9. Wie lange war Erhards Tochter schon verheiratet? 10. Wo hatte Erhard den Herrn Müller kennengelernt? 11. Wo verbrachte Erhard Grün mit seinen Freunden den Abend? 12. Wonach erkundigte sich Herr Müller? 13. Was wollte Frau Müller wissen? 14. Warum war Erhard Grüns Besuch so kurz? 15. Wann fuhr sein Zug ab?

Idiomatic Expressions

recht früh	bright and early
auf der Durchreise nach	passing through, on the way to
was machst du denn?	what are you doing?
wie geht es dir?	how are you?
schön grüßen lassen	to give kind regards
vor drei Jahren	three years ago
erst nach vier	not until after four
eine Reise machen	to take a trip
heute abend	this evening
zu Besuch	for a visit
zu Abend essen	to eat supper
Verspätung haben	to be late (*of trains, etc.*)
sich erkundigen über (*acc.*)	to inquire about
sich in Bewegung setzen	to start moving

EXERCISES

A. Combine two or more of the above expressions in six or seven German sentences.

B. Insert the proper German form of the English verb in its proper place in the sentence.

1. Am Dienstag der Briefträger (*rings*). 2. Er ihr ein Telegramm (*gives*). 3. Ihr Mann es (*opened*). 4. Sie ihn schön

13

begrüsste

(*greeted*). 5. Ich meinem Freunde (*have thanked*). 6. Was du mich (*have asked*)? 7. Er aus Frankfurt (*had come*). 8. Die Kinder sehr froh (*had been*). 9. Der Zug um sieben (*will arrive*). 10. Erhard nach Münster (*will travel*). 11. Herr Müller über die Verhältnisse (*will have inquired*). 12. Sie seine Familie wohl in Frankfurt (*will have made the acquaintance*).

C. Restate each sentence in the past, the past perfect, and the future.

1. Herr Braun reist am Montag. 2. In Deutschland bringt die Post alle Telegramme. 3. Sonderboten tragen gewöhnliche Telegramme aus. 4. Brieftelegramme nimmt der Briefträger mit. 5. Es kommt von Frankfurt. 6. Der Zug hat Verspätung. 7. Es geht ihm gut. 8. Sie fragt noch einmal nach ihm. 9. Sie essen in einem kleinen Gasthaus zu Abend. 10. Sie beschließen nichts. 11. Er weiß alles. 12. Der Zug setzt sich langsam in Bewegung.

D. Change each of the original sentences in C into a question with or without an interrogative.

E. Derive nouns or verbs respectively from the following words. EXAMPLE: klingeln (to ring) — die Klingel (bell).

klingeln	Briefträger	besorgen	Bewegung
eingehen	Durchreise	rufen	Zug
begrüßen	Besuch	wollen	Richtung

F. Use each of the derivatives from E in a German sentence. EXAMPLE: Die Klingel ist nicht in Ordnung.

Composition

1. Mr. Braun left on Monday and Erhard Grün arrived on Tuesday. 2. He was passing through on his way to Münster. 3. Mr. and Mrs. Müller had met Erhard and his wife two years ago in Frankfurt. 4. "Now," said Erhard, "my son is studying medicine and my daughter has been married almost a year." 5. Erhard was very glad to see his friends near Bonn. 6. But he did not stay long. 7. He arrived at four and Mr. Müller drove him to the station at seven. 8. "Next year we will visit you," said Mr. Müller to his friend. 9. "Meanwhile, please give our kind regards to your wife and children."

Variations

A. Write out in German the answers to the questions based on the second stanza of Goethe's poem, "Heidenröslein," reproduced below. **B.** With the aid of these answers rewrite the stanza in simple German prose.

> Knabe sprach: „Ich breche dich,
> Röslein auf der Heiden!"
> Röslein sprach: „Ich steche dich,
> Daß du ewig denkst an mich,
> Und ich will's nicht leiden."
> Röslein, Röslein, Röslein rot,
> Röslein auf der Heiden.

1. Wer sprach? 2. Was sagte der Knabe? 3. Was wollte der Knabe brechen? 4. Zu wem sprach der Knabe? 5. Wer antwortete dem Knaben? 6. Was sagte das Röslein? 7. An wen wird der Knabe denken? 8. Wer will es nicht leiden? 9. Wie ist die Farbe des Rösleins? 10. Wo wächst das Röslein?

Conversation — Im Postamt

Grün:	Bitte, geben Sie mir ein Telegrammformular!
Beamter:	Bitte schön! (Gibt Herrn Grün das Formular.)
Grün:	(Dankt, füllt das Formular aus, überreicht es wieder dem Mann am Schalter.) Bitte! Wann kommt das Telegramm in Berlin an?
Beamter:	Um sieben Uhr ist es bestimmt da.
Grün:	Um sieben ist das Büro aber schon geschlossen.
Beamter:	Dann geben Sie es als Brieftelegramm auf.
Grün:	Nun gut! Wieviel macht das?
Beamter:	(Zählt die Wörter und rechnet.) Zwei Mark, bitte.
Grün:	Als Brieftelegramm wird es dann morgen früh mit der Post im Büro abgegeben, nicht wahr?
Beamter:	Sie können sich darauf verlassen.
Grün:	Danke vielmals.
Beamter:	Bitte.

CHAPTER THREE

The Order of Subject and Verb

3.1 With reference to the position of the subject and the verb, German distinguishes three types of word order: (a) normal, (b) inverted, and (c) dependent.

(a) *NORMAL WORD ORDER*

3.2 As in English, the subject [1] in German is often the first unit in a simple declarative sentence.

Er ist hier.	He is here.
Mein Freund ist hier.	My friend is here.
Mein alter Freund ist hier.	My old friend is here.
Mein alter Freund aus Bonn ist hier.	My old friend from Bonn is here.

3.3 In English and in German the inflected part of the verb is the second unit in a simple declarative sentence.

Er zeigt mir das Buch.	He shows me the book.
Mein Freund zeigte mir das Buch.	My friend showed me the book.
Er hat mir das Buch gezeigt.	He has shown me the book.
Er wird mir das Buch zeigen.	He will show me the book.
Er steht frühmorgens auf.	He gets up early in the morning.

Note, however, the position of its "complementary" part (i.e. the infinitive, past participle, or separable prefix called adverb in English), in the two languages. In English the complementary part follows directly after the inflected part of the verb. In German it is at the end of the clause.

. . . hat . . . gezeigt.	. . . has shown . . .
. . . wird . . . zeigen.	. . . will show . . .
. . . steht . . . auf.	. . . gets up . . .

(b) *INVERTED WORD ORDER*

3.4 The order of the simple declarative statement is inverted in German when any element of the sentence other than the subject (conjunctions are not counted) [2] is in first place. The inflected

---

[1] That is, the noun or pronoun and its modifiers. [2] Interjections and particles are usually set off by a comma.

verb is in second place, as in normal word order, and the subject is in third place. (In English the verb is in third place instead.)

Gestern zeigte er mir das Buch.	Yesterday he showed me the book.
Morgen wird er mir das Buch zeigen.	Tomorrow he will show me the book.
Heute stand er um fünf Uhr auf.	Today he got up at five o'clock.

3.5 Similarly, in a question with an interrogative, the interrogative is in first place, the inflected part of the verb is in second place, and the subject is in third place in both languages.

Wann kommt er?	When is he coming?
Wann wird er ankommen?	When will he arrive?
Wer war es?	Who was it?

3.6 In questions beginning with the inflected part of the verb, the subject follows immediately after the verb in both English and German.

Geht er?	Is he going?
Wird er kommen?	Will he come?

3.7 In a main clause preceded by a dependent clause, the inflected verb is in first place and the subject in second in German.

Als er ging, ging ich mit.   When he went, I went along.

3.8 The subject (present or implied) also follows the inflected verb in:

(1) commands and exhortatory subjunctives, as in

Geben Sie (*or* Gib) mir den Apfel!   Give me the apple!
Gehen wir jetzt.   Let us go now.

(2) conditional clauses in which **wenn** is omitted, as in
Kommt er heute, so gehe ich morgen.
If he comes today, I'll go tomorrow.

(3) *as if*-clauses, in which **als** denotes *if*, as in

Er tat, als wüßte er nichts davon.
He acted, as if he knew nothing about it.

(4) for emphasis, followed by **doch,** as in
Er weiß alles, studiert er doch immer bis spät in die Nacht.
He knows everything; after all, he always studies far into the night.

17

(c) *DEPENDENT WORD ORDER*

3.9 In German the inflected part of the verb is at the end of a dependent [3] clause. (In English the sequence is conjunction-subject-verb or relative pronoun-subject-verb, etc., with the verb in third place, as in 3.4 on page 16.)

Als er nach Hause kam, . . .	When he came home, . . .
Wenn er mir morgen das Geld geben wird, . . .	If he will give me the money tomorrow, . . .
Da er es mir gegeben hatte, . . .	Since he had given it to me, . . .
Der alte Mann, den du sahst, . . .	The old man, whom you saw, . . .

3.10 In summary, with reference to the position of the verb in the sentence or clause, it may be said that German distinguishes the following three types of word order: (a) verb in first place, (b) verb in second place, (c) verb in last place.

(a) The inflected verb is first in (1) questions that do not begin with an interrogative, (2) imperatives, (3) conditional clauses not introduced by **wenn**.

Hast du ihm das Buch gezeigt?	Did you show him the book?
Zeig ihm das Buch!	Show him the book.
Hätte ich ihn doch gesehen!	If only I had seen him.

(b) The inflected verb stands in second place in (1) questions that begin with an interrogative, (2) clauses introduced by any other part of speech, including the subject, indirect object, direct object, adverb. It may be said to be in second place in a sentence in which the dependent clause precedes the main clause which begins with the inflected verb.

Warum hast du es ihm heute gezeigt?	Why did you show it to him today?
Heute hat er mir das Buch gezeigt.	Today he showed me the book.
Er hat mir das Buch heute gezeigt.	He showed me the book today.
Das Buch hat er mir heute gezeigt.	He showed me the book today.
Mir hat er das Buch heute gezeigt.	He showed the book to me today.

(c) The inflected verb stands in final position in dependent clauses.

Wenn er geht, gehe auch ich.	If he goes, I'll go too.

[3] Dependent clauses are introduced by subordinating conjunctions, relative pronouns, indefinite relative pronouns, and interrogatives in indirect discourse (Chapters XII, XIX, XXIII, XXIV).

BASIC PATTERNS

Am Dienstag gehen Herr und Frau Müller um zehn
Uhr zu Bett. An Wochentagen gehen sie immer früh zu
Bett, denn sie müssen immer früh auf sein. Am Mitt-
woch sind beide auch schon um sieben Uhr wach. Herr
Müller springt dann sofort aus dem Bett und geht ins 5
Bad, während seine Frau das Frühstück zubereitet.

Im Bad geht alles bei Herrn Müller wie mechanisch.
Er hängt den Schlafanzug an einen Haken und stellt sich
unter die Brause. Das macht ihn frisch. Er wäscht sich
gründlich mit Schwamm und Seife und trocknet sich mit 10
einem weichen Handtuch ab. Dann tut er Zahnpasta auf
die Zahnbürste und putzt sich die Zähne. Nachher
rasiert er sich, aber nicht mit einem elektrischen Rasierapparat. Er braucht noch Rasierpinsel, Rasierseife und
Rasierklingen. Nach dem Rasieren kämmt er sich das 15
Haar, zieht sich schnell an und geht zum Frühstück.

Herr und Frau Müller frühstücken morgens gewöhnlich um acht Uhr. Zum Frühstück trinken sie
meistens Kaffee mit Milch und Zucker und essen Brot
oder Brötchen mit Butter und Marmelade. Apfelsinen- 20
saft, wie ihn die Amerikaner trinken, trinken sie nicht
oder sehr selten. Wie die meisten Leute in Europa essen
die Müllers nur sonntags Kuchen. Hie und da essen sie
auch Eier zum Frühstück. Herr Müller hat dann weichgekochte Eier gern, während Frau Müller Spiegeleier
gern hat. Wenn sie Zeit hat, bäckt sie die Brötchen
lieber selbst. Aber das Brot kauft sie beim Bäcker.
Punkt halb neun legt Herr Müller seine Serviette beiseite,
und um neun Uhr ist er schon im Büro.

Questions

1. Wann gehen Herr und Frau Müller an Wochentagen zu Bett?
2. Warum gehen sie immer so früh zu Bett? 3. Wer von ihnen ist am
Morgen gewöhnlich zuerst wach? 4. Was tut Herr Müller, während
seine Frau das Frühstück zubereitet? 5. Um wieviel Uhr frühstücken
Herr und Frau Müller morgens? 6. Woraus besteht ein Frühstück bei

der Familie Müller? 7. Wie lange essen Herr und Frau Müller am Morgen? 8. Was essen die Müllers sonntags? 9. Warum legt Herr Müller seine Serviette um halb neun beiseite? 10. In wieviel Minuten ist Herr Müller im Büro?

Idiomatic Expressions

zu Bett gehen	to go to bed
wie mechanisch	mechanically
(frisch machen)	to refresh
sich (dat.) das Haar kämmen	to comb one's hair
zum Frühstück	to (or for) breakfast
frühstücken	to eat breakfast
die meisten	most of the
hie und da	now and then
gern haben	to like
lieber haben	to prefer
am liebsten haben	to like best

EXERCISES

A. Base a question and answer on each of the above expressions. EXAMPLE: Wann gehst du zu Bett? Ich gehe schon um zehn zu Bett.

B. In each of the following sentences change the normal word order to inverted word order.
1. Er fährt heute nach Wien. Er steht um acht Uhr auf. 2. Sie springen sofort aus dem Bett. Sie essen um halb acht Uhr Frühstück. 3. Frau Müller bereitet das Frühstück zu. Herr Müller stellt sich unter die Brause. 4. Er kämmt sich das Haar sofort. Er rasiert sich mit einem elektrischen Apparat. 5. Er ist um acht Uhr fertig. Er will um neun Uhr im Büro sein. 6. Herr Müller aß gestern ein Spiegelei. Er hat zum Frühstück weichgekochte Eier lieber.

C. Use the following conjunctions in German to make one of the sentences in each pair in B dependent upon the other: als, da, während, nachdem, denn, obgleich. EXAMPLE: Es ist noch früh. Mein Bruder fährt um sieben in die Stadt. Mein Bruder fährt um sieben in die Stadt, obgleich es noch früh ist.

D. In each of the sentences in C change the subject to the plural and the tense to the perfect. EXAMPLE: Meine Brüder sind in die Stadt gefahren, obgleich es noch früh ist.

E. Use each of the following phrases in a German sentence with normal word order and a subject with one or more modifiers: *ins Bad gehen, das Frühstück zubereiten, wie mechanisch gehen, sich unter die Brause stellen, zum Frühstück gehen, Kaffee mit Milch, Brötchen mit Butter, punkt halb neun, zum Frühstück essen.* EXAMPLE: Das kleine Kind geht früh zu Bett.

F. Explain in German: *Zahnbürste, Schlafanzug, Rasierpinsel, Handtuch, Wochentag.* EXAMPLE: Rasierseife ist Seife, mit der man sich vor dem Rasieren einseift.

Composition

1. Mr. and Mrs. Müller came home at six. 2. They ate supper at seven and went to bed at ten. 3. The next morning they were up again at seven. 4. They were always up at seven. 5. Mr. Müller was up first. 6. While Mrs. Müller prepared (the) breakfast, he stepped into the shower. 7. A shower always refreshed him. 8. Then he shaved with his electric razor, brushed his teeth, and combed his hair. 9. At half past seven he had finished. 10. (The) breakfast was already (standing) on the table. 11. As usual, it consisted of a glass [of] orange juice, a cup [of] hot coffee, two soft-boiled eggs, and two rolls. 12. At a quarter past eight Mr. Müller was in his car and on his way to the office.

Variations

A. Write out in German the answers to the questions based on the third stanza of Goethe's poem, "Heidenröslein," reproduced below. **B.** With the aid of these answers rewrite the stanza in simple German prose.

> Und der wilde Knabe brach
> 's Röslein auf der Heiden;
> Röslein wehrte sich und stach,
> Half ihm doch kein Weh und Ach,
> Mußt' es eben leiden.
> Röslein, Röslein, Röslein rot,
> Röslein auf der Heiden.

1. Wer war wild? 2. Wer brach das Röslein? 3. Was brach der Knabe? 4. Welches Röslein wehrte sich? 5. Welches Röslein brach der Knabe? 6. Wie wehrte sich das Röslein? 7. Wer stach den Knaben? 8. Was half dem Röslein nicht? 9. Wer mußte alles leiden?

Conversation — Beim Frisör

Frisör:	(Weist auf den Barbierstuhl.) Herr Müller, Sie sind an der Reihe. Bitte, nehmen Sie Platz. Was darf es sein?
Müller:	(Setzt sich und sagt:) Haarschneiden, bitte.
Frisör:	Wie wünschen der Herr [4] das Haar?
Müller:	Vorn (halb)lang und hinten ganz kurz.
Frisör:	Und an den Seiten?
Müller:	An den Seiten (schneiden Sie es) mit der Maschine.
Frisör:	(Schneidet emsig und fragt dann:) Ist (Ihnen) das so recht?
Müller:	(Sieht in den Spiegel.) Ausgezeichnet. Aber stutzen Sie bitte auch meinen Schnurrbart etwas.
Frisör:	Gern. (Stutzt. Nachher.) Etwas Pomade oder Kölnisches Wasser?
Müller:	Danke, nur ein bißchen Brillantine.
Frisör:	Jetzt sind wir fertig. Wenn ich bitten darf.

CHAPTER FOUR

The Order of the Other Parts of Speech

The order of the other parts of speech in German varies in some ways from that in English. The position of the adjective and the objects is the same in both languages. The position of the negative is generally the same. The sequence of adverbs differs in

---

[4] Note the form used to address a customer or patron.

English and in German. The separable prefix in German is always at or near the end of the clause.

(a) *ADJECTIVES*

4.1 In English and in German, limiting and descriptive adjectives precede the words they modify.

> Dein alter Freund ist hier.   Your old friend is here.

(b) *ADVERBS*

4.2 Adverbs and adverbial phrases are commonly arranged in German in the order of time, manner, place, with time always preceding place. The sequence differs in English.

Ich kam gestern mit dem Auto in Wien an.	I arrived in Vienna yesterday by car.
Er bleibt jetzt hier.	He is staying here now. *never between sub & verb*

4.3 An adverb of time or place always precedes an adverbial phrase of time or place in German, but not in English.

Er kommt heute um neun.	He is coming at nine today.
Sie muß hier im Zimmer bleiben.	She must stay here in the room.

(c) *OBJECTS*

4.4 When both objects are nouns, the indirect object precedes the direct object in German. It precedes in English, when the preposition *to* is omitted.

Er gab dem Mann das Geld.	He gave the man the money. He gave the money to the man.

4.5 When both objects are pronouns, the direct object generally precedes in both languages.

> Sie zeigte sie ihm.   She showed her to him.

4.6 When the indirect object is a noun and the direct object is a pronoun, the pronoun precedes the noun in English and in German.

> Er gab es dem Mann.   He gave it to the man.

*Heilige am Portal des Kölner Doms. Diese gotische
Kirche ist eine der schönsten in Europa.*

4.7 When the indirect object is a pronoun and the direct object is a noun, the pronoun generally precedes the noun in both languages.

Er gab ihr das Buch.   He gave her the book.

(d) *NEGATIVES AND SEPARABLE PREFIXES*

4.8 A negative generally precedes the word or phrase [1] it qualifies in German and in English.

Er wird nicht gehen.	He will not go.
Er hat es nicht gesagt.	He has not said it.
Es ist nicht schön.	It is not beautiful.
Er ist nicht zu Hause.	He is not at home.
Er ist nicht hier.	He is not here.

4.9 But the negative usually follows a simple clause in the present or past tense in German.

Er geht heute nicht.   He does not go today.

4.10 A separable prefix in German is placed at the end of a main clause in the present or past tense. In a compound tense it precedes the infinitive or the past participle of the verb. In a dependent clause it stands directly in front of the inflected form of the verb.

Er stand heute früh auf.	He got up early today.
Er war gestern früh aufgestanden.	He had got up early yesterday.
Er wird morgen früh aufstehen.	He will get up early tomorrow.
Als er heute früh aufstand, . . .	When he got up early today, . . .

BASIC PATTERNS

Am Sonnabend hatten die Müllers Gesellschaft. Nach Tisch wurde über allerlei geredet. Man kam auf alte Zeiten zu sprechen. Die einen erinnerten sich an die Zeit, wo sie zusammen in der Schule waren. Die anderen sprachen von ihren Kriegserlebnissen. Jeder 5 wußte etwas von den schweren Zeiten zu erzählen.

,,Ich erinnere mich noch deutlich an den Karl Schmidt,'' warf Herr Müller ein. ,,Schmidt war ein

[1] That is, an infinitive, a participle, a predicate adjective, an adverbial phrase, or an adverb.

famoser Kerl und hat mir die Geschichte selbst erzählt.
Er und ein gewisser Erich Meier waren alte Bekannte.
Beide waren bei derselben Firma angestellt, und beide
wurden eines Tages zugleich arbeitslos.   Da ging Meier
5 stempeln und hungerte sich mit seiner Familie nur so
durch.   Doch Schmidt blieb nicht untätig.   Er nahm
seinen letzten Sparpfennig, mietete sich einen kleinen
Wagen und verkaufte Würstchen vor dem Eingang einer
großen Bank.
10   Hier sah ihn Meier, als er an der Bank vorbeikam.
Es war um die Mittagszeit, und das Geschäft bei Schmidt
ging glänzend.   Schmidt hatte alle Hände voll zu tun.
Da trat Meier an ihn heran und sagte: ‚Dir geht es gut,
wie ich sehe.   Leider kann ich das nicht von mir behaup-
15 ten.   Sag mal, Schmidt,‘ meinte Meier dann nach einigem
Zögern. ‚Kannst du mir nicht fünf Mark leihen?‘
      ‚Es tut mir leid, lieber Meier, aber das darf ich nicht,‘
antwortete ihm darauf der geschäftige Schmidt.   ‚Ich
habe nämlich mit der Bank einen Vertrag abgeschlossen.
20 Die Bank darf keine Würstchen verkaufen, und ich darf
keinen Kredit geben.‘ ‚Heute,‘‘ schloß Herr Müller,
„ist der Schmidt Teilhaber der Firma Merck & Co.‘‘

Questions

1. Wann hatten die Müllers Gesellschaft? 2. Worüber wurde nach
Tisch geredet? 3. An wen erinnerte sich Herr Müller? 4. Bei wem waren
Schmidt und Meier angestellt? 5. Was tat Meier, als er arbeitslos wurde?
6. Wozu entschloß sich Schmidt? 7. Wo verkaufte Schmidt Würstchen?
8. Wer kam an der Bank vorbei? 9. Wie ging das Geschäft bei Schmidt?
10. Was wollte Meier von Schmidt? 11. Wie antwortete ihm Schmidt?
12. Warum gab Schmidt diese Antwort? 13. Was ist Schmidt heute?
14. Was ist aus Meier geworden?

Idiomatic Expressions

Gesellschaft haben	to have company
nach Tisch	after dinner
sich erinnern an (*acc.*)	to recall

26

stempeln gehen	to collect unemployment insurance
untätig bleiben	to remain idle
arbeitslos werden	to be laid off
um die Mittagszeit	around lunch time
das Geschäft geht glänzend	business is booming
alle Hände voll zu tun haben	to have all one can do to handle it
einen Vertrag abschließen	to make a contract
Kredit geben	to extend credit

EXERCISES

A. Use in a German sentence the noun or the verb from each of the above expressions. EXAMPLE: Zeig mir den Vertrag!

B. Replace one of the nouns in each of the following sentences with a suitable pronoun. EXAMPLE: Fritz dachte an seinen Bruder. Er dachte an seinen Bruder. Fritz dachte an ihn.

1. Die Müllers hatten Gesellschaft. 2. Die Freunde kamen auf alte Zeiten zu sprechen. 3. Frau Müller erinnerte sich an Karl Schmidt. 4. Beide waren bei der Firma angestellt. 5. Da ging Meier stempeln. 6. Doch Schmidt blieb nicht untätig. 7. Schmidt nahm seinen letzten Sparpfennig. 8. Er verkaufte dem Meier Würstchen. 9. Das Geschäft bei Schmidt ging glänzend. 10. Ich habe mit der Bank einen Vertrag abgeschlossen. 11. Die Bank darf Kredit geben. 12. Schmidt ist Teilhaber einer Firma.

C. Add one of the following adjectives or adverbs to each of the sentences in B: *berühmt, groß, gut, lang, schnell, neu, ganz, heiß, sofort.* EXAMPLES: Die Müllers hatten große Gesellschaft. Da ging Meier sofort stempeln.

D. Add an appropriate negative to each sentence in C. EXAMPLES: Sie hatten keine große Gesellschaft. Da ging er nicht sofort stempeln.

E. Complete each sentence, using one of the nouns in parenthesis as the direct object and the other as the indirect object.

1. Er verkaufte (Würstchen, Mann). 2. Schmidt lieh (Freund, Geld). 3. Ich gebe (Kredit, Junge). 4. Sie erzählte (Mädchen, Geschichte). 5. Meier schickte (Bank, Vertrag).

F. Form sentences in the present and present perfect tenses with each of the following expressions: *sich nicht erinnern, nicht arbeitslos werden, sich keinen Wagen mieten, nicht vorbeikommen* *an, keinen Vertrag abschließen, nicht zusammen in der Schule sein, nichts einwerfen, nicht herantreten an.*

Composition

1. Meier and Schmidt were old acquaintances. 2. Both were employed by the same company. 3. Both were laid off at the same time. 4. But only Meier collected his unemployment insurance. 5. Schmidt did not remain idle. 6. He rented a cart and began to sell wieners in front of the entrance of a large bank. 7. Business was booming and Schmidt had all he could do to handle it. 8. When Meier saw that, he said to Schmidt: "Couldn't you lend me five marks?" 9. "I'm sorry, but I am not allowed to," answered Schmidt. 10. "I have made a contract with the bank. 11. The bank isn't allowed to sell wieners and I am not allowed to extend credit."

Variations

A. Arrange the words in each line in their proper order.
B. Connect the sentences to form a brief anecdote.

1. prüft Physiklehrer der Studenten einen.
2. Kälte und der Wärme der Eigenschaften nennen Sie die.
3. lange überlegt Schüler der nicht.
4. aus Wärme dehnt die Körper die.
5. sie zieht Kälte die zusammen.
6. einige nennen Beispiele Sie.
7. kalt ist im es Winter.
8. Tage kurz sind die dann.
9. es ist warm Sommer im.
10. die lang sind dann Tage.

Conversation — Die Zeit

Herr Tieck:	Wieviel Uhr ist es?
Frau Tieck:	Es ist schon (drei Viertel fünf) 4.45 (Uhr).
Herr Tieck:	Geht deine Uhr auch genau?
Frau Tieck:	Ja, ich habe sie heute früh nach der Zeitansage im Radio gestellt.

Herr Tieck:	Dann geht der Wecker wohl falsch?
Frau Tieck:	Der Wecker geht fünf Minuten vor.
Herr Tieck:	Wann kann ich endlich meine Uhr wieder-haben?
Frau Tieck:	Deine Uhr kannst du dir schon morgen holen.
Herr Tieck:	Willst du mich bitte daran erinnern?

CHAPTER FIVE

Articles and Genders

English and German have two articles (definite and indefinite) and three genders (masculine, feminine, and neuter).

(a) THE DEFINITE ARTICLE

5.1 The definite article (Appendix I) is used more widely in German than in English. In German it must be used with the following:

(1) the days of the week, months, seasons, as

Am Montag war ich in Berlin.	On Monday I was in Berlin.
Im Juni kommt er nach Amerika.	In June he is coming to America.
Der Sonntag ist immer ein Ruhetag.	Sunday is always a day of rest.
Im Winter ist es kalt in Österreich.	In winter it is cold in Austria.

(2) the names of streets and the (feminine) names of coun-tries [1] ending in –ei, as

Er lebte einst in der Türkei.	He once lived in Turkey.
Jetzt wohnt er in der Goethestraße.	Now he lives on Goethe Street.

(3) the neuter names of countries and cities, as well as proper names, when modified by an adjective, as

Ich sah das schöne Wien (Deutschland, Gretchen).
I saw (the) beautiful Vienna (Germany, Gretchen).

[1] Note also *die Schweiz, das Elsaß,* as well as *die Vereinigten Staaten, die Nieder-lande,* and other plural names of countries.

29

(4) generic and abstract nouns,[2] as

Der Mensch ist sterblich.	Man is mortal.
Die Liebe ist blind.	Love is blind.

(5) parts of the body and clothing, instead of the possessive, when ownership is clear, as

Nehmen Sie den Hut ab!	Take off your hat!
Ich hob die Hand.	I raised my hand.

(6) various idiomatic expressions containing prepositions, as

Er geht in die Schule.	He goes to school.
Wir fahren mit dem Dampfer.	We are going by steamer.

5.2 In German the definite article is used instead of the indefinite article:

(1) in a distributive sense with nouns of weight and measure, as *per a pound not for a*

Er zahlte 20 Pfennig das Pfund.	He paid 20 pfennigs a pound.
Der Stoff kostet drei Mark das Meter.	The cloth costs three marks a meter.

(2) in certain idiomatic phrases containing prepositions, as

In der Regel rauche ich Zigarren.	As a rule I smoke cigars.

(b) THE INDEFINITE ARTICLE

5.3 The indefinite article (Appendix II) is used less frequently in German than in English. In German it is omitted:

(1) before predicate nouns denoting vocation, profession, rank, nationality, denomination, etc., which are not modified by an adjective, as

Sein Vater ist Kaufmann.	His father is a merchant.
Ihr Vater ist ein berühmter Chemiker.	Her father is a famous chemist.

(2) after **als,** meaning *as*

Er hat sie als Mädchen gekannt.	He knew her as a girl.

[2] Note, however, the omission of the article in certain sayings, such as

Arbeit ist keine Schande.	Work is no disgrace.
Liebe macht blind.	Love makes blind.

(c) *THE GENDER*

5.4 Grammatical gender is important in German, and yet it is to a great extent independent of natural gender. Therefore, the article reflecting the gender must be learned in each instance. However, the gender of a great many nouns may be identified easily in terms of their endings or the groups to which they belong (Chapter XIII). Very common are the masculine endings **–er, –ig, –ling;** the feminine endings **–heit, –keit, –schaft, –ung;** and the neuter endings **–chen, –lein,** and (with some exceptions) **–nis.**

5.5 An infinitive used as a noun is neuter, as **das Schwimmen.**

BASIC PATTERNS

„Kennst du den dunkelgrünen Opel unseres Nachbars?" fragte Frau Müller ihren Mann am Mittwoch beim Abendbrot. „Den Wagen mit der Nummer B 147148? Nun, der ist dem Herrn Schulz nämlich heute am hellen Tage in der Ringstraße gestohlen worden.   5

Es war so gegen fünf Uhr. Herr Schulz mußte noch einige Einkäufe machen. Da hatte er den Wagen auf der rechten Straßenseite am Gehsteig beim Zigarrenladen geparkt und war rasch in die Drogerie an der Ecke gesprungen. In der Eile hatte er vergessen, den Zünd-   10 schlüssel abzuziehen, und als er sich zwanzig Minuten später nach dem Wagen umsah, war er fort.

Fußgänger haben zu dieser Zeit einen jungen Mann beobachtet, der sich in der Nähe des Wagens aufgehalten hat. Die Polizei hat festgestellt, daß der verdächtige   15 junge Mann eine graue, karierte Jacke und eine dunkelbraune Hose anhatte. Er soll etwa 1,75 m groß sein, einen kleinen Schnurrbart und eine Brille mit einem dunklen Rand tragen. Ein Ladeninhaber will eine grüne Feder am hellbraunen, weichen Hute des jungen   20 Mannes gesehen haben. Weitere Nachrichten über die verdächtige Person oder über den gestohlenen Wagen bleiben jedoch aus."

Questions

1. Was für einen Wagen hatte Herr Schulz? 2. Welche Nummer trug der Wagen? 3. Wo hatte Herr Schulz den Wagen geparkt? 4. Wann ist er ihm gestohlen worden? 5. Wie lange blieb Herr Schulz in der Drogerie? 6. Wo war der Zündschlüssel? 7. Wen hatten Fußgänger in der Nähe des Wagens beobachtet? 8. Was für eine Jacke hatte der junge Mann an? 9. Wie groß war er? 10. Trug er einen Schnurrbart oder eine Brille? 11. Wer sah eine Feder am Hute des jungen Mannes? 12. Was hat die Polizei sonst festgestellt?

Idiomatic Expressions

am hellen Tage	in broad daylight
mir etwas stehlen	to steal something from me
so gegen	around, about
einige Einkäufe machen	to do some shopping
in der Eile	in the rush
sich umsehen nach (*dat.*)	to look (around) for
in der Nähe	in the vicinity
einen Schnurrbart tragen	to have a mustache
Brille mit dunklem Rand	dark-rimmed glasses

EXERCISES

A. Use each of the above expressions with *Er sah ihn . . .* or *Er lief . . .* or *Sie wollte . . .* EXAMPLE: Er sah ihn, mir das Geld stehlen.

B. Supply or add and combine (i.e. *an dem = am*) the appropriate article in the spaces indicated.

1. An —*m*— Mittwoch erzählte Frau Müller es ihrem Mann bei —*dem* Abendbrot. 2. *Der* Wagen *des* Herrn Schulz ist an *am* hellen Tage gestohlen worden. 3. Herr Schulz hatte *seinen* Wagen an *der* rechten Straßenecke geparkt. 4. Er war in *die* Drogerie an *der* Ecke gelaufen. 5. In *der* Eile hatte er *den* Zündschlüssel vergessen. 6. Er sah sich vergebens nach *dem* Wagen um. 7. Fußgänger sahen *einen* jungen Mann in *der* Nähe *des* Wagens. 8. *Ein* verdächtige Mann hatte *eine* graue Hose an. 9. Er trug *einen* kleinen Schnurrbart. 10. Weitere Nachrichten über *eine* verdächtige Person fehlen.

C. Wherever possible, change the sentences in B to the plural.

32

D. Form masculine, feminine, or neuter nouns based on: *Einkauf, kennen, Nachbar, dunkel, vergessen, Fußgänger, Zeit, Polizist, ein, Tag, einig, Inhaber, Frau, Feder, Hut.* EXAMPLES: Sitz — Sitzung, frei — Freiheit, Schlüssel — Schlüsselein.

E. Use each of the derivatives in D in a German sentence.

F. Translate, omit, or supply the words in parenthesis to complete the following sentences.

1. (*As a*) Regel geht mein Bruder (*on*) Montag nicht (*to*) Schule. Ich gehe jedoch jeden Tag (*to*) Schule. 2. (*In*) Juni kommt er (*by*) Dampfer nach New York. Bist du schon einmal (*by*) Eisenbahn gefahren? 3. (*In*) Winter fährt er oft (*to*) Schweiz, aber er stammt aus (*the*) Elsaß. 4. Ich hob (*my*) Hand, um (*my*) Hut abzunehmen. Er steckte jedoch (*his*) Hand in (*his*) Tasche. 5. Hast du ihn (*as a*) Kind gekannt? Ich kannte ihn (*as a*) Studenten. 6. Jetzt ist er (*a*) berühmter Chemiker. Sein Bruder ist (*a*) Physiker. 7. Sein Vater war (*a*) Kaufmann, und seine Mutter war (*a*) Lehrerin. 8. Wieviel hast du für (*a*) Pfund bezahlt? Ich habe drei Mark für zwei Dutzend (* of*) Eier bezahlt. 9. Drei Meter (*of*) Stoff sind nicht genug. Du wirst bestimmt noch (*a*) Meter (*of*) Stoff brauchen. 10. Ja, ( ) Liebe ist blind und ( ) Mensch ist sterblich.

Composition

1. When Mr. Müller came home on Wednesday, it was already seven. 2. At supper Mrs. Müller told her husband that Mr. Schulz' car had disappeared in broad daylight. 3. "It must have been around five o'clock," she said. 4. "Mr. Schulz had to do some shopping and parked the car at the curb near the drugstore. 5. When he looked for the car twenty minutes later, it was gone. 6. Pedestrians say that they saw a young man near the car. 7. 'He was about 1,75 m tall, had a small mustache and wore a pair of dark-rimmed glasses,' they say. 8. One storekeeper says, 'He wore a gray jacket, brown trousers, and a light brown hat.' 9. The police have not been able to find out anything else about the young man or the car."

Variations

A. Arrange the words in each line in their proper order.
B. Connect the sentences to form a brief anecdote.

1. Plum begegnet Plem Freund seinem.
2. trägt dieser Kopf Verband einen um den.
3. los was dir mit Plem ist?
4. gefallen bin ich Leiter zehn Meter hohen von einer.
5. Hals den du ja dir können brechen hättest.
6. nicht gerade das.
7. erst war ich nämlich der Sprosse auf vierten.

Conversation — In der Reparaturwerkstatt

Hugo Pochmann:	Guten Tag! Haben Sie nachgesehen, was am Motor in Unordnung ist?
Mechaniker:	Ja, wir müssen eine neue Zündkerze einsetzen.
Hugo Pochmann:	Und was ist mit dem Vergaser los?
Mechaniker:	Der Vergaser scheint nur verstopft zu sein.
Hugo Pochmann:	Haben Sie die Bremse und den Winker nachgeprüft?
Mechaniker:	Ich finde die Bremse in Ordnung, sie muß nur angezogen werden. Für den Winker brauchen sie eine neue Birne.
Hugo Pochmann:	Ist sonst alles in Ordnung?
Mechaniker:	Sonst ist mir nichts aufgefallen.
Hugo Pochmann:	Wann kann ich dann den Wagen wiederhaben?
Mechaniker:	Morgen nachmittag, wenn's Ihnen recht ist.

CHAPTER SIX

Special Uses of the Genitive

In English and in German the genitive is the case denoting ownership or relationship (Chapter I). In German the genitive case is also used with certain (a) prepositions, (b) verbs, (c) adjectives, and (d) in adverbial expressions of indefinite time and the time of customary action.

(a) *PREPOSITIONS*

6.1   The genitive case is used for the object of certain prepositions. The most common of these are:

(an)statt	instead of	**jenseits**	on the other side of
außerhalb	outside (of)	**trotz**	in spite of
innerhalb	inside (of)	**um ... willen**	for the sake of
oberhalb	on top of, above	**während**	during (the time of)
unterhalb	at the bottom of, below	**wegen**	on account of, because of
diesseits	this side of		

Er wohnt jenseits des Flusses.   He lives on the other side of the river.

Während des Sommers wohnte sie auf dem Lande.   During the summer she lived in the country.

Er kam trotz des Regens.   He came in spite of the rain.

(b) *VERBS*

6.2   The genitive case is used with certain verbs, including some reflexives, which have only one object. The most common are:

bedürfen	to (have) need (of)	**sich bedienen**	to make use of
gedenken	to remember	**sich erbarmen**	to take pity on
sich annehmen	to side with	**sich rühmen**	to boast (of)

Gedenke meiner!   Remember me!

Er rühmt sich immer seiner Kenntnisse.   He always boasts of his knowledge.

6.3   Among the verbs increasingly governing prepositions which require the accusative case rather than the simple genitive are:

denken (an)	to think of	**sich schämen**	to be ashamed of
sich erinnern (an)	to remember	**(über)**	

Ich erinnere mich des Vorfalls genau.   I clearly remember the incident.
Ich erinnere mich genau an den Vorfall.

(c) *ADJECTIVES*

6.4   Certain adjectives govern the genitive case. The most common of these are:

(handwritten margin notes: happy in; gen + froh; happy about; froh über; aware/worthy annotations)*

bewußt	aware (of)	**satt**	having enough (of)
fähig	capable (of)	**schuldig**	guilty (of)
froh	glad (of)	**sicher**	sure (of)
gewiß	certain (of)	**wert**	worthy (of)
müde	tired (of)		

Sind Sie seiner sicher?   Are you sure of him?
Er ist eines solchen Betruges nicht   He is not capable of such deception.
   fähig.

Note that these adjectives follow the words they govern in German, but not in English.

(d) *ADVERBS AND INDEFINITE TIME*

6.5   Adverbs (derived from the genitive case of nouns) and nouns in the genitive case are used adverbially to express customary action. Some common examples are: **morgens** — *mornings, in the morning;* **mittags** — *(usually) at noon;* **nachts** — *(usually) at night;* **sonntags** or **des Sonntags** — *(usually) on Sundays.*[1]

Morgens stehe ich um sieben Uhr   Mornings I rise at seven o'clock.
   auf.

6.6   The genitive case of nouns is used to express indefinite time, as **eines Tages** — *(of) one day.*

Eines Tages wirst du mir danken.   One day you will thank me.

(e) *NOTES*

6.7   A noun directly following a noun of number, weight or measure does not take the genitive case in German. English, however, uses the partitive.

Ich kaufte zwei Pfund [2] Kaffee und   I bought two pounds of coffee and
   eine Flasche Wein.   a bottle of wine.
Der Preis eines Pfundes Kaffee ist   The price of a pound of coffee has
   um drei Mark gestiegen.   gone up (by) three marks.

---

[1] Some adverbs derived from the genitive case of adjectives are: **neuestens** — *lately;* **spätestens** — *at the latest;* **bereits** — *already;* **rechts** — *to the right.*
[2] Note that such masculine and neuter nouns are not inflected in the plural in German.

Die Freie Universität Berlin.

wert

Es ist nicht der Mühe wert = gen only in idioms

Es ist einen Doller wert = acc

6.8 Note also the German usage in: **Die Stadt Hamburg** —
The city of Hamburg; **Der Monat Juni** — *The month of June;*
Der erste Mai — *The first of May.*

BASIC PATTERNS

„Na, wie geht es Ihnen," fragte Dr. Wohl, als er
Donnerstag gegen zehn trotz des Regens ans Bett des
Herrn Müller trat. „Leider schlecht," antwortete dieser.
„Die Kopfschmerzen sind nicht zum Ertragen. Ich habe
5 die ganze Nacht kein Auge zugetan."

„Nun, lassen Sie mal sehen," meinte der Arzt,
während er den Mantel ablegte. „Erst mal Ihren Puls
fühlen." Dann steckte er dem Kranken ein Thermometer in die Achselhöhle. „Jetzt," sagte darauf der Arzt,
10 „machen Sie den Mund auf! Ganz aufmachen, bitte,"
wiederholte er. Dabei beugte er sich über den Kranken
und sah ihm mit seiner Taschenlampe in den Mund.

„Ja, die Zunge ist belegt," stellte Dr. Wohl nun fest,
„und hinten im Hals haben Sie eine starke Rötung."
15 Sich das Thermometer besehend, fügte er hinzu: „Also,
etwas Fieber haben Sie auch." Herr Müller nickte nur
zu allem. Er stöhnte ein wenig, als der Arzt jetzt das
Hörrohr zur Hand nahm und sagte: „Bitte, richten Sie
sich nun auf und machen Sie sich oben frei. Ich will mal
20 Ihre Lungen abhorchen."

Nachdem Dr. Wohl dem Kranken das Hörrohr erst
an die Brust und dann an den Rücken gelegt hatte, erklärte er: „Herr Müller, es besteht kein Zweifel. Sie
haben die Grippe. Aber keine Sorgen. Die ist in einigen
25 Tagen überstanden, wenn Sie das Bett hüten. Inzwischen
verschreibe ich Ihnen zweierlei Tabletten. Die einen
werden Sie alle sechs Stunden nehmen. Die werden das
Fieber herabdrücken. Die anderen nehmen Sie stündlich.
Die lutschen Sie. Die werden Ihrem Hals guttun."
30 „So, jetzt muß ich aber eilen," sagte zuletzt Dr. Wohl
und reichte Frau Müller das Rezept. „Meine Sprech-

stunde beginnt morgens um elf, und mein Wartezimmer ist sicher voll von Patienten. Morgen komme ich noch einmal vorbei und sehe nach. Auf Wiedersehen. Gute Besserung, Herr Müller!"

Questions

1. Wen ließ Frau Müller am Donnerstag holen? 2. Worüber klagte Herr Müller? 3. Wie hatte Herr Müller geschlafen? 4. Was tat Dr. Wohl zuerst? 5. Womit sah er Herrn Müller in den Mund? 6. Was fehlte Herrn Müller? 7. Wie lange sollte er das Bett hüten? 8. Wann stöhnte Herr Müller? 9. Was für Tabletten verschrieb ihm Dr. Wohl? 10. Wie oft sollte Herr Müller die Tabletten nehmen? 11. Warum hatte der Arzt Eile? 12. Wann versprach er, noch einmal vorbeizukommen?

Idiomatic Expressions

holen lassen	to send for
zum Ertragen	bearable
klagen über (*acc.*)	to complain about
kein Auge zutun	not to sleep a wink
ihm in den Mund sehen	to look into his (*or* him in the) mouth
ganz aufmachen	to open wide
eine Rötung im Hals	an inflamed throat
Fieber haben	to have a temperature
sich oben freimachen	to open one's shirt
das Bett hüten	to stay in bed

EXERCISES

A. Form ten German sentences. In each combine one of the idiomatic expressions listed above with one of the following phrases: *innerhalb einer Stunde, trotz der Hitze, wegen der Hitze, trotz der Kälte, abends, eines Tages, dessen* (or *es*) *sicher, während der Nacht.* EXAMPLE: Er ließ ihn innerhalb einer Stunde holen.

B. Supply the appropriate genitive forms and endings.

1. Er kam trotz d— Regen—. 2. Er trat um zehn Uhr an das Bett d— Herr— Müller. 3. Er klagte ein— Tag— über heftige Kopfschmerzen. 4. Der Arzt steckte das Thermometer in die Achselhöhle d— Krank—. 5. Die Zunge d— Krank— war belegt. 6. Er stöhnte, als er das Hörrohr d— Arzt— sah. 7. Die-

39

ser verschrieb ihm ein Glas kalten Wein—. 8. Innerhalb ein— Woche ist er so weit. 9. Seine Sprechstunde beginnt morgen— um zehn. 10. Er nannte die Namen d— Patient—. 11. Sie war d— sicher. 12. Er besuchte ihn während d— Tag—.

C. Explain simply in German the components of each of the following compounds: *Kopfschmerzen, Achselhöhle, Taschenlampe, Höhrrohr, Wartezimmer, Wintermantel, Wiedersehen, Krankenzimmer.* EXAMPLES: Die Entzündung des Halses ist eine Halsentzündung. Eine Hausarbeit ist eine Arbeit, die man zu Hause macht.

D. Illustrate the use of the genitive with: *müde, bewußt, sich schämen, sich bedienen, oberhalb, wegen, nachts, sonntags.* EXAMPLE: Frau Müller war dessen (*or* es) müde.

E. Use each phrase in a sentence: *Monat Mai, Stadt Berlin, Pfund Butter, Glas Milch.* EXAMPLE: Der Plan der Stadt Berlin ist alt.

F. Derive at least one word from each of the words in D. EXAMPLES: müde — ermüden, Berlin — Berliner.

Composition

1. On Thursday Mr. Müller complained of a headache and Mrs. Müller sent for Dr. Wohl. 2. The doctor came and examined Mr. Müller. 3. "Your tongue is coated and your throat is inflamed," he said to the patient. 4. "You also have a slight temperature," he added. 5. "Yes, you have the grippe," declared Dr. Wohl. 6. "You will therefore have to stay in bed for a few days. 7. Here are two kinds of pills. 8. The red [ones] will bring down your fever. 9. Take them every six hours. 10. The white pills will help your throat. 11. Take one every hour and don't worry. 12. I'll look in [on you] tomorrow. 13. But now I must hurry. 14. My office is probably full of patients. 15. Goodby."

Variations

A. Arrange the words in each line in their proper order.
B. Connect the sentences to form a brief anecdote.

1. Dampfer der Hafen im liegt.
2. Deck die Passagiere spazieren auf.

3. die warten sie auf Abfahrt.
4. Radler heran ein rast Ferne in der.
5. Laufsteg den schon Matrosen fassen die.
6. ist schon jeder gespannt.
7. noch rechtzeitig springt der Radler als an Bord klatschen alle.
8. Abfahren er ruft.
9. Schiffes Kapitän denn er ist des.

Conversation — Der Arzt kommt

Dr. Wohl	Guten Tag, Frau Müller! Haben Sie nach mir geschickt?
Frau Müller:	Ja, Herr Doktor. Meinem Mann geht es gar nicht gut.
Dr. Wohl:	Was fehlt ihm denn?
Frau Müller:	Er hat furchtbare Schmerzen in der Brust.
Dr. Wohl:	Liegt er schon lange?
Frau Müller:	Drei Tage lang.
Dr. Wohl:	Und was haben Sie ihm gegeben?
Frau Müller:	Ich habe ihm dreimal täglich Tee gegeben.
Dr. Wohl:	Hat er Appetit?
Frau Müller:	Ja, aber ich habe ihm nichts zu essen gegeben.
Dr. Wohl:	Gut. Dann führen Sie mich zu dem Kranken. Sehen wir ihn uns mal an.

CHAPTER SEVEN

Special Uses of the Dative

In English and in German the dative is the case of the indirect object (Chapter I). In German the dative is also used with certain (a) prepositions, (b) verbs, (c) adjectives, and (d) other constructions.

41

(a) *PREPOSITIONS*

7.1 The dative case is always used for the object of certain prepositions. The most common of these are:

aus	from, out of	**nach**	to, for, after, toward, according to
außer	aside from, besides		
bei	at, near, at the home of	**seit**	since
		von	of, from, about, by
mit	with	**zu**	to, at [1]

Außer ihm kam niemand.   Besides him nobody came.
Er sprach mit seinem Bruder dar-   He spoke with his brother about it.
über.

7.2 The dative case is used for the object of the following prepositions, when the verb in the clause indicates the location of the object:

an	next to, on	**über**	over
auf	on (top of)	**unter**	under
hinter	behind	**vor**	in front of
in	in(side of)	**zwischen**	between
neben	next to, beside		

Es steht vor dem Hause.   It stands in front of the house.
Er ging zwischen mir und ihr.   He walked between me and her.

(b) *VERBS*

7.3 The dative case is used with certain verbs which have only one object. The most common of these are:

antworten	to answer	**gehören**	to belong to
befehlen	to order	**glauben**	to believe
begegnen	to meet	**helfen**	to help
danken	to thank	**passen**	to fit
dienen	to serve	**schaden**	to harm
drohen	to threaten	**scheinen**	to seem to
folgen	to follow	**trauen**	to trust
gehorchen	to obey	**trotzen**	to spite

Ich antwortete ihm ruhig.   I answered him calmly.

[1] **Entgegen** — *toward* and **gegenüber** — *opposite* are adverbial prepositions governing the dative. They follow the word they govern.

Er wohnt der Schule gegenüber.   He lives opposite the school.
Sie lief ihm entgegen.   She ran toward him.

7.4 Also common, but impersonal and (generally) translated idiomatically, are:

to be pleasing to

einfallen	to occur	**gelingen**	to succeed
fehlen	to lack	**geschehen**	to happen to
gefallen	to like	**mangeln**	to want for
Er gefällt ihr nicht.		She does not like him.	
Es gelang mir zweimal.		I succeeded in doing it twice.	
Es geschieht dir recht.		It serves you right.	

(c) *ADJECTIVES*

7.5 The dative case is used with certain adjectives. The most common of these are:

ähnlich	similar	**gleich**	like
angenehm	pleasant	**leicht**	easy
bekannt	known (to)	**möglich**	possible
böse	angry (with)	**nützlich**	useful
dankbar	grateful (to)	**treu**	true, faithful (to)
fremd	strange (to)	**verwandt**	related
Ist sie mir böse?		Is she angry with me?	
Ich bin dir dankbar.		I am grateful to you.	

Note that these adjectives follow the words they govern in German, but not in English.

(d) *OTHER CONSTRUCTIONS*

7.6 The dative case is also used in place of a possessive genitive, especially when referring to parts of the body or clothing.

Er sah dem Mädchen ins Gesicht.   He looked the girl in the face.

7.7 Time expressions often include prepositions governing the dative.

Er kommt am Abend (im Frühling).   He is coming in the evening (in spring).

BASIC PATTERNS

„Wir wollen alle besser leben," *resolved* ertönte es im Radio, als Herr Müller seinen Apparat auf dem Wege ins Büro einstellte. *tuned in* „Wir möchten gerne besser essen. Wir möchten uns besser kleiden und besser wohnen." Herr

43

Müller war sofort ganz Ohr und nickte dem Redner im Rundfunk zu, als dieser fortfuhr: „Aber ein Volk kann nur mehr verbrauchen, wenn es mehr erzeugt. Denn alles, was verbraucht werden soll, muß erst erzeugt wer-
5 den. Aber auf welche Weise können wir mehr erzeugen? Es gibt nur einen Weg, die Erzeugung zu erhöhen. Wenn wir die Erzeugung erhöhen wollen, müssen wir die Art der Produktion verbessern. Wir müssen mit bessern Maschinen und Werkzeugen arbeiten. Wir müssen die
10 Arbeit richtig einteilen und die besten Erfindungen benutzen. Dann werden wir mehr erzeugen können und auch mehr verbrauchen.

Dieser Gedankengang," erklärte der Redner, „wird eindeutig bewiesen durch die Erfahrung. Seit 150 Jahren
15 sind die Arbeitsverfahren ständig verbessert worden, und der Wohlstand ist seit dieser Zeit gewaltig gestiegen. Wir Deutsche verbrauchen dreimal soviel Fleisch, dreißigmal mehr Zucker, viermal soviel Bier, zwanzigmal soviel Baumwolle und Wolle. Es geht uns also wirtschaftlich
20 viel besser als unseren Urgroßeltern.

Aber wir dürfen nie glauben," mahnte der Redner seine Zuhörer, als Herr Müller seinen Wagen schon parkte und im Begriffe war, den Apparat auszuschalten, „wir dürfen nie glauben, daß eine bessere wirtschaftliche Lage
25 genügt, um die Menschen glücklich zu machen. Die Zufriedenheit hängt auch von andern Dingen ab. Der Mensch will seine seelischen Kräfte betätigen. Er will mit Freunden wandern, lachen und sich freuen und es am Feierabend behaglich haben."

Questions

1. Wann stellte Herr Müller seinen Apparat ein? 2. Wen hörte er im Radio? 3. Worüber sprach der Redner? 4. Wovon, sagte er, hängt der Verbrauch ab? 5. Wie wollte er die Erzeugung erhöhen? 6. Auf welche Güter kam er zu sprechen? 7. Seit wann, fragte er, sind die Arbeitsverfahren ständig verbessert worden? 8. Wie ist der Verbrauch seit damals gestiegen? 9. Wogegen warnte der Redner? 10. Wozu riet er? 11. Womit schloß er? 12. Was tat Herr Müller mit dem Wagen?

Idiomatic Expressions

jemand } *geht*
niemand } *s*

im Radio (*or* Rundfunk)	on the radio
ganz Ohr	all ears
es gibt (*acc.*)	there is (*or* are)
auf dem Wege	on the way
auf welche Weise	in what way
es geht mir besser	I am better (off)
im Begriffe sein	to be on the point of
jemandem zunicken	to nod to someone
abhängen von (*dat.*)	to depend on
(den) Liebhabereien nachgehen	to indulge in (*or* pursue) hobbies
am Feierabend	after work

EXERCISES

A. Use the above idioms to complete the following sentences.

1. Was sangt ihr . . . nach Hause? 2. Sie sagt, daß es von dir . . . 3. Ich hörte es . . . 4. Ich bin . . ., ihn anzurufen. 5. So etwas . . . hier nicht. 6. Es geht ihm . . . als seinem Bruder. 7. Als er sprach, war sie . . . 8. Am Wochenende geht er . . . 9. Ich weiß nicht, . . . wir mehr erzeugen können. 10. Ist er . . . immer so müde? 11. Die junge Dame hat ihm . . .

B. Include in each sentence below one of the prepositional phrases in the dative: *auf dem Lande, zu Hause, im Sommer, im Radio, im Garten, im Wagen, auf der Straße, im Winter, in Europa, von Baumwolle, bei der Arbeit, am Gehsieig.* EXAMPLE: Der Mann hieß Müller. Der Mann im Wagen hieß Müller.

1. Herr Müller stellte seinen Apparat ein. 2. Der Redner war sofort ganz Ohr. 3. Alle Menschen wollen mehr essen. 4. Frauen möchten sich besser kleiden. 5. Ein Volk kann dreimal soviel Güter verbrauchen. 6. Die Erzeugung hängt von bessern Maschinen ab. 7. Die Arbeitsverfahren werden ständig verbessert. 8. Wir müssen die Arbeit richtig einteilen. 9. Ein Mann will seinen Liebhabereien nachgehen. 10. Der Mensch will seine Kräfte betätigen. 11. Herr Müller parkte nachher seinen Wagen.

C. Form a brief sentence including a negative with each one of the following verbs: *antworten, begegnen, danken, drohen,* *folgen, gehören, glauben, helfen, schaden, gefallen, gelingen, zuhören, zunicken.* EXAMPLE: Sie antwortet mir nicht.

D. Use the following pairs as subject and object in sentences with: *bekannt, böse, dankbar, fremd, treu.* EXAMPLE: Der kleine Mann war dem Polizisten sofort verdächtig.

die junge Dame	der alte Mann
die kluge Frau	der berühmte Herr
der alte Soldat	der gute König
der neue Dichter	der dicke Lehrer
das große Buch	der fleißige Schüler

Composition

1. On the way to the office Mr. Müller was all ears when the speaker on the radio said: "We all want to live better. 2. We [should] like to eat more. 3. We [should] like to dress better and live more comfortably. 4. But to have more, we must produce more. 5. To produce more, we need better machines, better tools. 6. We must make use of the best inventions. 7. We must continue to improve our working methods. 8. But we must never believe that these things alone are enough to make man happy. 9. To be content, one must also have time to pursue his hobbies and to relax after work."

Variations

A. Write out in German the answers to the questions based on the first stanza of Uhland's poem, "Der gute Kamerad," reproduced below. **B.** With the aid of these answers rewrite the stanza in simple German prose.

> Ich hatt' einen Kameraden,
> Einen bessern find'st du nit.
> Die Trommel schlug zum Streite,
> Er ging an meiner Seite
> In gleichem Schritt und Tritt.

1. Wer hatte einen Kameraden? 2. Was hatte ich? 3. Wer findet keinen bessern Kameraden? 4. Was findest du nicht? 5. Was schlug? 6. Wozu schlug die Trommel? 7. Wo ging der Kamerad? 8. Wer ging an meiner Seite? 9. Wie ging der Kamerad? 10. Wer ging in gleichem Schritt und Tritt?

Conversation — In der Bank

Herr Meier:	Wechselt man hier amerikanisches Geld?
Bankbeamter:	Jawohl! Womit kann ich dienen?
Herr Meier:	Wie steht der Dollar heute?
Bankbeamter:	Der Kurs steht heute (auf) DM 4,20.
Herr Meier:	Dann möchte ich diesen Reisescheck einlösen.
Bankbeamter:	Gewiß. Unterschreiben Sie bitte hier unten.
Herr Meier:	Könnten Sie mir das Geld in Zwanzigmark-scheinen geben und den Rest in Silber?
Bankbeamter:	Wie Sie wünschen.
Herr Meier:	Nächstens möchte ich auch ein Scheckkonto anlegen.
Bankbeamter:	Dann gehen Sie bitte zu Schalter drei.
Herr Meier:	Besten Dank.
Bankbeamter:	Auf Wiedersehen.

CHAPTER EIGHT

Special Uses of the Accusative

In English and in German the accusative is the case of the direct object (Chapter I). But in German the accusative is also used with certain (a) prepositions, (b) verbs, and (c) adjectives, as well as (d) to express definite time or duration of time.

(a) *PREPOSITIONS*

8.1 The accusative case is always used for the object of certain prepositions. The most common of these are:

bis	until	**gegen**	against, contrary to, toward
durch	through	**ohne**	without
für	for	**um**	about, around

Der Junge lief durch den Wald.   The boy ran through the forest.
Der Apfel ist für mich.   The apple is for me.

8.2 The accusative case is used for the object of the following prepositions, when the verb in the clause indicates to(ward) what place the object is moving:

an	next to, on	**über**	over
auf	on (top of)	**unter**	under
hinter	behind	**vor**	in front of
in	in, into	**zwischen**	between
neben	near, beside		

Er setzte sich zwischen die zwei Mädchen. He sat down between the two girls.

Steck es in deinen Wagen. Put it into your car.

(b) *VERBS*

8.3 Certain verbs take two accusatives in German.

lehren	to teach	**schelten**	to call names
nennen	to call		

Sie nennt mich ihren Freund. She calls me her friend.

Er schalt mich einen Narren. He called me a fool.

Sie lehrte mich das Lied. She taught me the song (*or* She taught the song to me).

(c) *ADJECTIVES OF MEASURE*

8.4 The accusative is used with adjectives denoting extent of measure. The most common of these are:

breit	wide	**lang**	long
dick	thick	**tief**	deep
hoch	high		

Das Brett ist einen Zoll dick und einen Fuß breit.
The board is an inch thick and a foot wide.

(d) *DEFINITE TIME AND EXTENT OF TIME*

8.5 The accusative is used to denote definite time and extent of time, as in the following instances:

Ich habe ihn letzten Monat besucht. I visited him last month.

Es dauerte den ganzen Tag. It lasted all day.

Heute haben wir den dreizehnten Mai. Today is the thirteenth of May.

8.6 The accusative is also used to indicate the date in the heading of a letter.

Freitag, den (*or* d.) 16. Juni 1959 Friday, June 16, 1959

48

Berufsschüler an der Werkbank. Die Berufsschulen geben den jungen Leuten eine gründliche Ausbildung in ihrem Gewerbe.

BASIC PATTERNS

Frau Müller hatte in München eine Tante väterlicherseits, die eigentlich Irma Weiß hieß. Jedoch jeder nannte sie Tante Ida. Tante Ida war die Witwe eines Generals und in den Siebzigern. Sie lebte allein in der
5 großen Stadt und war noch ganz rüstig, nur wurde sie von Tag zu Tag schwerhöriger. Ihre Verwandten machten sich deshalb große Sorgen um sie und brüllten ihr endlich eines Tages mit vereinten Kräften ins Ohr: „Tante Ida, geh doch einmal zum Arzt."
10 Diese ließ sich das nicht zweimal sagen. Sie nickte und ging schon am nächsten Tage zu einem Facharzt. Dort setzte sie sich in das Wartezimmer, das glücklicherweise leer war, nahm ihr Strickzeug heraus und fing bald an zu stricken. Jedoch der Doktor ließ lange auf sich
15 warten.

Nach einiger Zeit kam die Frau des Doktors in das Wartezimmer und sagte zu Tante Ida, ihr Mann habe heute leider keine Sprechstunde. Doch die schwerhörige Frau Generalin verstand kein Wort. Sie nickte nur
20 freundlich, lächelte die Frau Doktor an und strickte munter weiter. Der Frau Doktor half auch kein Schreien. Zehn Minuten später war sie stockheiser, aber die gute Tante Ida strickte ruhig weiter.

Voller Verzweiflung nahm da endlich die Frau Dok-
25 tor einen Bleistift und ein Blatt Papier und schrieb darauf: „Heute keine Sprechstunde." Tante Ida nahm den Zettel, den ihr die Frau Doktor reichte, besah ihn und gab ihn dann freundlich lächelnd der Frau Doktor zurück. „Ach, Frau Doktor," sagte sie zu ihr, „lesen Sie mir das doch
30 bitte vor. Ich habe meine Brille vergessen."

Questions

1. Wer war Tante Ida? 2. Wie alt war sie? 3. Wo wohnte Tante Ida? 4. Warum hatten ihre Verwandten Sorgen um sie? 5. Zu wem schickten sie die Verwandten? 6. Was tat die Tante im Wartezimmer? 7. Was sagte die Frau des Arztes zur Generalin? 8. Warum verstand

Tante Ida die Frau des Arztes nicht? 9. Was versuchte die Frau des Arztes dann? 10. Was schrieb die Frau Doktor auf den Zettel? 11. Warum gab Tante Ida der Frau des Arztes den Zettel zurück? 12. Wo hatte Tante Ida ihre Brille vergessen? 13. Warum war die Frau des Arztes jetzt verzweifelt?

Idiomatic Expressions

in den Siebzigern	in her (or his) seventies
von Tag zu Tag	from day to day
sich Sorgen machen	to be concerned about
es sich nicht zweimal sagen lassen	not to wait to be told twice
(sie) auf sich warten lassen	to keep (her) waiting
Sprechstunde haben	to have office hours
es hilft mir nichts	it avails me nothing
voller Verzweiflung	in desperation
jemandem vorlesen	to read to someone

EXERCISES

A. Substitute the suggested words for the words in heavy type, and insert one of the following adjectives: *dick, schlank, alt, groß, hoch, jung, schön, lang, heftig.*

1. Die **Alte** ist in den Siebzigern. (Onkel, Frau, Fräulein) 2. Das ließ der **Junge** sich nicht zweimal sagen. (Lehrer, Bäuerin, Mädchen) 3. Sie macht sich Sorgen um ihre **Mutter**. (Vater, Tochter, Kind) 4. Der Arzt hatte keine **Sprechstunde**. (Antwort, Wagen, Geld) 5. Es half ihr kein **Schreien**. (Weinen, Mensch, Lüge) 6. Voller Verzweiflung rief sie den **Arzt** an. (Bruder, Mutter, Amt) 7. Das **Loch** wird von Tag zu Tag größer. (Baum, Schuld, Zahl) 8. Das Mädchen las der Mutter das **Gedicht** vor. (Geschichte, Märchen, Satz) 9. Der **Arzt** ließ lange auf sich warten. (Patientin, Kranke, Paar)

B. Use the suggested words or phrases to complete the sentences.

1. Der Junge lief mit . . . (Ball, Kind, Katze) 2. Die Frau lief durch . . . (Wald, Haus, Schule) 3. Der Schüler lief vor . . . (Wagen, Frau, Mädchen) 4. Das Kind lief in . . . (Haus, Schule, Garten) 5. Der Lehrer lehrte mich . . . (Lied, Name, Aufgabe) 6. Die Tante nannte mich . . . (Freund, Feindin, Kind) 7. Das

Loch war ... (Meter tief) 8. Der Baum war ... (Fuß hoch)
9. Der Stamm war ... (Zoll dick) 10. Sie wartete ... (ganze
Stunde, ganzer Tag, letztes Jahr)

C. Use the suggested words in the right-hand column to
form compounds like the words in the left-hand column.

väterlicherseits	Mutter
Siebziger	acht
Strickzeug	nähen
Wartezimmer	vor
glücklicherweise	vorsichtig
Sprechstunde	Abend
Bleistift	rot
Facharzt	Zahn

D. Form sentences with the new compounds in C.

E. Use each of the following accusatives in a German sentence beginning with an adverb: *eine Tante, sie, große Sorgen,
ins Ohr, in das Wartezimmer, keine Sprechstunde, einen Bleistift,
den Zettel, ihn, meine Brille.*

F. Derive verbs from: *Tag, Strickzeug, Sprache, Schrei,
Bitte, Gang, Leid, Hilfe, Ruhe, Blatt, Sage.* EXAMPLE: Blatt
— blättern.

G. Use each of the new verbs in F in a German sentence
with a negative.

H. Supply the appropriate forms of *ihr, Ihr, dein, euer.*

1. Gib es (*to her*)! 2. Ist es (*her*) Buch? 3. Ist das (*your*)
Buch, Herr Braun? 4. War es (*your*) Bruder, Karl? 5. Sind das
(*your*) Bleistifte, Kinder?

I. Explain in German: *schwerhörig, Wartezimmer, Strickzeug, Facharzt, stockheiser.* EXAMPLE: Ein stockheiserer Mensch
ist sehr heiser.

Composition

1. Mrs. Müller's aunt lived in Munich. 2. Although her
name was Irma, everybody called her Aunt Ida. 3. Aunt Ida was
in her seventies and getting harder‿of‿hearing every day. 4. One

day she therefore went to a specialist. 5. She sat down in his waiting room and began to knit. 6. After some time the wife of the doctor saw her in the waiting room and told her that her husband had no office hours (on) that day. 7. But Aunt Ida did not hear her. 8. She merely smiled and kept on knitting. 9. In desperation the wife of the doctor took a sheet of paper and wrote on it: "No office hours today." 10. Aunt Ida looked at the paper, but she handed it right back to the wife of the doctor. 11. Then she said: "Won't you please read that to me? 12. I forgot my glasses."

Variations

A. Write out in German the answers to the questions based on the second stanza of Uhland's poem, "Der gute Kamerad," reproduced below. **B.** With the aid of these answers rewrite the stanza in simple German prose.

> Eine Kugel kam geflogen:
> Gilt es mir oder gilt es dir?
> Ihn hat es weggerissen,
> Er liegt mir vor den Füßen,
> Als wär's ein Stück von mir.

1. Was kam geflogen? 2. Wo war die Kugel? 3. Wem galt die Kugel? 4. Wem galt die Kugel nicht? 5. Wen hat sie weggerissen? 6. Wo liegt der Kamerad? 7. Wer liegt mir vor den Füßen? 8. Wer steht auf den Füßen? 9. Was für ein Kamerad ist er?

Conversation — In einer fremden Stadt

Herr Bürger:	Herr Wachtmeister! Verzeihen Sie, führt diese Straße zum Karlsplatz?
Schutzmann:	Nein. Dies ist die Ludwigstraße.
Herr Bürger:	Wie komme ich bitte zum Karlsplatz?
Schutzmann:	Gehen Sie geradeaus bis zum Odeonsplatz, dann zwei Straßen rechts.
Herr Bürger:	Wie weit ist das zu Fuß?
Schutzmann:	Etwa zwei Kilometer.
Herr Bürger:	Kann ich mit der Straßenbahn hin?

Schutzmann:	Ja. Aber Sie müssen dann einmal umsteigen.
Herr Bürger:	Fährt der Autobus direkt?
Schutzmann:	Ja. Die nächste Haltestelle ist dort drüben an der Litfaßsäule.
Herr Bürger:	Danke vielmals.
Schutzmann:	Bitte.

CHAPTER NINE

The **der-***Words and* **ein-***Words*

Aside from descriptive adjectives (Chapters XVII and XVIII), there are so-called **der**-words and **ein**-words which delimit or restrict in some way the nouns they modify.

(a) **der-***WORDS*

9.1 In essence, **der**-words are declined like the definite article (Appendix I), and like the definite article they agree in gender, number, and case with nouns they modify. The **der**-words are:

dieser	this	**mancher**	many a; *pl.* some
jeder	each	**solcher**	such
jener	that	**welcher**	which, what

9.2 The **der**-words may be used as limiting adjectives,[1] as

Dieser Lehrer heißt Herr Braun.
This teacher is called Mr. Braun.

9.3 The **der**-words may also be used as pronouns, in which case they are usually followed in the singular by the word *one* in English translation, as

Ich ziehe diesen vor, aber er mag jenen.
I prefer this one, but he likes that one.

[1] Note that **manch, solch,** and **welch** are not declined when they precede an indefinite article. On the other hand, **jeder** and **solcher** are declined like descriptive adjectives when they follow an indefinite article.

Einen solchen Mann brauche ich nicht.	A man such as that I don't need.
Solch einen Mann brauche ich nicht.	Such a man I don't need.

9.4 As pronouns, referring to a more distant antecedent, **dieser** and **jener** are often translated as *the latter* and *the former*.

Ein Mann stand vor dem Hause, und ein Mann stand dahinter.	One man stood in front of the house and one man stood in back of it.
Dieser trug einen braunen Anzug, jener einen schwarzen.	The latter wore a brown suit, the former a black one.

(b) ein-*WORDS*

9.5 The **ein**-words are declined like the indefinite article in the singular and like the definite article in the plural (Appendix II), and like the articles they agree in gender, number, and case with the nouns they modify. The **ein**-words are: **ein** — *one*, **kein** — *no(one)*, and the possessives:

mein	my	**unser**	our
dein	your (*fam. sg.*)	**euer**	your (*fam. pl.*)
sein	his, its	**ihr**	their
ihr	her	**Ihr**	your (*pol. sg., pl.*)

9.6 The **ein**-words may be used as limiting adjectives, as

Mein Lehrer heißt Herr Braun.
My teacher is called Mr. Braun.

9.7 The **ein**-words may be used as predicate adjectives, without endings, except **ihr** and **Ihr,** which add **der**-endings that agree with the antecedent.

Das Buch ist mein.	That book is mine.
Der Bleistift ist ihrer.	That pencil is hers.
Dieses Haus ist ihres.	This house is theirs.

9.8 The **ein**-words may also be used as pronouns in which case they agree with their antecedents like **der**-words, i.e. by adding –**er** in the nominative singular masculine, and –**es** in the nominative and accusative singular neuter. (In the remaining cases they add the endings of the **ein**-word.)

Ich habe seinen Bleistift. Haben Sie meinen?	I have his pencil. Do you have mine?
Das ist mein Bleistift. Jener ist seiner.	This is my pencil. That one is his.

9.9 As indefinite pronouns, **ein** and **kein** also add the endings of the **der**-word.

Keiner ist so dumm.   Nobody is that stupid.

BASIC PATTERNS

Dr. med. Kraus war Herrn Müllers Neffe. Er war noch Junggeselle und befand sich eines Tages unter Kollegen bei einer Geburtstagsfeier. Bei dieser ging es hoch her. Ein Wort entlockte das andere, ein Glas folgte
5 dem anderen. Es war schon weit über Mitternacht, als der Doktor aufbrach. Er schwankte etwas — nicht viel, wie er meinte. Er sang vor sich hin — nicht laut, wie er glaubte. Und er lachte hin und wieder über die Witze, die er eben gehört hatte.
10 Zu Hause warf er sich müde in einen Sessel und kämpfte schon mit dem Schlaf, als das Telefon läutete, laut und herrisch. Gewohnheitsmäßig griff er nach dem Hörer. „Doktor Kraus," meldete er sich und nahm Haltung an. „Was?" rief er ins Telefon. „Da . . . Da
15 . . . Darmkolik? Ich ko . . . ko . . . komme . . ." Die Pflicht, die eiserne Pflicht rief ihn. Er ging in die Küche, setzte eine Flasche Sprudel an den Mund und hielt seinen dumpf surrenden Schädel unter den kalten Wasserstrahl. „Ich bin nüchtern . . . ich bin nüchtern . . . ich
20 bin nüchtern . . . ," versicherte er sich. Dann ging der Doktor, ganz aufrecht, zur Patientin.

„Zum Teufel, ich bin doch nicht nüchtern!" schimpfte er aber, als er über die Schwelle ins Haus seiner alten Patientin stolperte. „Ich bin blau, ganz schön blau."
25 Doch nahm er wieder Haltung an und trat aufrecht ans Bett seiner Dauerpatientin. Dort setzte er sich. Die Kranke sah er wie in weiter Ferne und griff dreimal vorbei, als er ihr den Puls fühlen wollte.

„Der verdammte Alkohol," murmelte er deshalb
30 ärgerlich vor sich hin, leise — wie er meinte. „Um Gottes willen!" jammerte da das ältliche Fräulein. „Verraten Sie doch bitte nichts, Herr Doktor. Ich war bei einer Geburtstagsfeier."

56

Questions

1. Wo traf sich Dr. Kraus eines Tages mit seinen Kollegen? 2. Was taten sie bei der Geburtstagsfeier? 3. Wie verließ Dr. Kraus die Feier? 4. Was tat er, als er nach Hause kam? 5. Warum griff er dann nach dem Hörer? 6. Wie wollte er nüchtern werden? 7. Warum stolperte er aber bei der Patientin über die Schwelle? 8. Was murmelte er, als er sich an ihr Bett setzte? 9. Was meinte er damit? 10. Was bedeuteten die Worte für die Patientin?

Idiomatic Expressions

bei einer Feier sein	to be at a party (*or* celebration)
es geht hoch her	spirits run high
weit über	way past
blau sein	to be tipsy
hin und wieder	now and again
lachen über (*acc.*)	to laugh about
greifen nach (*dat.*)	to reach for
Haltung annehmen	to brace up
an den Mund setzen	to put to one's lips
treten an (*acc.*)	to step up to
vor sich (*dat.*) hinmurmeln	to mumble to oneself

EXERCISES

A. Rewrite the Basic Patterns in the first person of the present tense.

B. (1) Substitute the suggested words for the words in heavy type. (2) Substitute one of the following nouns for the nouns which the **der-** or **ein-**words modify: *Gesellschaft, Vater, Mantel, Zeitung, Tochter.*

1. Ich war auf **dieser** Geburtstagsfeier. (jener, jeder) 2. Auf **dieser** ging es hoch her. (welcher, kein) 3. **Mein** Neffe rief mich hin und wieder. (dein, euer) 4. Sie lachten nicht über **ihren** Hut. (mein, dieser) 5. Er griff nach **solchen** Büchern. (mancher, unser) 6. **Ihr** Sohn nimmt Haltung an. (ein solcher, sein) 7. Sie trat an **meinen** Tisch. (jeder, dieser) 8. **Unsere** Sitzung dauert weit über Mitternacht. (jener, kein) 9. Er stellte die Flasche immer wieder auf **den** Tisch. (ihr, Ihr) 10. Ich sah **seine** Tante hin und wieder. (euer, ihr) 11. Der Bleistift ist **ihrer**. (mein,

dein) 12. Haben Sie **meinen**? (ihr, sein) 13. **Einer** von ihnen war doch so dumm. (kein, welcher) 14. Stellt man **eine solche** Frage? (solch ein, so ein)

C. Use in a sentence each of the components and at least five of the compounds of:

jung	Geselle	auf	recht
Geburt	Tag	drei	Mal
Wasser	Strahl	auf	brechen
Dauer	Patientin	Gewohnheit	mäßig

D. Complete the sentences by filling in the blank spaces.

1. Ich war —— einer Geburtstagsfeier. 2. Dort ging es —— her. 3. Es war weit —— Mitternacht. 4. Hin und —— sang er ein Lied. 5. Die anderen lachten —— ihn. 6. Da nahm er Haltung ——. 7. Er griff —— dem Hut. 8. Er setzte eine Flasche Sprudel an den ——. 9. Sie murmelte leise —— sich hin. 10. Dann trat er —— das Bett der Patientin.

E. Substitute the suggested **ein**-words for the words in heavy type.

1. Es ist der Bleistift **des** Neffen. (sein, ihr, unser) 2. Herr Müller half **dem** Onkel. (mein, dein, euer) 3. Er kennt **den** Arzt. (ihr, Ihr, kein) 4. Er warf sich in **einen** Sessel. (dein, Ihr, mein) 5. Er stolperte ins Haus **der** Patientin. (sein, dein, ihr)

F. (1) Rephrase the sentences with *richtete sich auf, nahm . . . ab, noch ledig, setzte sich, bei Freunden, ins Haus, lustig zu, wach, sehr gebeugt, ab und zu.* (2) Change the sentences into questions introduced by *warum.*

1. Er war Junggeselle. 2. Er befand sich unter Kameraden. 3. Es ging hoch her. 4. Er warf sich auf das Bett. 5. Sie lachte hin und wieder. 6. Wir gingen in die Küche. 7. Er griff nach dem Hörer. 8. Ich bin schon müde. 9. Das Mädchen ging ganz aufrecht. 10. Der Arzt nahm Haltung an.

G. Substitute one of the following subjects in sentences 1, 2, 4, 5, 6, 7, 9, 10 in F: *der Neffe des Herrn Müller, die Patientin des Arztes, die Kinder der Frau, der junge Dr. Kraus, der müde Arzt, der Patient.*

H. Discuss (a) **Eine Geburtstagsfeier** or (b) **Die Pflicht ruft.**

58

Composition

1. Mr. Müller's nephew lived alone. 2. His name was Dr. Kraus. 3. Dr. Kraus was still a bachelor. 4. One day he was at a birthday party. 5. Spirits ran high and it was way past midnight when he came home. 6. Although he was very tired, he answered the telephone. 7. A patient was calling. 8. "I'll come right away," he said to the patient. 9. But his head was spinning. 10. He stumbled over the threshold. 11. Yet he went. 12. "That cursed alcohol," he mumbled softly — (as) he thought — when he sat down by the bed of the patient. 13. But the patient heard him. 14. "You won't tell anyone, Doctor," she wailed. 15. "I was at a birthday party."

Variations

A. Write out in German the answers to the questions based on the third stanza of Uhland's poem, "Der gute Kamerad," reproduced below. **B.** With the aid of these answers rewrite the stanza in simple German prose.

Will mir die Hand noch reichen,
Derweil ich eben lad':
,,Kann dir die Hand nicht geben,
Bleib' du im ew'gen Leben
Mein guter Kamerad!"

1. Wer will mir die Hand reichen? 2. Was will der Kamerad mir reichen? 3. Wann will er mir die Hand reichen? 4. Wann lade ich? 5. Was kann ich nicht tun? 6. Wem kann ich die Hand nicht geben? 7. Wo soll der Kamerad bleiben? 8. Wer soll das ewige Leben haben? 9. Wer stirbt? 10. Wessen Kamerad ist er?

Conversation — An der Tankstelle

Tankwart:	Guten Tag! Womit kann ich dienen?
Herr Müller:	Füllen Sie den Tank (auf), bitte! (*or* Zwanzig Liter Benzin, bitte!)
Tankwart:	(Füllt auf.) Soll ich den Ölstand prüfen?
Herr Müller:	Ja, bitte. Sehen Sie auch nach, ob genug Wasser im Kühler (und in der Batterie) ist.

Tankwart:	(Sieht nach.) Das Wasser ist in Ordnung. Sie brauchen aber etwa zwei Liter Öl. Nehmen Sie schwer, mittel oder leicht?
Herr Müller:	Mittelschwer, bitte. Und möchten Sie auch die Reifen nachprüfen?
Tankwart:	Gerne. Wollen Sie den Wagen zur Luftpumpe fahren.
Herr Müller:	(Wartet und fragt:) Alles in Ordnung?
Tankwart:	Jawohl. Das macht 26 Mark 50 Pfennig.
Herr Müller:	(Zahlt.) Danke.
Tankwart:	(Ich) danke Ihnen. Auf Wiedersehn.

CHAPTER TEN

Personal, Impersonal, and Indefinite Pronouns

As in English, pronouns in German are words which are used in place of nouns.

(a) PERSONAL PRONOUNS

10.1 By and large, personal pronouns (Appendix VI) are used in German as they are used in English.[1]

Ich traf ihn im Konzert und ging mit ihm nach Hause.
I met him at the concert and went home with him.

They differ in usage in the two languages in the following ways:

10.2 In German (the second person singular) **du** is used to address in familiar terms one member, and (the second person plural) **ihr** several members of the family, relatives, children, and close friends called by first names. **Ihr** may be used to address a mixed group of friends and strangers, although **Sie** (the capital-

---

[1] As is the genitive case of masculine and neuter nouns in general, so is the genitive of personal pronouns also falling into literary disuse.

Herr, gedenke meiner.   Lord, remember me.
Es waren ihrer drei.   There were three of them.

ized form of the third person plural) is preferred. **Sie** is always used to address one or several persons with whom one is not on familiar terms.

Warst du auch im Konzert, Fritz? Were you too at the concert, Fritz?
Waren Sie auch dort, Herr Braun? Were you too there, Mr. Braun?

10.3 Since natural and grammatical genders do not always coincide, the personal pronouns of the third person singular (**er, sie, es**) must agree in gender and number with the nouns to which they refer. Their function in the sentence determines their case.

> Ich sah den Bleistift, aber er nahm ihn.
> I saw the pencil, but he took it.

10.4 Following a preposition governing the dative or the accusative, a pronoun which refers to a thing or state, an idea or action in a preceding clause is replaced by a compound of **da(r)** + preposition, as *thereon* in English.

Er nahm den Bleistift und schrieb damit.
He took the pencil and wrote with it (therewith).
Er sah die Bank und setzte sich darauf.
He saw the bench and sat down on it (thereon).

10.5 Following a preposition governing the genitive, forms of the demonstrative **derselbe** or **der**-compounds are commonly substituted instead of **da**-compounds.

Dann folgte eine Pause. Während derselben (*or* Währenddessen) rauchte er eine Zigarette.
Then a pause followed. During it he smoked a cigarette.

(b) *IMPERSONAL PRONOUN*

10.6 At the beginning of a sentence, **es,** meaning *there*, is frequently used as an introductory or anticipatory subject without regard to the gender or number of the actual subject following.

Es lebte ein König in Sachsen . . . There lived a king in Saxony . . .

10.7 If a subject, introduced by **es,** is definite, it follows **sein** in the nominative.

Es ist ein Schüler in der Klasse . . . There is one pupil in the class . . .
Es sind wenigstens zehn Leute . . . There are at least ten people . . .

Note that the **es** is omitted when the word order is changed.

Wenigstens zehn Leute sind da. At least ten people are here.

61

In the idiomatic phrase, **es gibt**, meaning *there is* or *there are*, **es** generally introduces an indefinite object which is in the accusative.

Es gibt solche Leute.   There are such people.

Es sind and **es gibt** are often confused in colloquial speech, as in

Es gab (*actually* waren) damals nur zwei Ärzte in der Stadt.
There were then only two doctors in town.

10.8 At the beginning of a sentence, **es** (meaning *it* in the singular, *they* in the plural) is used as the impersonal subject of the auxiliary verb **sein** without regard to the gender or the number of the noun following.

Es ist mein Apfel.   It is my apple.
Es ist deine Frau.   It is your wife.
Es ist ihr Wagen.   It is her car.
Es sind meine Bücher.   They are my books.

Note that **das** and **dies** are often used instead of **es**.

Dies sind meine Bücher.   These are my books.

10.9 **Es**, meaning *it*, may be the subject of an impersonal verb.

Es regnete gestern.   It rained yesterday.

10.10 In an idiomatic sense, the impersonal **es**, may also be used as the subject of many verbs requiring the dative, as **es fehlt mir nichts, es gefällt mir, es hilft mir, es gelingt mir, es geschieht mir,** etc.

Es hilft ihm nichts.   Nothing helps (avails) him.

These dative verbs are used without the impersonal **es**, when the sentence or clause begins with another part of speech.

Mir hilft nichts.
Nichts hilft mir.   Nothing helps me.
Hilft mir nichts?   Doesn't anything help me?

(c) INDEFINITE PRONOUNS

10.11 In addition to **einer** and **keiner** (Chapter IX), the indefinite pronouns in German are:

(et)was	something	**jemand**	somebody
nichts	nothing	**niemand**	nobody
man	one, they, you	**jedermann**	everybody

10.12 **Etwas** and **nichts** are indeclinable. **Jemand** and **niemand** may be declined. However, they are ordinarily declined only in the genitive, as is **jedermann** by adding –(e)s. **Man** itself is not declined. In the dative and accusative **einem** and **einen** are used in its place.

Jemand war hier, aber nichts ist fertig.	Somebody was here, but nothing is ready.
Man kann nie wissen, was einem zustößt.	You never know, what will happen (to you).

BASIC PATTERNS

Der Frühling stand schon vor der Tür, als Frau Müller endlich den Entschluß faßte, sich doch einen neuen Hut zu kaufen. Sie war ja letztes Jahr leer ausgegangen.

Herr Müller machte gerne mit, und Frau Müller fand schon im ersten Hutgeschäft in der Ringstraße viele   5
Hüte, die ihr auf den ersten Blick gefielen und die zu ihrem neuen Jackenkleid auch passen mochten. Als sie die Hüte aber aufprobierte, fand sie an jedem etwas auszusetzen. An dem einen gefiel ihr das Material nicht. Einen Strohhut wollte sie nicht. An den anderen waren   10
die Krempen zu breit oder zu schmal. Manche Hüte schienen ihr zu jugendlich. In manchen sah sie zu alt aus. Die einen hatten zu viele Bänder, die anderen zu viele Blumen oder zu viel Verzierung. Gefiel ihr ein Hut doch, so war er zu teuer. Die billigen waren ihr zu ge-   15
wöhnlich. Auch Gelegenheitskäufe wies sie dankend zurück, weil sie eben nicht die neueste Mode waren.

Im zweiten Geschäft um die Ecke war alles vornehmer. Das merkte man schon an den Preisen. Auch war die Auswahl viel größer. Hier probierte Frau Müller   20
vierunddreißig Hüte auf, bis sie endlich einen fand, den sie nehmen wollte. ,,Wunderhübsch,'' flüsterte sie nun aufatmend der geduldigen Verkäuferin zu. ,,Findest du nicht auch?'' fragte sie Herrn Müller. ,,Den schicken Sie mir bitte ins Haus.''   25

63

Erst die Arbeit, dann das Spiel.

„Sofort . . . meine Dame. Selbstverständlich," nickte das Fräulein erstaunt. „Wir tun alles für unsere Kunden. Nur darf ich Sie darauf aufmerksam machen, daß dies der Hut ist, den Sie aufhatten, als Sie hereinkamen . . ."

Questions

1. Welchen Entschluß faßte Frau Müller im Frühling? 2. Warum wollte sie einen neuen Hut haben? 3. Wie ging sie dabei zu Werke? 4. In welchem Geschäft gefielen ihr viele Hüte schon auf den ersten Blick? 5. Doch wie viele kaufte sie da? 6. Was fand sie an diesen Hüten auszusetzen? 7. Wie viele Hüte probierte Frau Müller im zweiten Geschäft auf? 8. Welcher Hut gefiel ihr da am besten? 9. Welchen ließ sie sich ins Haus schicken? 10. Was sagte dazu die Verkäuferin? 11. Wen überraschte das wohl am meisten?

Idiomatic Expressions

vor der Tür stehen	to be just around the corner
den Entschluß fassen	to make up one's mind
leer ausgehen	to go empty-handed
mitmachen	to be game, to go along
auf den ersten Blick	on first sight
es gefällt mir	I like it
es paßt zu meinem Hut	it matches my hat
er setzt an mir immer etwas aus	he always finds fault with me (*or* something to criticize about me)
es sagt mir zu	it suits my taste
einem anmerken	to tell by looking at a person
findest du nicht auch	don't you think so too
ins Haus schicken	to (have) deliver(ed)
aufmerksam machen auf (*acc.*)	to call attention to

EXERCISES

(A) Change the figurative sentences to the present tense and the literal sentences to the past perfect tense.

1. Der Frühling stand vor der Tür. Der Mann stand vor der Tür.

2. Ich habe seine Hand gefaßt. Ich habe einen Entschluß gefaßt.

3. Sie ist wieder leer ausge-   Sie ist wieder hungrig ausgegangen.   gangen.
4. Machten Sie beim Spiel mit?   Machten Sie die Aufgabe mit?
5. Fanden Sie die Antwort gut?   Fanden Sie das neue Buch?

B. Form sentences in which the expressions in the right- and left-hand columns may be used interchangeably. EXAMPLE: Das Buch gefällt mir nicht. Das Buch mag ich nicht.

auf den ersten Blick	sofort
es gefällt mir	ich mag es
es sagt mir zu	ich habe es gern
aufmerksam machen auf	hinweisen auf
den Entschluß fassen	sich entscheiden

C. Replace all nouns with personal pronouns or their substitutes. EXAMPLE: Die Frau stand im Zimmer. Sie stand darin.

1. Der Mann stand vor der Tür. 2. Frau Müller faßte seine Hand. 3. Das Mädchen kaufte den Hut. 4. Herr Müller machte gerne mit. 5. Die Frau fand Hüte im Hutgeschäft. 6. Das Jackenkleid gefiel der Frau nicht. 7. Dann probierte die Dame die Hüte auf. 8. Den Strohhut wollte die Witwe auch nicht. 9. Der Hut sagte der Tante zu. 10. Im Geschäft probierte die Schwester Hüte auf. 11. Fritz flüsterte dem Vater etwas zu. 12. Kaufleute tun alles für Kunden. 13. Der Mann setzte sich auf die Bank. 14. Der Schüler schrieb mit der Feder.

D. (1) Supply the appropriate anticipatory pronoun subject. (2) Rephrase sentences 2, 4, 5, 10 without it. EXAMPLE: Es ist einer, der sie kennt. Einer kennt sie.

1. —— war einmal ein König. 2. —— lebte eine Frau in der Nähe. 3. —— ist einer, der sie kennt. 4. —— sind wenigstens zehn, die mit ihr sprechen. 5. —— gibt aber auch einige, die sie nicht kennen. 6. —— ist Herrn Müllers Frau. 7. —— ist der vierundzwanzigste Mai. 8. —— donnert jeden Tag. 9. —— geht mir besser. 10. —— half ihm nichts.

E. Supply the appropriate indefinite pronouns and comment, or answer the question. EXAMPLE: Niemand durfte ihr helfen? Nein, keiner durfte ihr helfen.

1. —— wollte sie sehen? 2. —— hilft ihm? 3. Kann ——, wenn man will? 4. Schadet ihm ——? 5. Ist —— mehr

als nichts? 6. Warum will —— es ihm sagen? 7. —— muß es doch wissen! 8. —— weiß er?

F. Answer in complete sentences in German.

Was kauft man . . . im Hutgeschäft, im Schuhladen, in der Drogerie, in der Apotheke, im Zigarrenladen, beim Bäcker, vor der Bank, auf dem Markt?

G. (1) List the verbs of the first two paragraphs in the Basic Patterns. (2) Use each in a sentence in the perfect tense.

Composition

1. It was March when Mrs. Müller decided to buy a new suit. 2. Now spring was almost around the corner. 3. However, she still had no hat. 4. "Are you coming with me?" she asked Mr. Müller. 5. "I must buy a new hat." 6. Mrs. Müller had looked at a number of hats in one store which might go well with her new suit. 7. But she hadn't liked any [of them]. 8. Some were not [in] the latest style. 9. The prettier [ones] were too expensive and the cheap [ones] were too ordinary. 10. Some [of the] hats had too many ribbons. 11. In the second store Mrs. Müller found that the selection was much greater. 12. However, here, too, she had to try on thirty-four hats before she found one which she liked. 13. "This [one] is very pretty," she said to the salesgirl. 14. "Don't you think so?" she asked her husband. 15. "Would you please have this one delivered," she asked the girl. 16. "At once," replied the latter. 17. "May I, however, call to your attention the fact that this is the hat you wore when you came in."

Variations

A. Arrange the words in each line in their proper order.

B. Connect the sentences to form a brief anecdote.

1. ein Patientin eine einmal behandelte alte Arzt berühmter.
2. besser es ging schon ihr.
3. in da fuhr Urlaub Arzt der.
4. besuchen die mußte Patientin daher Arzt anderen einen.
5. schlechter nun immer Patientin der ging es.
6. kurz starb Patientin des die nach Arztes Rückkehr der berühmten.

7. aus da füllte Totenschein dieser wütend den.
8. Rubrik Todesursache in schrieb er die.
9. Ärzte zwei.

Conversation — An der Theaterkasse

Dr. Kempe:	(Steht Schlange. Ist endlich an der Reihe.) Zwei Plätze im ersten Rang, bitte.
Fräulein an der Kasse:	Es tut mir leid. Der erste Rang ist ausverkauft.
Dr. Kempe:	Dann geben Sie mir bitte zwei Plätze im Parkett.
Fräulein an der Kasse:	Siebte Reihe links, oder achte Reihe rechts?
Dr. Kempe:	Haben Sie keine Mittelplätze?
Fräulein an der Kasse:	Nein. Die Vorstellung ist heute fast ganz ausverkauft.
Dr. Kempe:	Dann nehme ich die achte Reihe rechts.
Fräulein an der Kasse:	(Reicht ihm die Karten.) Sie sehen von dort alles sehr gut.
Dr. Kempe:	(Bezahlt.) Danke. Im Notfall habe ich ja auch mein Opernglas. (Eilt mit Susi ins Theater.)

CHAPTER ELEVEN

Demonstrative Adjectives and Pronouns

11.1 Either as adjectives or as pronouns, demonstratives are words which point out or designate.

ADJECTIVES AND PRONOUNS	ADJECTIVES	PRONOUNS
der	this, that	this one, that one
derjenige	the (very)	the (very) one
derselbe	the (very) same	the (very) same one
dieser	this	this one
jener	that	that one

68

11.2 As a demonstrative pronoun, **der** is declined like the relative pronoun **der** (Appendix III), but it is spoken with greater stress. In the genitive plural, however, it has the added form **derer**, which is used when it precedes a relative pronoun.

Nimm einige Äpfel es gibt deren genug

Der gefällt mir nicht.	I don't like that one.
Die Kinder derer, die arm sind . . .	The children of those who are poor . . .

Ee ist ein Freund derer, die ihm helf

11.3 As a demonstrative adjective, **der** is declined, with some exceptions, like the definite article **der** (Appendix I), but it is spoken with greater stress.

Der Mann ist kein Fremder.   That man is no stranger.

11.4 Dieser and **jener** are also declined like the definite article **der** (Appendix I). They may be used as demonstrative pronouns or as adjectives.

Dieser Mann gefällt mir nicht.	I don't like this man.
Gefällt Ihnen jener?	Do you like that one?

11.5 Derjenige and **derselbe** are compounds of the definite article plus an adjective (Appendix IV) and both parts are declined accordingly. They may also be used as pronouns and adjectives.

Derjenige, der es findet, behält es.	The (very) one who finds it keeps it.
Er ist derselbe Mann, der gestern hier war.	He is the (very) same man who was here yesterday.

BASIC PATTERNS

Die Geschichte von Papenbrink wollte Herrn Müller nicht aus dem Sinn. *since* *care* Herr Papenbrink tat alles mit Bedacht, auch wenn ihm ein Mädchen gefiel. Er war immer vorsichtig. *careful* Er holte zuerst Auskunft ein, und ging dann *first made inquiries, and then would go* *on a date* *information office be paid 10 mark in advance* zum Stelldichein. In der Auskunftei zahlte er dann zehn 5 Mark im voraus und, da er seinen eigenen Namen nicht nennen wollte, noch fünf Mark extra. Genau acht Tage später erhielt er dann die gewünschte Auskunft.

„Also es stimmt alles," sagte ihm der Mann vom Auskunftsbüro. „Fräulein Brigitte Hornung ist die 10

Tochter eines Postinspektors. Zur Zeit zählt sie zweiundzwanzig Jahre. Sie besuchte die höhere Handelsschule und ist jetzt bei der Firma Strauß & Co. als Aushilfssekretärin angestellt.

5 „Na ja, das ist alles nicht so wichtig," unterbrach Papenbrink den Mann ungeduldig. „Das habe ich Ihnen ja selbst gesagt. Höchstens das mit dem Alter ... Daß es stimmt, ist mir von Interesse. Aber was ich wissen wollte, das ist ja ... Sie wissen doch ... Ich wollte
10 etwas von ihrem Vorleben wissen."

„Damit haben sich unsere Leute sehr viel Mühe gegeben," versicherte der Mann vom Büro dem Papenbrink und sah den Bericht weiter ein. „Also bisher war auch nicht das Geringste über Fräulein Hornung zu sagen.
15 Sie hat immer zurückgezogen gelebt und ist immer nur mit ihren Eltern ins Theater oder ins Kino gegangen."

„Fast zu schön, um wahr zu sein!" bemerkte Papenbrink nun zufrieden. „Das wollte ich ja wissen." „Einen Augenblick bitte," rief jedoch der Herr von der Auskunf
20 tei. „So war es bis jetzt. Doch in letzter Zeit wurde sie in Begleitung eines Herrn gesehen. Der Herr ist von zweifelhaftem Charakter und steht als Geschäftsmann in schlechtem Ruf."

„Also doch!" rief nun Papenbrink ärgerlich aus.
25 „Das hätte ich nicht gedacht! Mit einem zweifelhaften Menschen ... Diesen Kerl möchte ich mir mal ansehen! Wie heißt er denn? Kennen Sie seinen Namen?" „Sein Name ...," sagte der Mann vom Büro und las den Bericht zu Ende. „Der Herr mit dem zweifelhaften
30 Charakter heißt Papenbrink."

Questions

1. Was für ein Mensch war Herr Papenbrink? 2. Weshalb ging er zur Auskunftei? 3. Wieviel mußte er hier im voraus bezahlen? 4. Wann erhielt er die gewünschte Auskunft? 5. Was fand er am Bericht von Interesse? 6. Wie stellte er sich zu Brigittes Vorleben? 7. In wessen Begleitung wurde sie in letzter Zeit gesehen? 8. Was war dieser Herr von Beruf? 9. In welchem Ruf stand dieser Herr? 10. Wie hieß er?

Idiomatic Expressions

es will mir nicht aus dem Sinn	I cannot get it out of my mind
Auskunft einholen	to seek (*or* gather) information
im voraus	in advance
zur Zeit	at present
zehn Jahre zählen	to be of the age of ten
angestellt sein bei (*dat.*)	to be employed by
es ist mir von Interesse	it is of interest to me
sich Mühe geben mit (*dat.*)	to take (the) trouble with
zurückgezogen leben	to lead a sheltered (*or* secluded) life
in schlechtem Ruf stehen	to have a bad reputation

EXERCISES

A. Form sentences with *der Mann, dieses Fräulein, jene Frau, derselbe Geschäftsmann* as subjects, and the idiomatic expressions listed above.

B. Explain these idiomatic expressions in simple terms in German. EXAMPLE: Er steht in schlechtem Ruf. Er steht in keinem guten Ruf *or* Er ist nicht beliebt *or* Man hat ihn nicht gern *or* Man hält nicht viel von ihm.

C. Substitute the suggested words for the words in heavy type, and insert *nur* somewhere in each sentence.
1. **Der** Herr tut alles mit Bedacht. (dieser, jener)   2. Sie fragt jetzt **einen** Mann. (derselbe, der)   3. **Eine** gefällt mir nicht. (der, dieser)   4. Es ist die Tochter **dieses** Mannes. (jener, derselbe)   5. Der Name **des** Mädchens ist Brigitte. (dieser, derjenige)

D. (1) Supply a demonstrative. (2) Vary the gender and, if possible, the number of the demonstrative and modify the sentence accordingly. EXAMPLE: Er ist ein und derselbe Mann. Sie ist ein und dieselbe Frau. Es ist ein und dasselbe Mädchen. Sie sind ein und dieselben Leute.
1. Geben Sie es ——, der es mag.   2. Dieser gefällt mir, —— gefällt ihr.   3. Ist das —— Mann, den sie gestern gesehen hat?   4. Ich bin in —— Monat geboren.   5. ——, der es findet, behält es.   6. Es ist ein und —— Mann.

E. Note the relationship of the words in columns one, two, and three.   Use each word in a sentence.

Bedacht	bedenken	denken
vorsichtig	Vorsicht	sehen

ungeduldig *impatient* Geduld *patience*   dulden *to endure*
Aushilfe *help*   aushelfen *help out*   helfen *help*
zurückgezogen *to pull back* zurückziehen   ziehen
zweifelhaft *questionable* Zweifel *doubt*   zweifeln *to doubt*

F. Complete the following sentences.

1. Der vorsichtige Herr Papenbrink war ... 2. Die hübsche Brigitte war ... 3. Der alte Postinspektor war ... 4. Strauß & Co. war ... 5. Der Herr mit dem zweifelhaften Charakter war ... 6. Die junge Dame mit den Eltern war ... 7. Die höhere Handelsschule war ... 8. Das mit dem Alter war ...

Composition

1. Mr. Papenbrink was a businessman. 2. He was also very careful and made inquiries about Brigitte Hornung. 3. Brigitte was twenty-two years old. 4. She had taken a business course in high school and was now employed by the firm (of) Strauss and Co. as [a] secretary. 5. Until recently she had led a sheltered life. 6. She had never gone out alone. 7. She had gone to the movies and to the theater only with her parents. 8. Lately, however, she had been seen in the company of a gentleman. 9. But that gentleman did not have a good reputation as [a] businessman. 10. Mr. Papenbrink was therefore very (much) annoyed. 11. "I would like to see that fellow," he said. 12. But the man from the information bureau replied: "The man's name is Papenbrink."

Variations

A. Arrange the words in each line in their proper order.
B. Connect the sentences to form a brief anecdote.

1. der gegeben Rechtsanwalt hatte Mühe alle sich.
2. aussichtslos war aber Prozeß der.
3. verloren in wurde letzter auch er Instanz.
4. Mühe dankte dem Anwalt für Klient der die.
5. leid tut mir es.
6. umsonst Sie bemüht haben sich.
7. umsonst vergebens nicht ja aber.

Conversation — Das Wetter

Herr Funck:	Was sagt der Wetterbericht?
Freund:	Der Bericht ist nicht sehr günstig.
Herr Funck:	Die Sonne scheint doch!
Freund:	Ja, aber das Barometer fällt.
Herr Funck:	Dann nehmen wir Regenmäntel und Gummischuhe mit.
Freund:	Regnet es hier oft im Frühling?
Herr Funck:	Es regnet Bindfäden im Frühling.
Freund:	Und wie ist das Klima im Sommer?
Herr Funck:	Im Sommer haben wir meistens schönes Wetter.
Freund:	Wird es bei euch sehr heiß?
Herr Funck:	Nein. Im Sommer steht das Thermometer im Durchschnitt auf fünfundzwanzig Grad (Celsius).
Freund:	Dann komme ich lieber her. Bei uns ist die Hitze nicht zum Ertragen.
Herr Funck:	Ich wäre froh, wenn du uns nächsten Sommer besuchen könntest.
Freund:	Abgemacht.

CHAPTER TWELVE

Interrogatives and Relative Pronouns

In general, interrogatives and relative pronouns are used in German as they are used in English.

(a) *INTERROGATIVES*

12.1 In addition to **welcher** (Chapter IX), which may also be used either as an adjective, meaning *which* or *what*, or as a pro-

73

noun, meaning *which one(s)* or *which*, the interrogatives in German are: **wer** — *who*, **was** — *what*, and **was für** — *what kind of.*

Welcher Hut gefällt Ihnen?	Which hat do you like?
Welchen mögen Sie?	Which one do you like?

12.2 **Wer** is used as a pronoun in speaking of persons, for both genders and numbers. Its genitive, dative, and accusative are: **wessen** — *whose*, **wem** — *to whom*, **wen** — *whom.*

Wer ist der Mann?	Who is that man?
Wen hast du gerufen?	Whom did you call?
Wem folgen die Leute?	Whom are these people following?
Wessen Geld ist das?	Whose money is that?

12.3 In the nominative and accusative case, **was** is used as a pronoun in speaking of an inanimate object or objects. Its genitive, **wes**, survives commonly only in **wes**-compounds. Its dative and accusative are commonly replaced by **wo**-compounds, as *wherewith, whereupon* in English.

Was liegt auf dem Tisch?	What is lying on the table?
Weswegen weint sie?	On account of what does she cry?
Womit tat er es?	With what did he do it?
Was hält er in der Hand?	What does he hold in his hand?
Worauf warten Sie?	What are you waiting for?

12.4 The phrase **was für** is used pronominally and adjectivally.[1] In the singular it adds the forms of **ein.**

Was für ein Wagen ist das?	What kind of a car is this?
Mit was für einem Ball spielt er?	With what kind of a ball is he playing?
Was für Federn sind dies?	What kind of pens are these?
Was für eine hat er?	What kind does he have?

12.5 Some interrogative adverbs are: **wo** — *where*, **wohin** — *where(to)*, **wie** — *how*, **warum** — *why.*

Wo bist du?	Where are you?
Wohin gehst du?	Where(to) are you going?
Wie gefällt es dir?	How do you like it?
Warum wartest du?	Why are you waiting?

---

[1] In this phrase **für** does not function as a preposition and hence does not require an accusative.

(b) *RELATIVE PRONOUNS*

12.6 The relative pronouns in German are **der** and **welcher**. With the exception of the genitive, they are usually used interchangeably [2] and correspond to *who, which,* and *that* in English. Their parallel forms are:

Case	SINGULAR			PLURAL
	Masculine	*Feminine*	*Neuter*	*All Genders*
Nom.	**der**	**die**	**das**	**die**
	welcher	**welche**	**welches**	**welche**
Gen.	**dessen**	**deren**	**dessen**	**deren**
Dat.	**dem**	**der**	**dem**	**denen**
	welchem	**welcher**	**welchem**	**welchen**
Acc.	**den**	**die**	**das**	**die**
	welchen	**welche**	**welches**	**welche**

12.7 In both languages the relative pronouns agree in some way with their antecedents. In English, *who* refers to live objects, *which* to lifeless objects, and *that* to both. In German, the relationship is more specific: <u>der and welcher agree in gender and number with the nouns to which they refer, and their case is determined by their use in the clause.</u>

Der Junge, der (*or* welcher) vorne steht, ist mein Schüler.	The boy who stands in front is my pupil.
Der Junge, dessen Vater Sie sahen, ist mein Schüler.	The boy whose father you saw is my pupil.
Der Junge, dem (*or* welchem) ich den Bleistift gab, ist mein Schüler.	The boy to whom I gave the pencil is my pupil.
Der Junge, den (*or* welchen) Sie sahen, ist mein Schüler.	The boy whom you saw is my pupil.

12.8 At times the relative pronoun is omitted in English. It is never omitted in German.[3]

Er ist der Junge, den Sie sahen.   He is the boy you saw.

---

[2] As a relative pronoun **welcher** is not used in the genitive.   [3] Note that all relative clauses in German are dependent clauses which are always set off by commas.

12.9 The forms of **der** and **welcher** referring to a lifeless object may be replaced by **wo(r)**-compounds, as *wherein, wherewith* in English.

Das Zimmer, in dem (*or* worin) ich schlafe, ist kleiner.
The room in which (*or* wherein) I sleep is smaller.

12.10 **Was** is used instead of **das,** when the antecedent is: ① an indefinite neuter pronoun like **alles, das, etwas, manches, nichts, vieles;** ② a neuter adjective used as a noun; ③ or an entire clause.

Alles, was er sagt, ist falsch.	Everything (that) he says is wrong.
Es ist das Beste, was ich vermag.	It is the best (that) I can do.
Er mußte um sieben aufstehen, was ihm gar nicht gefiel.	He had to rise at seven, which he didn't like at all.

12.11 **Wer** and **was** are used as indefinite relative pronouns which contain their own antecedents (*he who* or *whoever, that which* or *whatever*).

Wer mich braucht, wird mich rufen.	Whoever needs me will call me.
Was er sagt, ist falsch.	Whatever he says is wrong.

BASIC PATTERNS

„Liebe Schwester," schrieb Frau Krause der Frau Müller. „Ein Wunder ist geschehen. Susi hat endlich Beine.

Du weißt doch noch, wie scheu sie war, und wie
5 überzeugt sie davon war, krumme Beine zu haben. Auf dem Heimweg vom Büro merkte sie nun zufällig, wie sich ein Herr auf der Straße nach ihr umdrehte. ‚Was gibt es denn an meinen Beinen zu sehen,' meinte Susi. ‚Sie sind plump und krumm und reizlos.'

10 Doch der eine Blick genügte. Susi sah in ein Schaufenster und fand ihre Beine gar nicht häßlich. Sie begann etwas langsamer zu gehen und den Kopf nicht so gesenkt zu halten. Viele Männer lächelten Susi nun an, und mit der Zeit lächelte auch Susi. Natürlich mehr nach innen
15 hinein. Susi blickte an sich herab. ‚Ja, es stimmt,' sagte

76

Oben: Die Insel Rügen in der Ostsee.
Unten: Badestrand an der Nordsee.

sie sich. ‚Ich trage diese schönen, neuen Schuhe.' Zu Ehren der neuen Schuhe hatte sie auch ihre besten Strümpfe
angezogen. Und ein feines Gewebe hebt den Reiz.
Auf einmal bekam sie nun Mut. Ihr Wohlgefallen
5 an sich selbst stieg. ‚Warum sollten denn die Herren
mir auch eigentlich nicht nachsehen,' dachte sie jetzt.
Sie ging hocherhobenen Hauptes ihren Weg weiter. Da
blieb ihr plötzlich beinahe das Herz stehen, denn der
junge Doktor vom Hause gegenüber kam ihr entgegen.
10 Susi liebte den Doktor heimlich, aber er hatte nie einen
Blick für sie und Susi nur immer einen verstohlenen Blick
für ihn. Aber jetzt lächelte Susi ihn an, und der junge
Doktor lächelte auch, als er an ihr vorüberging. Susi
konnte es jedoch fühlen, wie er sich nach ihr umdrehte,
15 und wandte unwillkürlich den Kopf nach ihm um. Er
grüßte. Sie dankte. Darauf machte der junge Arzt
kehrt. Er holte sie ein und stellte sich als Fritz Kempe
vor. Dann fragte er, ob er ein Stück mitgehen dürfe, und
begleitete Susi nach Hause. Beim Abschied bat er sie um
20 ein Stelldichein. Als Susi nach Hause kam, fiel sie mir
um den Hals. Doch jetzt merkte ich ein faustgroßes
Loch in Susis rechtem Strumpf. ‚Mein Gott,' schrie ich
auf, ‚die Leute müssen dir ja nachgeblickt haben.' ‚Ja,
das haben sie auch getan,' antwortete mir Susi nach-
25 denklich . . .“

Questions

1. Warum war Susi scheu? 2. Was bemerkte sie auf dem Heimweg? 3. Wie fand sie ihre Beine im Schaufenster? 4. Wie ging sie nun
über die Straße? 5. Wann bekam sie noch mehr Mut? 6. Wer kam Susi
jetzt entgegen? 7. Wie war sie dem jungen Arzt früher begegnet?
8. Wann stellte er sich ihr vor? 9. Warum fiel Susi ihrer Mutter um den
Hals? 10. Was sah Susis Mutter jetzt?

Idiomatic Expressions

überzeugt sein von (*dat.*)	to be convinced of
sich umdrehen nach (*dat.*)	to turn to look
man sieht es ihr an	one can tell by looking at her

78

mit der Zeit	in time
an sich herabblicken	to glance down at oneself
zu Ehren	in honor of
auf einmal	suddenly, at once
Mut bekommen	to take courage
hocherhobenen Hauptes	head held high
er kommt mir entgegen	he comes toward (or to meet) me
vorbeigehen an (dat.)	to walk past
den Kopf wenden nach (dat.)	to turn one's head to look
bitten um (acc.)	to ask for
um den Hals fallen	to throw one's arms around the neck
es bleibt mir das Herz stehen	my heart stops (beating)

EXERCISES

A. Supply the appropriate interrogative.

1. —— war davon überzeugt? 2. —— überzeugte er? 3. Nach —— drehte er sich um? 4. Zu —— Ehren zog sie die neuen Strümpfe an? 5. —— bekam sie? 6. ——wegen ging sie hocherhobenen Hauptes? 7. Nach —— wandte er den Kopf? 8. Mit —— einem Strumpf ging sie ins Büro? 9. Was —— ein Loch war es? 10. Um —— bat er sie?

B. Relate one sentence to the other. EXAMPLE: Frau Krause schrieb ihrer Schwester. Frau Krause wohnt in Frankfurt. Frau Krause, die ihrer Schwester schrieb, wohnt in Frankfurt.

1. Susi war auf dem Heimweg. Sie bemerkte einen Herrn. 2. Der Herr lächelte. Er drehte sich nach ihr um. 3. Susi begann etwas langsamer zu gehen. Sie hielt den Kopf hoch. 4. Susi trug neue Schuhe. Sie waren schön. 5. Sie hatte neue Strümpfe und Schuhe angezogen. Davon bekam sie Mut. 6. Die Herren sahen Susi nach. Susi hatte ein Loch im Strumpf. 7. Sie warf ihm einen verstohlenen Blick zu. Er lächelte. 8. Susis junger Mann grüßte. Sie dankte. 9. Susis Mutter war froh. Susi schrie auf.

C. Supply the missing words.

1. Susi tat alles, —— ihre Mutter ihr sagte. 2. —— sie auch ruft, ruft mich. 3. —— sie ihm sagt, sagt er mir. 4. Er redete immer, —— ihr an ihm nicht gefiel. 5. Es war das Schönste, —— er sagte. 6. Sie war die Schönste, —— er sah. 7. Sie will alles, —— du hast.

79

D. Add any relative clause to complete the sentence.

1. Frau Müller war die Schwester, der... 2. Susi war das Mädchen, welches... 3. Die Strümpfe waren neu, die... 4. Dumm war die Frau nicht, die... 5. Die Schuhe waren schön, zu deren... 6. Es war der rechte Strumpf, worin... 7. Der Blick war verstohlen, welchen... 8. Es war ein Stelldichein, worum... 9. Sie lächelte dem jungen Mann zu, den... 10. Er kannte den Arzt, dessen...

E. Supply the appropriate German equivalent for "where" in each sentence.

1. —— warst du gestern? 2. —— geht er morgen? 3. —— werde ich ihn finden? 4. —— wollen sie ihn schicken? 5. Sag mir, —— er ist.

F. Change the modifier into a relative clause. EXAMPLE: Der neue Strumpf ist schön. Der Strumpf, der neu ist, ist schön.

1. Die gute Schwester schreibt oft. 2. Die braunen Schuhe waren auch alt. 3. Die lachenden Herren waren zufrieden. 4. Der junge Arzt begleitete sie nach Hause. 5. Das faustgroße Loch war im rechten Strumpf. 6. Die glückliche Mutter weinte. 7. Die erstaunte Schwester antwortete sofort. 8. Der nachdenklichen Susi sah niemand nach.

Composition

1. Susi was not only shy. 2. She was also convinced that her legs were unattractive. 3. On the way home from the office, however, she noticed accidentally that a gentleman turned‿to‿ stare‿at her. 4. That gave her courage. 5. She began to walk more slowly. 6. As other gentlemen smiled at her, she too began to smile. 7. When she saw the young doctor who lived across‿ the‿street‿from her house, her heart almost stopped [beating]. 8. She was secretly in love with him. 9. She smiled at him and he smiled at her. 10. Then he introduced himself as Fritz Kempe. 11. He asked whether he might walk with [her] a ways and walked her home. 12. At home Susi threw‿her‿arms‿around‿ her‿mother's‿neck and shouted: "Mother, he likes me!"

Variations

   A. Arrange the words in each line in their proper order.
B. Connect the sentences to form a brief anecdote.

   1. ein Offizier junger Zug einen bestieg.
   2. langsam dieser Zug sehr fuhr.
   3. Schaffner den der da Offizier fragte.
   4. können Endstation Sie schneller kommen nicht zur.
   5. Antwortete gemütliche der Schaffner.
   6. Dienstvorschrift gegen das ist meine.
   7. darf ich Zug den Fahrt während der verlassen nicht.

Conversation — Ein Ferngespräch

Herr Müller:	(Wählt die Fernamtnummer. Nimmt den Hörer ab.)
Telefonistin:	Hier Fernamt.
Herr Müller:	Ich möchte Herrn Braun in Berlin sprechen.
Telefonistin:	Welche Nummer, bitte.
Herr Müller:	Charlottenburg 23840 (zwo — drei — acht — vier — null).
Telefonistin:	(Verbindet.) Wie ist Ihre Nummer, bitte? (Dann:) Bitte, sprechen Sie!
Walter Braun:	(Am anderen Ende der Leitung.) Hier Walter Braun. Wer dort?
Herr Müller:	Hier Müller. Guten Morgen, Herr Braun.
Walter Braun:	Schön, daß Sie anrufen. Wann darf ich Sie erwarten?
Herr Müller:	Morgen um dreizehn Uhr zwanzig.
Walter Braun:	Gut. Dann kommen Sie gleich in die Bank.
Herr Müller:	Also, bis morgen.
Walter Braun:	Grüßen Sie indessen von Haus zu Haus.

CHAPTER THIRTEEN

The Declension of Nouns

As in English, nouns in German are declined by adding some endings in (a) the singular and (b) the plural (Appendices VII, VIII).

(a) *THE SINGULAR*

13.1 Only one significant case or inflectional ending remains in the singular in English and in German. The *s* may be added to nouns to form the genitive or possessive case in English. However, only masculine or neuter nouns [1] and feminine names [2] add (e)s to form the genitive or possessive case in German.[3]

	MASCULINE	FEMININE	NEUTER
N.	der Mann	die Frau	das Buch
G.	des Mannes	der Frau	des Buches
D.	dem Mann	der Frau	dem Buch
A.	den Mann	die Frau	das Buch

des Mannes Buch	the man's book
des Kindes Mutter	the child's mother
das Buch des Mannes	the book of the man
die Mutter des Kindes	the mother of the child
Annas Buch	Anna's book

13.2 To indicate the dative case, currently an –e is commonly added to masculine or neuter nouns of one syllable which end in **b, d, g,** or **s.**

	MASCULINE	FEMININE	NEUTER
D.	dem Diebe	der Frau	dem Hause

(b) *THE PLURAL*

There are several ways in which nouns form their plural in English.[4] In German there are basically four classes into which nouns may be divided according to their plural endings.

---

[1] Exceptions are the masculine nouns in Class IV and the "irregular" nouns listed under (b). [2] Names ending in –s add an apostrophe or –ens in German, as **Hans'** or **Hansens.** [3] Feminine names ending in –e add –ns in German, as **Mariens.** [4] Cf. book — books, wolf — wolves, man — men, sheep — sheep, apex — apices, etc.

13.3 The nouns in Class I add no ending to form the plural, but they often add umlaut, as **der Vogel, die Vögel** and **der Vater, die Väter** in 13.3(1); **die Mutter, die Mütter** and **die Tochter, die Töchter** in 13.3(5). To Class I belong:

(1) masculine and neuter nouns (of more than one syllable) ending in –el, –er, –en, as **der Vogel, der Wagen, der Vater, das Segel, das Leben, das Alter;**

(2) a dissyllabic masculine noun, **der Käse;**

(3) (neuter) diminutives terminating in –chen, –lein, as **das Märchen, das Kindlein;**

(4) all collective (neuter) nouns with the prefix **ge**– and the suffix –e, as **das Gebäude, das Gebirge.** (The –e may be missing, as in **das Gewässer.**)

(5) (only two) feminines, **die Mutter, die Tochter.**

13.4 The nouns in Class II add –e to form the plural and often add umlaut, as **die Stadt, die Städte** and **der Stand, die Stände** in 13.4(1). To Class II belong:

(1) masculine, feminine, and a few neuter nouns of one syllable, as **der Arm, der Stand, die Stadt, das Gas;**

(2) nouns of more than one syllable terminating in (the masculine endings) –ich, –ig, –ling, (the feminine ending) –kunft, and (the largely neuter, sometimes masculine endings) –nis,[5] –sal, as **der Rettich, der König, der Frühling, die Ankunft, das Ereignis, das Schicksal.**

13.5 The nouns in Class III add –er to form the plural and always add umlaut, where possible, as **das Glas, die Gläser.** To Class III belong:

(1) no feminines;

(2) most monosyllabic neuter and a few masculine nouns of one syllable, as **das Buch, der Rand;**

(3) (masculine or neuter) nouns of more than one syllable ending in –tum, as **der Irrtum, das Eigentum;**

(4) a few miscellaneous neuter nouns of more than one syllable, as **das Spital, das Gesicht.**

---

[5] Nouns of more than one syllable ending in –s add an additional s in the plural to keep the pronunciation voiceless, as **das Ereignis, die Ereignisse.**

13.6 The nouns in Class IV add –(e)n (nouns ending in –in take –nen) to form the plural, but they never add an umlaut. To Class IV belong:

(1) feminine nouns of one syllable, as **die Frau;**

(2) feminine nouns of more than one syllable ending in –e, –ei, –ie, –in, –ik, –tät, –heit, –keit, –schaft, –tion, –ung, –ur, as **die Farbe, die Rederei, die Harmonie, die Schülerin, die Romantik, die Einheit, die Fruchtbarkeit, die Eigenschaft, die Nation, die Frisur;**

(3) a few masculine nouns, including **der Herr, der Mensch, der Junge, der Knabe.** These nouns also add –(e)n in the genitive, dative, and accusative singular, as **der Herr, des Herrn, dem Herrn, den Herrn; der Mensch, des Menschen, dem Menschen, den Menschen.**

13.7 In addition to the nouns in Classes I, II, III, and IV there are a few nouns which are sometimes classified as (a) "mixed" and (b) "irregular." Mixed nouns add an –(e)s in the genitive singular, as do nouns in Classes I, II, III, and an –(e)n to form the plural, as do nouns in Class IV. The most common of the "mixed" nouns are: **der Doktor, der Professor, der Pastor, der Schmerz, das Auge, das Ohr, das Bett** (Appendix VII). The most common of the "irregular" nouns which add –(e)ns in the genitive, –(e)n in the dative, and –(e)n in the accusative singular, if masculine, and which add an –(e)n to form the plural are: **der Name, der Friede, das Herz** (Appendix VII).

13.8 The plurals of loanwords vary with their degree of "naturalization." Accordingly, some add –e (Class II) or –er (Class III) to form the plural, as **das Hospital, die Hospitale** or **Hospitäler.** Others add –ien or change the ending to –en and are therefore conveniently grouped with the "mixed" nouns, as **das Material, die Materialien** and **das Museum, die Museen.** Still others add –s to form the plural, as **das Auto, die Autos,** while some, as **der Kaktus, die Kakteen,** seem to defy classification. (The plural of **der Autobus, die Autobusse,** is patterned after the plural of nouns in 13.4(2), footnote 5.)

13.9 While there are no case endings in the plural in English, nouns in German add –n to the regular plural ending in the dative plural (as **den Vätern**), unless the noun itself ends in an –n in the plural.

13.10 The last part of a compound noun generally determines its gender and its declension, but the first part retains the primary accent, as in **das Klássenzìmmer.** *duzen – to address someone informly*

BASIC PATTERNS

dat ref sage mir

„Man muß Glück haben," sagte sich Hans Bürger. Er ging durch den dünnen, kalten Regen die lange Straße hinunter. Die Uhr drüben am Platz zeigte 9 Uhr 50. Aber die Lampen brannten noch. Die Scheinwerfer der Autos glitten trübe über den nassen Asphalt. In zehn 5 Minuten mußte er beim Direktor sein, und sicher bekam doch wieder ein anderer den Posten.

„Man muß Glück haben," sagte sich Bürger. Und dann passierte es. *happened* Eine alte Frau links vor ihm rutschte plötzlich aus und lag hilflos auf der Straße. Ihr Stadt- 10 koffer sprang auf und streute seinen Inhalt auf die Fahr- bahn hinaus. „Mein Arm!" stöhnte *groaned* die Frau. „Und mein Koffer, das Geld, die Papiere..." Sie versuchte ächzend aufzustehen. *achzen = ach!*

„In fünf Minuten muß ich beim Direktor sein," 15 dachte Bürger. Aber da war er schon auf der Straße, um *in order to* den Koffer, eine Wachstuchtasche und irgend etwas *gather* Papierenes aus der Nässe aufzusammeln. Er sah, daß weiter unten an der Kreuzung das rote Licht verschwand, und eine Reihe Wagen in Bewegung kam. Die Frau 20 mußte sofort herunter von der Fahrbahn. Aber als er ihr in die Höhe helfen wollte, jammerte sie und wurde weiß im Gesicht. Da war wohl etwas gebrochen.

„In drei Minuten muß ich auf der Direktion sein," seufzte Bürger und sah sich aufgeregt um. Kam denn 25 kein Mensch? War er der einzige, der helfen sollte? Sollte

85

2. mußte sofort herunter — had to get off imediately

etwas
nichts
viel wenig } *neuter adj alwas*
allerlei } *capitalized*

er deshalb die Verabredung versäumen, von der doch so viel abhing, die neue Stellung, seine ganze Zukunft vielleicht? Sollte er denn niemals Glück haben?

Die Frau stand endlich auf dem Gehsteig. Bürger
5 stützte sie und sah nach der Uhr. Zwei Minuten vor zehn. Donnerwetter! Konnte die Alte denn nicht besser aufpassen! „Sei anständig!" sagte eine Stimme in ihm. Aber eine andere sagte dagegen: „Soll der Dicke dort in dem grauen Mercedes doch mal anständig sein! Warum immer
10 ein armer Kerl wie du!"

Der graue Mercedes stoppte wirklich, und der dicke Mann stieg aus. Er hatte ein gutmütiges Gesicht und fragte, ob er helfen könne. Als der Mercedes wieder anfuhr, in der Richtung Sanitätswache, schlug es gerade
15 zehn, und Bürger ging resigniert auf das Direktionsgebäude zu. Zwei Bewerber saßen schon im Vorzimmer; aber sie mußten alle warten, weil der Herr Direktor sich verspätet hatte.

Als Bürger hineingerufen wurde, erhob sich hinter
20 dem Schreibtisch ein dicker Mann mit gutmütigem Gesicht. „Wir kennen uns ja schon von vorhin," sagte er freundlich. „Denken Sie, die arme Frau hat wirklich einen Oberarmbruch."

„Glück muß man haben," dachte Bürger vergnügt,
25 als er wieder die lange Straße hinunterging. „Und ich muß der lieben Frau ein paar Blumen in die Klinik bringen."

Questions

1. Was sagte sich Hans Bürger auf dem Wege zur Direktion?
2. Wie war das Wetter, als er die Straße hinunterging? 3. Warum brannten die Lampen noch? 4. Wen sah Bürger plötzlich auf der Straße?
5. Warum mußte die Frau herunter von der Fahrbahn? 6. Wer half der Frau endlich in die Höhe? 7. Warum hatte Bürger solche Eile? 8. Wer kam ihm im letzten Augenblick zu Hilfe? 9. Wann erreichte Bürger erst die Direktion? 10. Weshalb bekam er aber die Stellung?

86

Idiomatic Expressions

Glück haben	to be lucky
in Bewegung kommen	to start to move
in die Höhe helfen (*dat.*)	to help (get) up
auf der Direktion	in the director's (*or* main) office
sehen nach (*dat.*)	to look at
in der Richtung	in the direction of
ein paar	a few, some
abhängen von (*dat.*)	to depend on
besser aufpassen	to be more careful, to pay more attention
es schlägt zehn	the clock strikes ten

EXERCISES

A. Change subject and verb to the plural.

1. Der Mann hatte Glück. 2. Der Wagen kam in Bewegung. 3. Der Herr half der Dame in die Höhe. 4. Der Bewerber mußte um zehn Uhr auf der Direktion sein. 5. Die Frau sah nach der Uhr. 6. Das Auto fuhr in der Richtung Sanitätswache. 7. Der Junge nahm ein paar Bücher. 8. Die Stellung hängt von ihm ab. 9. Der Bewerber muß besser aufpassen. 10. Die Uhr geht nach.

B. Relate one odd-numbered to one even-numbered sentence in A. EXAMPLE: Der Bewerber, dessen Uhr nachgeht, muß besser aufpassen.

C. Change the objects to the plural.

1. Die Männer gingen die lange Straße hinunter. 2. Er sah die Lampe. 3. Die Papiere lagen auf dem Fahrdamm. 4. Er versäumte die Verabredung. 5. Die Frauen standen auf dem Gehsteig. 6. Die Leute saßen schon im Vorzimmer. 7. Er sah einen Schreibtisch. 8. Ich kenne ihn. 9. Die Frau hat einen Oberarmbruch. 10. Er brachte ihr eine schöne Blume.

D. Include a demonstrative in each sentence in C. EXAMPLE: Er sah jene Lampe.

E. Change the plurals to the singular.

1. In die Kliniken bringt man oft Blumen. 2. An den Gesichtern erkennt man die Kinder. 3. Die Bewerber sprachen

mit den Direktoren.　4. Auf den Schreibtischen liegen Papiere.
5. In den Koffern waren Gelder.　6. Die Frauen hörten Männer-
stimmen.　7. Die Dicken laufen den Schlanken nach.　8. Die Lich-
ter an den Kreuzungen waren rot.　9. Die Fahrbahnen waren
naß.　10. Auf den Straßen sah man Studenten.

F. Add one of the following expressions of time to the sentences in E: *am Abend, während des Tages, gestern früh, oft.*

G. Substitute the suggested words for the words in heavy
type.

1. Der Koffer des **Mannes** ist groß.　(Mädchen, Frau)
2. Die Scheinwerfer der **Autos** leuchten stark.　(Wagen, Omnibus)　3. Die Bücher des **Fritz** sind hier.　(Marie, Hans)　4. Der
Name des **Nachbars** ist Krause.　(Herr, Student)　5. Das Pflaster
der **Fahrbahn** ist glatt.　(Gehsteig, Straße)

H. Use the subjects in G as objects of *Er sieht . . .*

I. Substitute the suggested words for the words in heavy
type.

1. In den **Koffern** lagen Papiere.　(Schreibtisch, Tasche)
2. Es waren viele Leute in den **Straßenbahnen.**　(Auto, Wagen,
Zug)　3. Sie fuhren mit **Straßenbahnen.**　(Schiff, Flugzeug)
4. Er kommt in fünf **Minuten** wieder.　(Stunde, Tag, Woche)
5. Sie folgte den **Studenten.**　(Kind, Mann, Frau)

J. Substitute pronouns for the nouns in four of the five sentences in I.

Composition

1. It was fifty minutes past nine when Mr. Bürger walked
through the fine, chilling rain.　2. The streetlights were still
burning.　3. Only an old lady walked in front of him.　4. Suddenly she slipped and lay helpless in the street.　5. Her attaché
case snapped open and its contents scattered [6] on the pavement.
6. After he had gathered up the papers, Mr. Bürger tried to help
the lady up.　7. But she groaned and grew white in the face.
8. When she was finally up, a heavy-set gentleman in a Mercedes
stopped and drove the lady to the nearest clinic.　9. It was therefore past ten when Mr. Bürger arrived at the main office.　10. Two

[6] *Translate* and scattered its contents.

88

other candidates were already waiting. 11. Mr. Bürger was almost certain that one of them would therefore get the new job. 12. But when the director arrived, he recognized Mr. Bürger. 13. "We know‿one‿another, don't‿we," he said to him cordially. 14. "You just have to‿be‿lucky," thought Mr. Bürger, as he walked down the street again. 15. The sun was now shining, and he looked confidently [in] to the future.

Variations

A. In addition to several basic meanings, some German words have a flavor of their own that is not readily reproduced. In the latter sense they are referred to as Füllwörter or Färbewörter which are best understood in their German context. Suggested English equivalents are often mere approximations.

aber *but*

Aber, for example, may express contrast, emphatic contrast or it may register surprise. Ich rief ihn, aber (but) er kam nicht. Ich rief Karl und Fritz, Fritz aber (however) kam nicht. Jetzt wurde ich aber (really) wütend. „Du hast mich doch gehört," fragte ich ihn da. „Aber (of course) ja," antwortete er ärgerlich. „Aber (but) Fritz!" sagte ich. „Von dir hätte ich das aber (certainly) nicht erwartet."

auch *also*

Auch may be equated with *ebenfalls* or *wirklich* or have a pejorative connotation. Ich bat ihn zu kommen, und er kam auch (actually). Er kam und seine Frau auch (also *or* too). Ich freue mich, und auch (too) meine Frau freut sich. Er hat es gesagt, und so ist es auch (actually). Soll das auch (really) etwas Neues sein?

da *there*

Da may mean *hier, in diesem Augenblick, aus diesem Grund, in diesem Fall* or *unter diesen Umständen*, and *im anderen Fall*. „Wo sind meine Schlüssel?" fragte er. „Da (here) liegen sie," sagte sie. Da (at that point) unterbrach er sie. Sie wollte sie ihm geben. Da (instead) nahm er sie selbst. Was tat sie da (then)? Gut, daß er endlich nachgab. Da (there) hätte es einen Krach gegeben. Er kam, da (because) er krank war. Da (since, as) er morgen arbeitet, müssen wir uns beeilen.

B. Simplify the Basic Patterns and, in the appropriate places, include variants of *aber, auch, da* and *geschehen, der Turm, das Pflaster, ausgleiten, sich erheben, erbleichen, haltmachen, erfreut.*

89

Conversation — Im Hotel

Dr. Krause:	Guten Abend. Kann ich ein Zimmer mit Bad haben?
Hotelbeamter:	Haben Sie vorausbestellt?
Dr. Krause:	Ja. Aus Hamburg.
Hotelbeamter:	(Sieht nach.) Stimmt. Sie haben ein Zimmer im ersten Stock.
Dr. Krause:	Ich hoffe, daß es ruhig ist.
Hotelbeamter:	Es geht auf den Garten hinaus.
Dr. Krause:	Wie hoch ist der Preis?
Hotelbeamter:	18 Mark pro Tag.
Dr. Krause:	Gut. Dann nehme ich es.
Hotelbeamter:	Bleibt der Herr länger hier?
Dr. Krause:	Ich denke, ungefähr eine Woche.
Hotelbeamter:	Hier ist Ihr Schlüssel. Ich lasse Ihr Gepäck auf Ihr Zimmer bringen.

CHAPTER FOURTEEN

The Indicative of Weak Verbs

Weak verbs in German correspond to regular verbs in English.
Both have six basic tenses, with six forms each, and are conjugated
without any change in the stem vowel. With few exceptions, verbs
with **ä, ö, ü, u, eu,** or **au** in the stem are weak in German, as are
verbs ending in **–igen, –ieren, –eln, –ern.**

(a) *THE PRINCIPAL PARTS*

14.1   The principal parts or key forms of a regular verb in English are based on the infinitive. The key forms of a weak verb in
German are based on the infinitive stem, that is, the infinitive
without the infinitive ending **–en,** sometimes **–n.** The key forms

include: (1) the infinitive, (2) the present tense stem, (3) the past tense stem, and (4) the past participle. Examples are:

INFINITIVE	PRESENT TENSE STEM	PAST TENSE STEM [1]	PAST PARTICIPLE
frag –en	**frag**	**frag –t**	**ge– frag –t**
wart –en	**wart**	**wart –et**	**ge– wart –et**
reis –en	**reis**	**reis –t**	**ge– reis –t**
to ask	ask	ask –ed	asked
to wait	wait	wait –ed	waited
to travel	travel	travel –ed	traveled

14.2 These key forms or principal parts are formed as follows:

infinitive without –(e)n = present tense stem

frag – en	**frag**
to ask	ask

present tense stem + **t** = past tense stem [1]

frag + t	**fragt**
ask + ed	asked

ge + past tense stem = past participle

ge + fragt	**gefragt**
asked	asked

14.3 To form the past tense stem and the past participle, a connecting or glide vowel –e– is inserted before the **t** when the present tense stem ends in –**t**, –**d**, or –**m**, –**n**, preceded by a consonant other than l or r. (Cf. **arbeite, arbeitete, gearbeitet,** but **lerne, lernte, gelernt.**)

14.4 Verbs ending in –**ieren,** as **addieren,** and verbs with inseparable prefixes, as **be–** (**beginnen**), **emp–** (**empfangen**), **ent–** (**entstehen**), **er–** (**erhalten**), **ge–** (**gelingen**), **ver–** (**verlangen**), **zer–** (**zerbrechen**), omit the **ge–** prefix in the past participle.

(b) *THE PRESENT AND THE PAST TENSE*

14.5 The present tense and the past (or preterite or imperfect) tense of the indicative of weak verbs are formed by adding almost

---

[1] The past tense stem is frequently, but inaccurately, said to consist of the present tense stem + –**te,** to which personal endings (–, –**st**, –, –**n**, –**t**, –**n**) are added.

identical sets of personal endings to the present and past tense stems, respectively (Appendix XII).

PERSON	PRESENT	PAST [2]
ich	–e	–e
du	–(e)st	–est
er, sie, es	–(e)t	–e
wir	–en	–en
ihr	–(e)t	–et
sie, Sie	–en	–en

14.6 As in some present tenses in English,[3] in the present tense in German, the **e** shown in parentheses above is used as an aid to pronunciation after –**d,** –**t,** or –**m,** –**n,** preceded by a consonant other than **l** or **r.** The **s** of the second person singular ending in German is omitted if the present tense stem ends in **s, ß, sch, z,** as in **du reist** (you travel).

(c) THE PRESENT PERFECT AND THE PAST PERFECT

14.7 The present perfect of the indicative is a combination of the present tense forms of **sein** or **haben** and the past participle of the verb (Appendix XII).[4]

er hat gesagt	he (has) said [5]
er ist gereist	he (has) traveled [5]

14.8 The past perfect of the indicative is a combination of the past tense forms of **sein** or **haben** and the past participle of the verb (Appendix XII).[4]

er hatte gesagt	he had said
er war gereist	he had traveled

(d) THE FUTURE AND THE FUTURE PERFECT

14.9 The future indicative is a combination of the present tense forms of **werden** (Appendix XI) and the infinitive of the verb.

er wird sagen	he will say
er wird reisen	he will travel

---

[2] Cf. Footnote 1. [3] Compare *he works* and *he passes* with **er arbeitet** and **er geht.**
[4] Most weak verbs take **haben.** Only intransitive verbs of motion, as **reisen,** or change of condition, as **erblinden,** take **sein.** [5] Cf. Chapter I, "The Principles of Tense."

14.10 The future perfect indicative is a combination of the present tense forms of **werden,** the past participle of the verb, and the infinitive of its auxiliary (Appendix XII).

er wird gesagt haben	he will have said
er wird gereist sein	he will have traveled

(e) *THE IMPERATIVE*

14.11 Unlike English, German has three imperative forms: (1) a familiar singular, (2) a familiar plural, and (3) a polite form for both singular and plural. The imperative forms of the weak verb are formed as follows:

(present tense stem)	**sag** [6]	(familiar singular)	say
(present tense stem + **t**)	**sagt**	(familiar plural)	say
(present tense stem + **en** + **Sie**)	**sagen Sie**	(polite singular and plural)	say

(f) *THE PRESENT PARTICIPLE*

14.12 The present participle, ordinarily used in German as an adjective, is formed by adding –**d** to the infinitive, as in **sagend** (saying), **reisend** (traveling). At the same time, an –**e**– is inserted, if it is missing in the infinitive ending, as in **tun — tuend, sein — seiend.** The –**e**– is not inserted before an –**n** preceded by an **l** or **r,** as in **wackeln — wackelnd, zwinkern — zwinkernd.**

Er fiel vom fahrenden Zug.   He fell from the moving train.

(g) *IRREGULAR WEAK VERBS*

There are eight so-called irregular weak verbs in German which deviate slightly from the pattern of the regular German weak verb (Appendix XVI).

14.13 In six of them the stem vowel –**e**– of the infinitive and the present tense changes to –**a**– in the past tense and the past participle, as in **brennen, brennt, brannte, gebrannt.** They are: **brennen** (to burn), **kennen** (to know), **nennen** (to name), **rennen** (to run), **senden** (to send), and **wenden** (to turn).

[6] Many grammarians still insist on an additional –**e.** Duden does not.

14.14 In two of them, **bringen** (to bring) and **denken** (to think), the stem vowel, –i– or –e– respectively, of the infinitive and the present tense changes to –a– in the past tense and the past participle, and the consonant following it, g or k respectively, changes to **ch** as follows:

INFINITIVE	PRESENT TENSE	PAST TENSE	PAST PARTICIPLE
bringen	bringt	brachte	gebracht
denken	denkt	dachte	gedacht

BASIC PATTERNS

Frau Müller hatte etwas Herzklopfen, als sie das Amtsgericht betrat, denn sie sollte zum erstenmal als Schöffe in einem Prozeß mitwirken. Doch als sie den Eid geleistet hatte und mit dem Richter und dem anderen
5 Schöffen am Richtertisch saß, war sie völlig bereit, sich unparteiisch und unvoreingenommen ein Bild von dem Angeklagten und seinem Vergehen zu machen.

Der Angeklagte hieß Martin Grube. Er hatte keine frohe Kindheit gehabt. Seine Eltern hatten sich wenig
10 um ihn gekümmert. Er hatte auch keinen Beruf erlernt. Als Soldat wurde er im Krieg schwer verwundet. Fünf Jahre lang wurde er von einem Lazarett ins andere geschickt. Viele Operationen waren notwendig, um das rechte Kniegelenk zu retten. Als man ihn dann endlich
15 entließ, stand er als vierundzwanzigjähriger Invalide heimatlos und ohne Familie auf der Straße. Seit dieser Zeit ist er nur hin und wieder beschäftigt gewesen.

Im Landbezirksamt hatte man ihm zuletzt gesagt, man könnte ihn nur einstellen, wenn er ein Fahrrad hätte.
20 Da war ihm der Gedanke gekommen, sich das Rad zu besorgen, das bei einem alten Gemüsehändler im Schuppen stand und nicht gebraucht wurde. Jetzt bereute er seine Tat und bat das Gericht um ein mildes Urteil.

Die Nachbarn schilderten Grube als einen stillen,
25 ordentlichen Menschen, der sich immer hilfsbereit gezeigt hatte. Doch der Staatsanwalt bestand darauf, daß

*Weinlese an der Mosel. Die
Weine von Rhein und Mosel sind
in der ganzen Welt berühmt.*

Grube nach Paragraph 243 des Strafgesetzbuches wegen schweren Diebstahls zu bestrafen sei. Er beantragte sechs Monate Gefängnis. --

Frau Müller meinte aber bei der Beratung mit dem
5 Richter und dem anderen Schöffen, eine solche Strafe wäre zu hart. Unter Zubilligung mildernder Umstände wurde Grube dann zu fünf Monaten Gefängnis verurteilt. Er hatte die Kosten des Verfahrens zu tragen. Die Vollstreckung der Strafe wurde aber auf die Dauer von
10 zwei Jahren zur Bewährung ausgesetzt.

Questions

1. Wer war Martin Grube? 2. Was war er mit 24 Jahren?
3. Weshalb hatte er keinen Beruf erlernt? 4. Wo wurde er schwer verwundet? 5. Wie lange hatte er im Lazarett gelegen? 6. Wozu brauchte er ein Fahrrad? 7. Bei wem fand er eines? 8. Warum stand er aber vor Gericht? 9. Wie schilderten die Nachbarn den Angeklagten? 10. Welche Strafe beantragte der Staatsanwalt? 11. Warum schien die Strafe der Frau Müller zu hart? 12. Wozu wurde Grube daher verurteilt?

Idiomatic Expressions

einen Eid leisten	to take an oath
sich ein Bild machen	to get a picture
sich kümmern um (*acc.*)	to care about
auf der Straße stehen	to be without a roof over one's head
es kommt mir der Gedanke	the thought strikes me
um ein mildes Urteil bitten (*acc.*)	to ask for leniency
sich hilfsbereit zeigen	to be ready to help
bestehen auf (*dat.*)	to insist on
wegen Diebstahls bestrafen	to convict of theft
unter Zubilligung mildernder Umstände	in view of extenuating circumstances

EXERCISES

A. Change each of the sentences to the past, perfect, and future tenses.

1. Frau Müller leistet den Eid mit Herzklopfen. 2. Der Richter macht sich ein Bild von dem Vergehen. 3. Der Staats-

anwalt kümmert sich nicht um ihn. 4. Der Invalide wandert heimatslos umher. 5. Der Angeklagte sagt hin und wieder ein Wort. 6. Es kommt dem Schöffen dabei der Gedanke. 7. Der Junge steht ohne Familie auf der Straße. 8. Er bittet um ein mildes Urteil. 9. Der Nachbar zeigt sich immer hilfsbereit. 10. Man bestraft so kein Kind.

B. In each of the sentences in A change the regular word order to inverted word order. EXAMPLE: Mit Herzklopfen leistete Frau Müller den Eid.

C. Complete the main clause and the relative clause.

1. Frau Müller, die den Eid... 2. Der Richter, der sich ein Bild... 3. Der Staatsanwalt, der sich um... 4. Der Invalide, der heimatlos... 5. Der Angeklagte, der hin und wieder... 6. Der Schöffe, dem dabei der Gedanke... 7. Der Junge, der auf der Straße... 8. Der Mann, der um ein mildes Urteil... 9. Der Nachbar, der sich immer hilfsbereit... 10. Die Frau, die so ein Kind...

D. Give the key forms of the following simple and complex verbs.

wirken *to effect, work*	bewirken	mitwirken
lernen *learn*	verlernen	umlernen
schicken *send*	verschicken	einschicken
zeigen *to show*	bezeigen	vorzeigen
sagen *to say*	versagen	zusagen

E. Use the following present or past participles as descriptive adjectives. EXAMPLES: Er nahm das weinende Kind bei der Hand. Das eingeschickte Angebot ist zu hoch.

weinend	eingeschickt
suchend	verwundet
grüßend	belebt
wandernd	verdient
mildernd	verurteilt

F. Substitute the verbs in parentheses for the verbs in the sentences.

1. Frau Müller betrat das Amtsgericht zum erstenmal. (besuchen) 2. Der Schöffe schwor einen Eid. (leisten) 3. Der Staatsanwalt erhob die Anklage. (einreichen) 4. Der Richter

97

ging an den Tisch. (sich setzen)   5. Der Angeklagte sprach von seiner Jugend. (erzählen)   6. Grube hatte keinen Beruf. (erlernen)   7. Eine Kugel traf den Soldaten. (verwunden)   8. Der Arzt operierte das rechte Kniegelenk. (retten)   9. Das Landbezirksamt hat ihn entlassen. (einstellen)   10. Der Junge hat sich ein Rad gekauft. (sich besorgen)

G. (1) Form sentences with the words in the left-hand column. (2) Explain in German their antonyms in the right-hand column. EXAMPLE: Frau Müller war unparteiisch. Aber der andere Schöffe war etwas parteiisch.

unparteiisch	parteiisch
voreingenommen (gegen)	eingenommen (für)
wenig	viel
beschäftigt	arbeitslos
unordentlich	ordentlich
Strafe	Belohnung

Composition

1. Martin Grube had not had a happy childhood.   2. His parents had paid little attention to him.   3. He had not even learned a trade.   4. When he was severely wounded in the war, he was sent from one field hospital to the next.   5. It took many operations to save his right knee.   6. And when he was finally discharged at the age of twenty-four, he found himself all alone and without a roof over his head.   7. Since then he had been employed off and on.   8. When he was therefore told that he could be employed in the County Office, if he had a bicycle, he did not know what to do.   9. He finally hit on the idea of taking the bicycle that was standing in an old shed.   10. At that moment nobody was using it.   11. He now regretted his deed and begged the court for leniency.

Variations

A. In addition to some basic meanings, some little German words have a flavor of their own that is not readily reproduced. At times they are therefore referred to as Füllwörter or Färbewörter, and are best understood in their German context. Suggested English equivalents are often mere approximations.

doch

As indicated in the successive sentences, *doch* may express contrast, emphasis, affirmation (in answer to a negative question), and surprise, ranging from "but" to "still" or "yet" to "indeed." Ich erwartete ihn, doch (but) er kam nicht. Das ist doch (nonetheless) wahr. Das ist doch (but) wahr! Das ist doch (isn't it) wahr? Käme er doch (only)! Wenn er doch (only) da wäre! Sie meinen, es ist nicht wahr? Doch (indeed)! Ich glaube es. Er wollte kommen und kam doch (yet) nicht. Aber sie wollte nicht kommen und kam doch (still).

eben

The basic meaning of *eben* is cognate to the English meaning "even" or "flat," as in *Das Land ist eben*. On the other hand, it may underscore an unalterable fact or also mean *vor ganz kurzer Zeit* or *im gleichen Augenblick*. So ist es eben (just). Ich bin eben (just) nach Hause gekommen. Ich wollte dich eben (about) anrufen und es dir sagen, als das Telefon klingelte. Was kann man tun? Er ist eben (after all) mein Freund.

erst

The adjective *erst*, meaning "first," must not be confused with the adverb. The latter may mean *zuerst* or *als erstes*. It may also suggest *nicht mehr als* or *nicht länger als*. It may mean "not until" or indicate emphasis. Geschieht das zum ersten (first) Male? Gut. Mach erst (first) deine Aufgabe, dann kannst du gehen. Du bist erst (only) eine Stunde da. Ich komme erst (not . . . until) morgen. Dann sollst du erst (wait till) sehen.

B. Simplify the Basic Patterns and, in the appropriate places, include variants of *doch, eben, erst* and *das Herz klopft mir, eintreten in* (acc.), *das Krankenhaus, der Eingriff, anstellen, einem einfallen, verlangen*.

Conversation — Am Bahnhof

Herr Feist:	Wann fährt der nächste Zug nach Köln?
Bahnbeamter:	Der nächste Zug nach Köln fährt um 5.14 ab.
Herr Feist:	Und wann kommt er in Köln an?
Bahnbeamter:	Um 12.47 Uhr.
Herr Feist:	Das dauert ja eine Ewigkeit. Gibt es keinen schnelleren?
Bahnbeamter:	Ja. Einen Eilzug um 8.58 und einen Schnellzug um 9.44.

Herr Feist:	Und wie lange dauert die Fahrt mit dem Schnellzug?
Bahnbeamter:	Drei Stunden und 48 Minuten.
Herr Feist:	Hat der Zug Aufenthalt in Bonn?
Bahnbeamter:	In Bonn hält der Zug 2 Minuten, aber in Koblenz hält er 5 Minuten.
Herr Feist:	Gut. Dann geben Sie mir bitte eins zweiter und zurück.
Bahnbeamter:	Die Rundreisekarte kostet 44 Mark.
Herr Feist:	Können Sie mir auf hundert Mark herausgeben?
Bahnbeamter:	Jawohl. Hier ist Ihre Karte, und hier sind 56 Mark.

CHAPTER FIFTEEN

The Indicative of Strong Verbs

Strong verbs in German generally correspond to irregular verbs in English. Both have six basic tenses, with six forms each, and are conjugated with a change in stem vowel.

(a) THE PRINCIPAL PARTS

15.1 The principal parts or key forms of the irregular verb in English are based on the infinitive with certain changes in the stem vowel. The key forms of the strong verb in German are based on the infinitive stem with certain changes in the stem vowel.

15.2 In German the key forms of strong verbs frequently include: (1) the infinitive, (2) the present tense stem of the first person singular, (3) the past tense stem, (4) the past participle, and (5) the present tense stem of the third person singular, where it differs from that of the first person. In German grammars, dictionaries, and vocabularies, the third person singular is often given in parenthesis, together with the other key tense vowels, as **sprechen, a, o (i)**. Regular verbs are listed simply, as **sagen**. Examples are:

INFINITIVE	PRESENT TENSE STEM(S)	PAST TENSE STEM	PAST PARTICIPLE
sing –en	sing	sang	ge– sung –en
sprech –en	sprech (sprich)	sprach	ge– sproch –en
geb –en	geb (gib)	gab	ge– geb –en
to sing	sing	sang	sung –
to speak	speak	spoke	spoke –n
to give	give	gave	give –n

15.3   The principal parts are formed very much the way they are formed in English. The infinitive without the infinitive ending –(e)n is the present tense stem of the first person singular.

INFINITIVE	PRESENT TENSE STEM
sing –en	sing
to sing	sing

15.4   In the present tense, an –e– in the stem of most strong verbs changes in the second and third person singular to –i(e)–, and an –a– changes to –ä–. Examples are:

ich gebe	ich sehe	ich nehme	ich fahre
du gibst	du siehst	du nimmst	du fährst
er gibt	er sieht	er nimmt	er fährt

15.5   Sometimes an adjoining consonant is also modified, as in **er nimmt** (he takes), **er ißt** (he eats).[1]

15.6   A change in stem vowel indicates a change in tense from present to past.[2]

PRESENT TENSE STEM	PAST TENSE STEM
sing	sang
sing	sang

15.7   A **ge–** prefix and an **–en** suffix are used to form the past participle, often with still another change in vowel.[2] Verbs with

---

[1] A number of changes in the present tense stem of strong verbs are tabulated in Appendix XIII.   [2] A number of vowel patterns of strong verbs are tabulated in Appendix XVI.

inseparable prefixes, as **be–, emp–, ent–, er–, ge–, ver–, zer–**, omit the **ge–** prefix, as **zerbrochen** (broken).

(b) *THE PRESENT AND THE PAST*

15.8 The present and past (or imperfect or preterite) tenses of the indicative of strong verbs are formed in a manner similar to those of weak verbs, by adding almost identical sets of personal endings to the present and past tense stems (Appendix XIII).

PERSON	PRESENT	PAST
ich	**–e**	–
du	**–st**	**–st**
er, sie, es	**–t**	–
wir	**–en**	**–en**
ihr	**–t**	**–t**
sie, Sie	**–en**	**–en**

15.9 The –s– of the second person singular ending is omitted in the present tense when the verbal stem ends in **s, ß, sch, z**, as in **du sitzt** (you sit), **du ißt** (you eat).

(c) *THE PRESENT PERFECT AND THE PAST PERFECT*

15.10 The present perfect of the indicative is a combination of the present tense forms of **sein** or **haben** and the past participle of the verb.[3]

er hat gesungen	he has sung
er ist gefahren	he has journeyed

15.11 The past perfect of the indicative is a combination of the past tense forms of **sein** or **haben** and the past participle of the verb.

er hatte gesungen	he had sung
er war gefahren	he had journeyed

---

[3] Most strong verbs take **haben**. Only a few take **sein**. These include intransitive verbs of motion, such as **fahren, fallen, folgen, laufen, gehen, kommen, reiten, springen**, or change of condition, as **einschlafen**. In addition, **sein, werden, bleiben, geschehen, gelingen** also take **sein**.

(d) *THE FUTURE AND THE FUTURE PERFECT*

15.12 The future indicative is a combination of the present tense forms of **werden** (Appendix XI) and the infinitive of the verb.

er wird singen	he will sing
er wird fahren	he will journey

15.13 The future perfect indicative is a combination of the present tense forms of **werden,** the past participle of the verb, and the infinitive of its auxiliary.

er wird gesungen haben	he will have sung
er wird gefahren sein	he will have journeyed

(e) *THE IMPERATIVE*

15.14 The three imperative forms (cf. Chapter XIV) of strong verbs which do not change their vowel in the present tense stem are formed as follows:

(PRESENT TENSE STEM UNCHANGED)	**komm**	(fam. sg.)	come
(PRESENT TENSE STEM UNCHANGED + **t**)	**kommt**	(fam. pl.)	come
(PRESENT TENSE STEM UNCHANGED + **en** + **Sie**)	**kommen Sie**	(pol. sg. and pl.)	come

15.15 If the stem vowel of the present tense (first person singular) is an **a** which changes to **ä** in the second and third person singular, the three forms of the imperative are based on the stem of the first person singular as follows:

(PRESENT TENSE STEM UNCHANGED)	**fahr**	(fam. sg.)	journey
(PRESENT TENSE STEM UNCHANGED + **t**)	**fahrt**	(fam. pl.)	journey
(PRESENT TENSE STEM UNCHANGED + **en** + **Sie**)	**fahren Sie**	(pol. sg. and pl.)	journey

15.16 If the stem vowel of the present tense (first person singular) is an **e** which changes to **i** or **ie** in the second and third person singular, the familiar form singular of the imperative is based on the stem of the second (or third) person singular, and the other two forms are based on the stem of the first person singular, as follows:

(PRESENT TENSE STEM CHANGED)	**sprich**	(fam. sg.)	speak
(PRESENT TENSE STEM UNCHANGED + **t**)	**sprecht**	(fam. pl.)	speak
(PRESENT TENSE STEM UNCHANGED + **en** + **Sie**)	**sprechen Sie**	(pol. sg. and pl.)	speak
(PRESENT TENSE STEM CHANGED)	**lies**	(fam. sg.)	read
(PRESENT TENSE STEM UNCHANGED + **t**)	**lest**	(fam. pl.)	read
(PRESENT TENSE STEM UNCHANGED + **en** + **Sie**)	**lesen Sie**	(pol. sg. and pl.)	read

(f) *THE PRESENT PARTICIPLE*

15.17 The present participle of the strong verb, ordinarily used as an adjective in German, is formed by adding –**d** to the infinitive, as **singend** (singing), **fahrend** (journeying).

BASIC PATTERNS

Karl Pechmann hatte die Fahrprüfung bestanden. Aber Karl war eine schüchterne Seele. Als er daher die erste Überlandsfahrt ohne Fahrleiter antreten sollte, sprach er erst ein stilles Gebet. Dann setzte er sich ans
5 Steuer seines Wagens.

Aus der Garage ging's noch gut. Aber auf einer Großstadtstraße lauern tausenderlei Gefahren. Eben schaffte es ein altes Mütterchen noch, den Fahrdamm vor dem heransausenden Pechmann zu überqueren. Wie
10 gut, daß das Auto eine Hupe hatte, und daß das Mütterchen nur alt, nicht aber schwerhörig war. „Du lieber Himmel, das war knapp!" seufzte der frischgebackene Ritter des Steuers. Als sich Karl der Querstraße näherte,

murmelte er ängstlich: „Herrgott, wenn die Ampel doch endlich grünes Licht zeigen würde!" Und siehe da! Der sie bedienende Schutzmann schaltete flugs auf grün und gab ihm freie Fahrt. Nun war eine Straßenbahn zu überholen. Doch der 5 Platz dafür schien außerordentlich spärlich bemessen. Aber ein tiefer Seufzer, und die Elektrische bog in eine Seitenstraße ab, noch bevor Karl heran war. An der nächsten Kreuzung spielte eine Schar Kinder auf dem Damm. Alles Hupen erwies sich als vergeblich. „Herr 10 im Himmel, nimm diese unschuldigen Kinder da weg!" flehte der Mann im Auto in höchster Not. Da verschwanden die Kinder plötzlich von der Straße, wie von unsichtbarer Hand hinweggefegt.

Kurz vor dem Stadtrand türmte sich noch ein neues 15 schreckliches Hindernis auf, in Gestalt eines entgegenkommenden Fernlastwagens mit Anhänger. Wie sollte er es mit dem Ungetüm aufnehmen? Du oder ich, diese beiden Möglichkeiten gab es nur, und der Lastwagen war bei weitem der Stärkere. „Mein Gott, laß ihn ausweichen 20 oder anhalten!" stöhnte Karl und wollte eben die Augen zumachen, da fuhr der Lastwagen gehorsam an den Gehsteig und stoppte.

„So, bis hierher hätten wir's gemeinsam geschafft, lieber Gott. Ich danke dir!" sagte Karl aufatmend, als 25 die menschenleere Ausfallstraße wie ein langes gerades Band vor ihm lag. „Jetzt werde ich die Sache allein in die Hand nehmen. Solch schwierige Kunst ist das Autofahren letzten Endes ja doch nicht!" Er hatte den Satz noch nicht ganz ausgesprochen, da platzte plötzlich ein 30 Reifen, und Karl landete kopfüber im Straßengraben.

Questions

1. Was für ein Mensch war Karl Pechmann? 2. Mit wem trat er seine erste Überlandsfahrt an? 3. Wo lauerten Gefahren auf ihn? 4. Was geschah an der ersten Querstraße? 5. Warum konnte Pechmann die Straßenbahn nicht überholen? 6. Wo lief ihm eine Schar Kinder in den

Weg? 7. Wo kam Pechmann ein Lastauto entgegen? 8. Warum schien ihm der Lastwagen gefährlich? 9. Wo atmete er endlich auf? 10. Wie endete Pechmanns erste Überlandsfahrt?

Idiomatic Expressions

eine Prüfung bestehen	to pass an examination
freie Fahrt geben (*dat.*)	to give the right of way
sich erweisen als	to prove to be
es aufnehmen mit (*dat.*)	to cope (*or* compete) with
fahren an (*acc.*)	to drive up to
aufatmend	breathing a sigh of relief
in die Hand nehmen	to take matters in hand

EXERCISES

A. Arrange the sentences in the approximate order of their degree of similarity. EXAMPLE: Seine Karte erwies sich als falsch. Seine Karte war gefälscht. Seine Karte war meiner nachgeahmt worden. Seine Karte war gültig.

1. Sie hat die Prüfung bestanden.
   Sie hat das Examen gemacht.
   Sie ist durchgefallen.
   Sie ist mit ihrem Studium zu Ende.
2. Der Schutzmann gab ihm freie Fahrt.
   Der Schutzmann schaltete das Licht auf rot.
   Der Schutzmann fuhr ihm aus dem Wege.
   Der Schutzmann ließ ihn vorfahren.
3. Die Antwort erwies sich als richtig.
   Die Antwort war kaum richtig.
   Die Antwort schien richtig.
   Die Antwort war nicht falsch.
4. Er nimmt es mit zweien auf.
   Er ist stärker als drei.
   Er fürchtet sich vor jedem.
   Er überwindet zwei bestimmt.
5. Der Wagen fuhr an den Gehsteig.
   Der Wagen parkte.
   Der Wagen stand am Gehsteig.
   Der Wagen machte nicht halt.

6. Sie lehnte sich aufatmend gegen die Tür.
Sie lehnte sich etwas beruhigt gegen die Tür.
Sie lehnte sich zitternd gegen die Tür.
Sie stand bleich an der Tür.
7. Er will die Sache selbst in die Hand nehmen.
Er will davon nichts wissen.
Er macht es selbst.
Er will sich selbst darum kümmern.

B. Give the principal parts of the following verbs: *sein, stehen, treten, gehen, geben, nehmen, weichen, halten, liegen, sprechen.*

C. (1) Use the verbs in B to form verbal compounds with *an, auf, mit,* or *vor.* EXAMPLES: *aufsein, aufstehen, antreten.* (2) Use each compound in an original German sentence. EXAMPLE: Ich bin schon um sieben auf.

D. (1) Use the words in parentheses as adjectives or adverbs. (2) Replace all articles with demonstrative adjectives.

1. Der Mann sah den fallenden Jungen. (laufend, schwimmend) 2. Das Mädchen trat singend ins Zimmer. (essend, schreiend) 3. Der Apfel lag am Boden. (abgefallen, zertreten) 4. Die lachende Frau wies auf die erwachsenen Mädchen. (erschrocken, verstummt) 5. Der erwachsene Junge ist gut angezogen. (singend, erzogen)

E. Correct the statements.

1. Pechmann war bei der Fahrprüfung durchgefallen.
2. Er war ein tapferer Mensch.
3. Er trat die Überlandsfahrt mit dem Fahrleiter an.
4. Dabei schimpfte er laut.
5. Er kam nicht aus der Garage.
6. Ein alter Mann fiel vor dem Wagen auf den Damm.
7. Die Ampel zeigte rot.
8. Der Schutzmann schaltete auf grün.
9. Die Straßenbahn überholte Pechmann.
10. Die Kinder hörten die Hupe.

F. Use each of the components of the six compounds in a sentence with a negative. EXAMPLE: (außerordentlich) Außer mir war keiner da. Ich habe ihn nie ordentlich ausgeschimpft.

Großstadtstraße	Schutzmann	Fernlastwagen
frischgebacken	Stadtrand	Autofahren

107

Composition

1. After he had passed his driver's test, Karl Pechmann set out on his first cross country trip. 2. But since he was a bit timid, he uttered a silent prayer before he sat down at the wheel of his car. 3. When an old lady crossed the street in front of his car, he blew his horn with all his might. 4. At the first intersection he mumbled softly: "Good God, if only that light were green!" 5. At the second intersection a flock of children were playing in the street. 6. Again he blew his horn, but it proved to be almost in vain. 7. Pechmann sighed even more heavily when a streetcar loomed up ahead of him. 8. But the streetcar turned off into a side street. 9. Pechmann's last obstacle was a long distance moving van which stopped at the curb before he even got to it. 10. Heaving a sigh of relief Pechmann now said: "Thank you, dear God. 11. Now I'll take matters in my own hands." 12. Suddenly, however, a tire blew out and Pechmann landed headfirst in the ditch.

Variations

A. In addition to some basic meanings, some little German words have a flavor of their own that is not readily reproduced. At times they are therefore referred to as Füllwörter or Färbewörter, and are best understood in their German context. Suggested English equivalents often are mere approximations.

etwas

Etwas may mean "some," "something," "anything," "a bit," or "a while." Möchten Sie etwas (some) Tee? Darin ist etwas (something). Hat er etwas (anything) gesagt? Ich bitte Sie, etwas (a while) zu warten. But its meaning may also be elusive. Na, so etwas (. . . of all things)! Er wird es noch zu etwas (somewhere) bringen.

noch

Noch has several basic meanings and a number of extended connotations. It may mean "else" or "still." Was wünschen Sie noch (else)? Regnet es noch (still)? With numerals it means "more." Wünschen Sie noch ein Paar? Kann ich noch eine Tasse Tee haben? Other combinations are: *noch einmal* (once more), *noch nicht* (not yet), and *noch nie* (never before). Versuchen Sie es noch einmal. Ich bin noch nicht fertig. Ich war noch nie dort.

108

schon

The common equivalents of *schon* are: "already," "all right," "very," "yet." Ich habe es ihm schon (already) zweimal gesagt. Er weiß schon (all right) warum. Schon (very) der Gedanke daran plagt mich. Ist er schon (yet) gekommen? Es ist schon (already) spät, aber ich rufe ihn doch an. Note, however: Hast du es schon (... so soon) wieder vergessen? Na, wenn schon (... so what)! Schon (very) gut!

B. Simplify the Basic Patterns and, in the appropriate places, include variants of *etwas, noch, schon* and *der Mensch, gelingen, Fahrer, schnell, müssen, Fahrdamm, sich hinstrecken, machen, beenden.*

Conversation — Anmeldung im Hotel

Hotelbeamter:	Haben Sie sich schon angemeldet?
Herr Roth:	Noch nicht.
Hotelbeamter:	Darf ich Ihnen dann an die Hand gehen?
Herr Roth:	Ja, bitte.
Hotelbeamter:	(Nimmt die Feder in die Hand.) Also. Familien- und Vorname?
Herr Roth:	Roth, Richard.
Hotelbeamter:	Beruf?
Herr Roth:	Rechtsanwalt.
Hotelbeamter:	Ständiger Wohnort?
Herr Roth:	New York.
Hotelbeamter:	Straße und Hausnummer?
Herr Roth:	Parkstraße 25.
Hotelbeamter:	Geburtsort und Geburtstag?
Herr Roth:	New York, den 10. Mai 1930.
Hotelbeamter:	Voraussichtliche Dauer des Aufenthalts?
Herr Roth:	Zwei Wochen.
Hotelbeamter:	Gut. Wollen Sie gütigst hier unterschreiben?
Herr Roth:	Danke bestens.

CHAPTER SIXTEEN

The Modal Auxiliaries

Besides the three auxiliary verbs of tense (**sein, haben,** and **werden**),[1] there are in German six auxiliary verbs of mood (Appendix XIV). Of this number only four or possibly five remain in English (*can, may, must, shall,* and perhaps *will*).

(a) *FORMS*

16.1 In English the modals are defective. Of the verb *must*, for example, only a present tense form survives. In German, on the other hand, the modals are irregular (or appear to be)[2] only in the present tense of the indicative. Their past tense and past participle are formed on the analogy of weak verbs. Their key forms are:

Infinitive:	**dürfen**	**können**	**mögen**	**müssen**	**sollen**	**wollen**
3rd Sg. Past:	**durfte**	**konnte**	**mochte**	**mußte**	**sollte**	**wollte**
Past Part.:	**gedurft**	**gekonnt**	**gemocht**	**gemußt**	**gesollt**	**gewollt**
3rd Pl. Pres.:	**dürfen**	**können**	**mögen**	**müssen**	**sollen**	**wollen**
Past Part. Inf.:	**dürfen**	**können**	**mögen**	**müssen**	**sollen**	**wollen**
3rd Sg. Pres.:	**darf**	**kann**	**mag**	**muß**	**soll**	**will**

(b) *MEANINGS*

16.2 In general, the six modals express, respectively, the idea of permission, ability, possibility, compulsion, obligation, and intention. But some of their meanings are contiguous; in some cases they even overlap.

dürfen [3] (may)

to be allowed	Ich darf es tun.	I am allowed to do it.
(to be permitted)	Darf er?	May he?

können (can)

to be able	Ich konnte es nicht lesen.	I could not read it.
(to be permitted)	Ich konnte es nicht lesen.	I was not able (permitted) to read it.

---

[1] Cf. Chapters XIV and XV. [2] The seemingly irregular present tense forms are in fact past tense forms of verbs that were "strong" at one time. [3] With a negative **dürfen** means *must not*, as in **Das dürfen Sie nicht tun** (You must not do that).

	mögen (may)	
(to be possible)	Das mag sein.	That may be.
to like (to) [4]	Mag sie's tun?	Does she like to do it?

	müssen (must)	
to have to	Er muß nicht warten.	He does not have to wait.
(to be compelled to)	Muß ich singen?	Must I sing?

	sollen (shall)	
(to be supposed to)	Du sollst nicht stehlen.	Thou shalt not steal.
to be said to	Er soll gestohlen haben.	He is said to have stolen.

	wollen [5] (will)	
to want to	Er will Arzt werden.	He wants to become a doctor.
to claim to	Er will Arzt sein.	He claims to be a doctor.
to intend to	Er will Arzt werden.	He intends to become a doctor.

(c) *USES*

16.3 In English and in German modal auxiliaries are normally used with dependent infinitives.

(1) Such dependent infinitives are used without **zu** in German (and without *to* in English). Otherwise, dependent infinitives with **zu** in German generally correspond to the use of the infinitive with *to* in English.

> Er kann viel tun.
> He can do much.
>
> Er hat heute viel zu tun.
> He has much to do today.

(2) In clauses expressing purpose such infinitives with **zu** and *to* are introduced by the preposition **um** and *in order to*, respectively

> Ich arbeite, um Geld zu verdienen.
> I work (in order) to earn money.

---

[4] **Mögen,** meaning *to like,* functions like a transitive verb. [5] Note that **wollen,** meaning *to will* or *intend,* must not be confused with **werden,** meaning *shall* or *will* as the auxiliary of the future tense.

111

(3) The prepositions **anstatt** (*instead of*) and **ohne** (*without*) are also followed by an infinitive with **zu** in German, but not in English.

> Er nahm es, ohne ein Wort zu sagen.
> He took it without saying a word.

(4) If the dependent infinitive is a verb of motion, it is often omitted in German when the meaning is clear from the context.

> Jetzt muß ich nach Hause (gehen).
> Now I must go home.

(5) In the present and past perfect tenses of modals, a form of the past participle identical with the infinitive is used with a dependent infinitive. The result is a so-called double infinitive. That form, too, may be used without a dependent infinitive.

> Hat sie gehen wollen?
> Did she want to go?
>
> Nein, sie hat nicht gewollt (*or* wollen).
> No, she did not want to.

(6) In a dependent clause, the auxiliary of the verb precedes the double infinitive.

> Da sie zuerst nicht hatte gehen wollen, . . .
> Since she had not wanted to go at first, . . .

(d) *RELATED VERBS*

16.4 The verbs **heißen** (to bid, to command), **helfen, hören, lassen, sehen** always require a double infinitive construction and a dependent infinitive without **zu** (cf. 16.3 and 16.5).

Ich habe ihn kommen sehen.   I saw him coming (*or* come).

16.5 The verbs **brauchen** (to need to), **fühlen, lehren, lernen,** and **machen** sometimes function like modals and require a double infinitive construction and a dependent infinitive without **zu.**

Er hatte mich fallen lassen.   He had let me fall.

16.6 The verb **wissen** is conjugated like a modal auxiliary. It is (or seems to be) [6] "irregular" in the present indicative (**ich**

---

[6] Its present tense forms are, in fact, past tense forms of a verb that was "strong" at one time. Cf. 16.1 (footnote 2 above).

weiß, du weißt, er weiß, wir wissen, ihr wißt, sie wissen)
but regular in the remaining tenses (er wußte, er hat gewußt).
Wissen means *to know a fact*, wissen von *to know about*. It must
not be confused with kennen. Kennen means *to know a person*
or *a thing*. Note:

Ich weiß die Antwort.	I know the answer.
Was wissen Sie von ihm?	What do you know about him?
Kennt sie den Herrn?	Does she know the gentleman?
Kennt er diese Marke?	Does he know that brand?

16.7 The verb kennen, meaning *to know* (a person), must not
be mistaken for the modal auxiliary können, meaning *to be able*.
Ich kann Deutsch (*I know German*) is an idiomatic abbreviation
of Ich kann Deutsch sprechen (*I can speak German*).

BASIC PATTERNS

„Ich werde Landwirt," sagte Andreas, der älteste
unter den Jungen, zu Felix. „Ich muß mit etwas Lebendi-
gem zu tun haben. Auf dem Lande habe ich auch Abwechslung ..." „Ja, zwischen Kühen und Ochsen," fiel
ihm da Felix ins Wort. Doch Andreas ließ sich nicht   5
beirren. „Red nicht so dumm," sagte er. „Ein Landwirt
muß heute viel verstehen: vom Boden, vom Düngen, von
Landmaschinen und Schleppern, von Getreidearten und
Futterpflanzen, von der Tierzucht und von noch so
manchem. Dafür hat er auch sein eigenes Reich und   10
braucht nicht die Klinken fremder Leute zu putzen."
„Mag sein," entgegnete Felix. „Aber ich werde
Tankwart. Der Tankwart ..." „Was ist das mit dem
Tankwart," fragte jetzt Herr Müller, der zu den Jungen
in den Hof trat. „Wir streiten uns über künftige Berufe,   15
Onkel," antwortete Felix. „Ich sagte eben, ich werde
Tankwart. Denn der Tankwart in unserer Nachbarschaft
ist jedem gut bekannt, und seine Tankstelle ist besonders
beliebt." „Aber immer nur Benzin einfüllen, wird das
nicht langweilig?" warf nun Andreas ein.   20
„Keine Spur," meinte Felix. „Zum Tankwart ge-

113

Oben: Marktfrauen in Ulm.
Unten: Arbeiter am Hochofen.

hört schon mehr als einen Wagen bedienen. Da kommt
zum Beispiel ein schwarzer Mercedes vorgefahren, und
der Besitzer verlangt zehn Liter. Aber ich weiß bei
jedem Wagen, wieviel der Tank faßt. Da blicke ich unauffällig auf die Benzinuhr, die angibt, wieviel noch im 5
Tank ist, und sage höflich: ,Es gingen auch dreißig Liter
'rein.' Dazu sagt der Herr am Steuer gewöhnlich:
,Meinetwegen, so viel 'reingeht.' Während ich Scheiben,
Scheinwerfer und Stopplicht reinige, frage ich dann, ob
sonst alles in Ordnung wäre. Wenn der Wagen nicht 10
auf das richtige Tempo kommt oder der Motor unregelmäßig geht und leicht klopft, kann ich Verschiedenes
vorschlagen. Entweder müssen die Düsen gewechselt
werden, oder die Zündkerzen müssen ersetzt werden.
Vielleicht muß man die Benzinleitung durchblasen. 15
Vielleicht ist es gar schlechter Treibstoff. Haben die
Reifen zu wenig Druck, muß man sie auffüllen. Gelegentlich sind auch Pannen zu reparieren und andere kleine
Reparaturen vorzunehmen. Außerdem muß man sich
auf der Karte auskennen und Auskunft geben können 20
wie ein Reisebüro, und den besten Weg für den Kunden
herausbringen. Und wenn man sich eine schöne Tankstelle pachtet, mit Zapfanlage, Abschmiervorrichtungen,
Hebebühne, Waschanlagen und dergleichen, kann man
es mit Fleiß schon zu etwas bringen." 25

Questions

1. Worüber stritten Andreas und Felix? 2. Warum wollte Andreas
Landwirt werden? 3. Was dachte er von einem Tankwart? 4. Wieviel
muß ein Landwirt heute verstehen? 5. Was gehört zu einem Tankwart?
6. Warum wird mancher aber lieber Landwirt als Tankwart? 7. Welcher
Beruf bietet mehr Abwechslung? 8. Wie kann ein Tankwart es zu etwas
bringen? 9. Was gehört zu einer guten Tankstelle? 10. Inwiefern ist
eine Tankstelle ein Reisebüro?

Idiomatic Expressions

einem ins Wort fallen	to interrupt a person; to break into his conversation
sich beirren lassen	to be dissuaded

die Klinken fremder Leute	to depend on the whim of others;
putzen	to ring doorbells
sich streiten über (*acc.*)	to argue about
keine Spur	not at all
dazu gehört viel	that takes a lot
Auskunft geben	to give information
es zu etwas bringen	to get somewhere
ich werde es zu etwas bringen	I'll amount to something
hat er es zu etwas gebracht	does he amount to anything

EXERCISES

A. Relate the following sentences to the idiomatic expressions listed above. EXAMPLE: „Bringen Sie mir das Glas, bitte," sagte sie zu dem jungen Mann, der es zu etwas gebracht hatte.

1. Bringen Sie mir das Glas, bitte. 2. Er hatte den Streit angefangen. 3. Wo bekomme ich Auskunft? 4. Das Wort ist schwer zu verstehen. 5. Er fand ihre Spur sofort. 6. Ich putze mir die Schuhe. 7. Der Ball fällt ins Wasser. 8. Das Buch gehört nicht mir. 9. Die Tür hat keine Klinke. 10. Sie irrt sich nicht.

B. Fit a modal auxiliary into each sentence in A. EXAMPLE: Sie müssen mir das Glas bringen.

C. (1) Substitute the words in parentheses in the past perfect tense for the words in heavy type. (2) Change the number of each subject from the singular to the plural or vice versa.

1. Ein Landwirt **muß** so manches wissen. (können, sollen) 2. Ihr **solltet** Benzin einfüllen. (dürfen, müssen) 3. Er **soll** die Reifen auffüllen. (wollen, können) 4. Sie **mochten** das nicht. (wissen, kennen) 5. Er **will** reich sein. (sollen, müssen) 6. Lassen Sie ihn doch **gehen.** (fahren, laufen) 7. Hat er es tun **müssen?** (dürfen, sollen) 8. Warum hat sie nicht **gesollt?** (wollen, müssen) 9. Sie blieb zu Hause, da er hatte **gehen wollen.** (helfen können) 10. Er hat es **fühlen können.** (sagen sollen)

D. (1) Change the tenses to the perfect tense and use a demonstrative pronoun, wherever possible. (2) Start each sentence or question with *wer* or *was*.

1. Wie konnte ich es wissen? 2. Könnte ich ihn nur kennen! 3. Braucht sie es zu nehmen? 4. Sie hörte ihn singen. 5. Sie

116

ließ es nicht fallen. 6. Ich lasse ihn holen. 7. Kann er Deutsch? 8. Ich kenne den Herrn. 9. Sie weiß die richtige Antwort. 10. Kennt er die Marke?

E. List the principal parts of the verbs from which the following nouns derive: *Bedarf, Vermögen, Soll, Wille, Kenner.*

F. Explain in German: *Landwirt, Futterpflanze, Landmaschine, Getreideart, Tankwart, Reisebüro.*

G. Form nominal compounds of the words in the two columns and use the compounds in original sentences.

Tier	Tank
Stelle	Werfer
Schein	Werkstätte
Benzin	Zucht
Reparatur	Uhr

H. Supply the missing infinitives with or without **zu.**

1. Man muß fleißig arbeiten, um es zu etwas . . . 2. Er hätte dir nicht ins Wort fallen . . . 3. Anstatt es selbst . . . , habe ich es ihn tun . . . 4. Er las es, ohne ein Wort . . . 5. Soll ich den Arzt rufen . . .? 6. Müssen Sie schon nach Hause . . .? 7. Ich habe ihm helfen . . . , aber er lehnte es ab. 8. Wenn du nicht willst, brauchst du sie nicht . . . 9. Er wollte mich tanzen . . . 10. Es wäre schön, wenn er hätte . . . können.

Composition

1. You will probably ask why Felix wanted to become a gas station attendant? 2. Firstly, because he knew the gas station attendant in his neighborhood, who was very well liked, and whose gas station was very popular. 3. Moreover, Felix knew that it takes more than just pumping gas to be a good gas station attendant. 4. At the age of sixteen the boy knew that it takes more than cleaning windows, headlights, and tail lights. 5. "A good gas station attendant," he said to his uncle, "has to know how much each tank holds. 6. If he wants to, he can change spark plugs and make minor repairs. 7. But he must always be prepared to put air into tires and to repair flat tires. 8. Besides all that he must know his way around on the map." 9. "A good gas station attendant will also want to find the best routes for his customers," Felix explained to his friends.

117

10. "In short," he said, "I know that a gas station attendant can amount to something, if he works diligently. 11. However, I also know that he must be courteous and know a great deal."

Variations

Match and arrange in their proper order the portions of the familiar sayings listed in the two columns and explain their meaning in German.

alles gut	wer sucht
armer Mann	viel Segen
Gott lenkt	heute mir
morgen dir	Ende gut
viel Kinder	kranker Mann
der findet	der Mensch denkt
morgen tot	der mäht
wer sät	heute rot

Conversation — In Ferien

Hans Kahl:	Wann haben Sie Ferien?
Inge Roth:	Im August. Und Sie?
Hans Kahl:	Ich gehe im Juli in Urlaub.
Inge Roth:	Fahren Sie wieder an die See?
Hans Kahl:	Gewiß. Schwimmen ist meine Leidenschaft.
Inge Roth:	Nun, ich mache eine kleine Seereise.
Hans Kahl:	Doch nicht nach England?
Inge Roth:	Ja, auf zwei Wochen.
Hans Kahl:	Wie schön, da beneide ich Sie.
Inge Roth:	Nicht doch. Denn es gilt, recht gut Englisch zu lernen.
Hans Kahl:	Aber die Gelegenheiten!
Inge Roth:	Auf die freue ich mich auch.
Hans Kahl:	Fahren Sie allein?
Inge Roth:	Nein, meine Kusine macht mit.
Hans Kahl:	Dann wünsche ich euch beiden gute Reise.
Inge Roth:	Danke schön, lassen Sie sich's auch gut gehen.
Hans Kahl:	Auf Wiedersehen.

CHAPTER SEVENTEEN

Descriptive Adjectives and Adverbs

As in English, descriptive adjectives in German may be used predicatively or attributively.

(a) *PREDICATE ADJECTIVES*

17.1 When used predicatively (in an adjectival or adverbial sense),[1] descriptive adjectives never take endings in German. The superlative form (Chapter XVIII) may be considered an exception.

Das Mädchen ist jung.	The girl is young.
Er arbeitet schwer.	He works hard.
Wir arbeiten am schwersten.	We work hardest.

(b) *ATTRIBUTIVE ADJECTIVES*

17.2 When used attributively, that is, to modify nouns they precede, descriptive adjectives always take endings.[2]

(1) Singly or in series,[3] they take the so-called strong endings of the **der**-word,[4] when neither an inflected **der**-word nor an inflected **ein**-word precedes (Appendix VIII).

Armer Mann, kranker Mann.	Poor man, sick man.
Ein gutes Buch ist ein guter Freund.	A good book is a good friend.
Sie haben ein schönes, altes Haus.	They have a nice old home.
Er hat drei entzückende Kinder.	He has three charming children.

[1] In English, too, the word following the verb is an adjective, if it describes the subject, as in "He looks sad." It is an adverb, if it designates the manner of action of the verb, as in "She looks sadly at the broken plate." [2] They never take endings when they follow the noun they describe.

Wolken, dunkel und schwer, verdeckten den Himmel.
Clouds, dark and heavy, covered the sky.

[3] In colloquial speech only the first adjective takes strong endings. The adjectives that follow take weak endings. [4] Except in the genitive singular, masculine and neuter, where –**en** has supplanted the original –**es.**

Das ist alten Mannes Rede.   That is old man's talk.

(2) Singly or in series, they take the so-called weak –**en** endings,[5] when they are preceded by an inflected **der**-word or **ein**-word (Appendix VIII).

Er gab es dem alten Mann.	He gave it to the old man.
Sie las es in einem alten Buch.	She read it in an old book.

17.3 Capitalized adjectives used as nouns are subject to the same rules (1 and 2).

Er ist kein Fremder.	He is no stranger.
Ich traf einen Bekannten.	I met an acquaintance.

17.4 After the indefinite numerals **viele, wenige, andere, einige, manche, mehrere** descriptive adjectives, as in a series, take the so-called strong endings, except in the genitive plural, where –**en** is used instead of the original –**er**. After **alle,** all endings of the descriptive adjective are –**en.**

Es gibt viele gute Leute.	There are many good people.
Er hat alle guten Bücher gelesen.	He has read all good books.

17.5 Adjectives used as nouns after **allerlei** (*all kinds of*), **etwas, nichts, viel, wenig** are capitalized and take strong endings.

Das Buch enthält viel Neues.	The book contains much that is new.

17.6 When inflected, adjectives ending in –**el,** –**en,** –**er** usually drop the –**e**– of the ending.

Er aß trock(e)nes Brot.	He ate dry bread.

17.7 As indicated in (a) above, in the predicate in German, the uninflected form of the adjective is used adverbially to describe the manner of the action of the verb. (In English –*ly* is usually added to the adjective to change it into an adverb.)

Wir warten geduldig.	We are waiting patiently.
Sie fährt langsam.	She drives slowly.

[5] Except in five instances in the singular (the nominatives of the masculine, feminine, neuter and the accusatives of the feminine and neuter), where the ending is –**e** after inflected **der**-words.

Das scheue Mädchen sagte kein Wort.	The shy girl did not say a word.

17.8 Adverbs, which never double as adjectives, are relatively few in number in German. The most common are: **da, hier, dort, jetzt, hin, her, nun, schon, doch, noch, dann.**

Es ist jetzt Zeit.	It is time now.
Sie wartet noch.	She is still waiting.

BASIC PATTERNS

Jeder kannte Herrn Böckle nur zu gut. Herr Böckle litt nämlich an zwei weitverbreiteten Zeitkrankheiten. Er hatte erstens keine Zeit. Zweitens hatte er eine Vorliebe für alle ärgerlichen und verdrießlichen Seiten des Lebens. Gleich zu Tagesbeginn stellte Herr Böckle fest, daß der 5 Wecker ihn wieder einmal eine Viertelstunde zu früh geweckt und ihm fünfzehn kostbare Minuten Schlaf gestohlen hatte. Die mußte er nun untätig daliegen, während alle Sperlinge der Nachbarschaft zusammenkamen, um ihn mit ihrem Geschrei zu ärgern. Vor Ärger 10 merkte er so natürlich nicht, wie schnell die Minuten davonrasten, und mußte dann verzweifelte Versuche machen, sich gleichzeitig zu rasieren, den Schlips zu binden, das Frühstück zu verschlingen und die Morgenzeitung zu durchfliegen. 15

Draußen setzte sich der Ärger fort. Sobald die Straßenbahn ihn atemlos herbeistürzen sah, fuhr sie höhnisch klingelnd davon. Und kam eine zweite endlich nach fünfzehn Minuten, fuhr sie so langsam, daß Herr Böckle immer zu spät ins Büro kam. 20

Da las er eines Tages in einer Zeitschrift über die Bekämpfung der Zeitkrankheiten: „Nimm dir Zeit, wenn dir das Leben lieb ist, und mach das Beste daraus!" Und weil er sein Leben herzlich lieb hatte, sagte er am nächsten Morgen zu sich: „Nimm dir Zeit, Böckle!" 25 Als der Wecker klingelte, stieg er langsam aus dem Bett. Er rasierte sich langsam und ging erfrischt zum Frühstück, das ihm besonders gut schmeckte. Stand doch in der Zeitung, daß die Eier trotz der hohen Futterpreise erfreulich billig waren. 30

Herr Böckle war fast ein wenig froh, als die Straßenbahn auch diesmal davonfuhr, bevor er einsteigen konnte. „Nimm dir Zeit, Böckle," sagte er zu sich. „Mach das Beste daraus. Atme zehn Minuten länger die frische
5 Morgenluft ein." Der nächste Wagen war zwar ungewöhnlich voll, und sein Nebenmann machte sich mit seiner entfalteten Zeitung auch noch breit. Doch Herr Böckle blieb ruhig. Und als der Nebenmann sich sogar als sein allerhöchster Vorgesetzter herausstellte, der ihm
10 freundlich zunickte, gratulierte sich Böckle insgeheim. „Böckle, du bist ein famoser Kerl," sagte er zu sich. „Du machst schon das Beste daraus."

Questions

1. An welchen Zeitkrankheiten litt Herr Böckle? 2. Warum hatte er nie Zeit? 3. Was ärgerte ihn besonders? 4. Wo fand Böckle eines Tages ein Mittel gegen Zeitkrankheiten? 5. Was tat er nun jeden Morgen? 6. Warum störte ihn die Straßenbahn nicht mehr? 7. Was tat er, wenn jemand sich neben ihm in der Straßenbahn breit machte? 8. Wer nickte ihm einmal in der Straßenbahn zu? 9. Wie kam er jetzt ins Büro? 10. Warum gratulierte sich Böckle?

Idiomatic Expressions

leiden an (*acc.*)	to suffer from
zu Tagesbeginn	at the beginning of the day
vor Ärger	in (his) anger
lesen über (*acc.*)	to read about
nimm dir Zeit	take your time
mir ist das Leben lieb	I love life
sich breit machen	to spread oneself out
sich herausstellen als	to turn out to be
das Frühstück schmeckt mir gut	I like my breakfast

EXERCISES

A. Use the above expressions in sentences with adjectival or adverbial modifiers. EXAMPLE: Er litt an Zeitkrankheiten. Er litt an den neuesten Zeitkrankheiten. Er leidet neuestens an Zeitkrankheiten.

122

B. (1) Use the words in parentheses to complete the sentences. (2) Include a modal auxiliary in each sentence. 1. Der —— Müller kannte den —— Böckle. (ärgerlich, ruhig) 2. Er hat eine —— Vorliebe für die —— Seiten des Lebens. (stark, verdrießlich) 3. Die —— fünfzehn Minuten Schlaf waren ——. (letzt-, kostbar) 4. Alle —— Sperlinge kamen dann im —— Garten zusammen. (klein, jung) 5. Die —— Straßenbahn fuhr —— davon. (langsam, klingelnd) 6. Dem —— Herrn Böckle war das Leben ——. (lieb, müde) 7. Am —— Morgen holte er ihn —— ab. (nächst-, schnell) 8. Die —— Eier waren trotz der —— Futterpreise billig. (groß, hoch) 9. Er atmete die —— Morgenluft —— ein. (frisch, lange) 10. Die —— Zeitung störte den —— Böckle. (freundlich, entfaltet)

C. Supply the missing endings.

1. Arm— Mann, krank— Mann. 2. Schön— Mutter, schön— Tochter. 3. Alt— Haus, billig— Haus. 4. Sie haben ein schöner— Haus als wir. 5. Ist das eine neu— Tankstelle? 6. Ich nehme einen rot— Bleistift. 7. Nehmen Sie einen schwarz—. 8. Das ist eine freundlich—, alt— Dame. 9. Solch ein groß— Haus habe ich noch nicht gesehen. 10. Ein solch— Haus habe ich noch nicht gesehen. 11. Die Dächer viel— alt— Häuser sind aus Stroh. 12. Alle alt— Dächer sind hier aus Stroh.

D. (1) Pattern after the example questions and answers which include the following phrases: *eine weitverbreitete Zeitkrankheit, ein unerwarteter Tagesbeginn, hohe Futterpreise, eine ungewöhnliche Morgenzeitung, ein verdrießlicher Nebenmann, ein verzweifelter Fluchtversuch, eine langweilige Viertelstunde.* EXAMPLE: Was ist eine weitverbreitete Zeitkrankheit? Es ist eine Krankheit der Zeit, die weit verbreitet ist. (2) Derive at least one verb from each phrase and give its principal parts. EXAMPLE: hohe Futterpreise — füttern, preisen, erhöhen.

E. Correct the following statements and modify each noun or noun phrase with an adjective.

1. Herr Müller kannte Herrn Böckle nicht. 2. Herr Müller litt an zwei Zeitkrankheiten. 3. Herr Böckle las ein Buch beim Frühstück. 4. Als der Wecker klingelte, sprang Herr Böckle aus dem Bett. 5. Er ließ sich rasieren. 6. Die Eier waren sehr teuer. 7. Herr Böckle stieg in den ersten Straßenbahnwagen. 8. Die

123

Straßenbahn war leer. 9. Der Nebenmann las in einem Buch.
10. Der Nebenmann sah Herrn Böckle nicht an.

F. (1) Form nouns by combining: (a) the endings *–heit* or
–keit with (the adjectives) *schön, dankbar, frei, heiter, lustig,
dumm*; (b) the endings *–ei* or *–schaft* with (the nouns) *Bruder,
Bäcker, Ort, Schlosser, Herr, Nachbar, Ziegel, Maler*; (c) the
endings *–er* or *–ung* with (the verbal stems of) *wandern, heizen,
schreiben, zahlen, sprechen, wenden, rechnen, lehren.* (2) Use one
example from each of (a), (b), and (c) in a complete sentence.
EXAMPLES: (a) selten — die Seltenheit; (b) der Freund — die
Freundschaft; (c) kreuzen — die Kreuzung. Ein Elefant ist
bei uns eine Seltenheit. Auf seine Freundschaft lege ich großen
Wert. Der Wagen hielt vor der Kreuzung.

Composition

1. Because Mr. Böckle liked⌣himself⌣very⌣much, he said
to himself: "Take your time." 2. When the alarm rang, he no
longer jumped out of bed. 3. Instead he got out of bed slowly.
4. He didn't make a desperate effort to shave and tie his bow⌣tie
at⌣the⌣same⌣time. 5. He even shaved himself slowly every
morning and enjoyed his good breakfast. 6. Outside he breathed⌣
in the fresh morning⌣air and waited patiently for the second streetcar, when the first rushed⌣off. 7. When it finally came⌣along, he
got⌣on even when it was unusually full. 8. He even stayed calm
when the man⌣next⌣to⌣him (then) unfolded his large newspaper.
9. He then merely said to himself again and again: "Böckle, make
the best of it." 10. On a certain day he was really glad⌣of⌣it
when the man⌣next⌣to⌣him turned out to be (i.e. when it turned
out that the man⌣next⌣to⌣him was) his superior who nodded to
him cordially. 11. Böckle could then really congratulate himself
and say to himself quietly: "Böckle, you are a fine fellow. 12. I
know you are making the best of it."

Variations

Match and arrange in their proper order the portions of the
familiar sayings listed in the two columns and explain their meaning in German.

so schläft man auch	hilf dir selbst
eines Mannes Rede	wie man sich bettet

fleißiger Lehrer	ohne Leid
keine Freud	dem wird gegeben
das Leben ist kurz	die Kunst ist lang
andere Sitten	keines Mannes Rede
wer hat	fleißiger Schüler
so hilft dir Gott	andere Länder

Conversation — Im Lebensmittelgeschäft

Verkäufer:	Was darf's heute sein, Frau Strauß?
Frau Strauß:	Vor allem ein Pfund Butter bitte, ein halbes Pfund Schweizerkäse und einen Karton Eier.
Verkäufer:	Sonst etwas?
Frau Strauß:	Ist der Spargel frisch?
Verkäufer:	Ja, ganz frisch, von heute morgen. Außerdem haben wir frischen Spinat und Blumenkohl.
Frau Strauß:	Dann geben Sie mir ein Kilo Spargel und ein Pfund Spinat.
Verkäufer:	Darf ich Ihnen unsere frischen Tomaten empfehlen? Sie sind diesmal besonders schön.
Frau Strauß:	Wieviel kostet das Kilo? Schön sind sie ja.
Verkäufer:	Nur dreißig Pfennig das Kilo.
Frau Strauß:	Gut, dann nehme ich zwei Kilo.
Verkäufer:	Haben gnädige Frau sonst noch einen Wunsch?
Frau Strauß:	Nein, danke. Wieviel schulde ich? (Bezahlt. Empfiehlt sich.)
Verkäufer:	Danke vielmals. Schönen guten Tag.

CHAPTER EIGHTEEN

Comparison of Adjectives and of Adverbs

As in English, there are three degrees of comparison in German:
positive, comparative, and superlative.

125

(a) COMPARISON OF ADJECTIVES

18.1 In English, adjectives of more than one syllable are usually compared with *more* and *most*, whereas adjectives of one syllable are usually compared by adding *–er* and *–(e)st* to the positive. In German, only **–er** and **–(e)st**,[1] and a possible umlaut, are used to form the comparative and superlative of adjectives.[2] (The umlaut is usually added in the comparative and superlative to the stem vowel, **a, o,** or **u,** of adjectives of one syllable.)

POSITIVE	COMPARATIVE	SUPERLATIVE
klein	kleiner	kleinst–
jung	jünger	jüngst–

18.2 Among the very common adjectives which have different or irregular forms or deviations in spelling in the comparative and superlative in German are: **gut (besser, der beste), hoch**[3] **(höher, der höchste), nah (näher, der nächste), viel (mehr, der meiste),** and **groß (größer, der größte).**

18.3 As in the positive degree, descriptive adjectives in the comparative and superlative degree may be used either attributively or predicatively.

18.4 Attributively, the comparative forms in **–er** and the superlative forms in **–(e)st** are declined like ordinary adjectives.

Sein älterer Bruder war hier.	His older brother was here.
Ist er der jüngste?[4]	Is he the youngest?
Fritz ist der jüngste.[4]	Fritz is the youngest.

18.5 Attributively, the inflected comparative (and adverbially the uninflected superlative) is sometimes used in an absolute manner to express a very high degree without actual comparison.

Der ältere Herr zeigte mir ein höchst interessantes Buch.
The elderly gentleman showed me a highly interesting book.

---

[1] The **–e–** is inserted after **s, sch, ß, z, t, d,** but not **isch, nd: weisest, heißest, fadest,** but **närrischst, brennendst.** [2] The analytic form of the comparative is used in German only to compare two qualities of one and the same noun, as in **Das Bild ist mehr grausig als schön** (The picture is more gruesome than it is beautiful). [3] In the positive **hoch** also drops the c when inflected, as in **der hohe Baum.** [4] In these examples the noun **(Bruder)** is distinctly understood.

18.6 Predicatively, the comparative (adjective or adverb) forms in –**er**,[5] and the superlative (adjective or adverb) forms, introduced by **am** and ending in –**sten,** add no other endings.

Welche Stadt ist größer?	Which city is larger?
Wer fährt langsamer?	Who drives more slowly?
Welche Stadt ist am größten?	Which city is (the) [6] largest?
Wer fährt am langsamsten?	Who drives most slowly?

(b) *COMPARISON OF ADVERBS*

18.7 As indicated above and in Chapter XVII, most adjectives in German can be used predicatively, and in their predicate form they can serve as adverbs (of manner), not only in the positive, but also in the comparative and superlative degrees.

Er schreibt schön, sie schreibt schöner, aber Marie schreibt am schönsten.
He writes beautifully, she writes more beautifully, but Marie writes most beautifully.

18.8 To express a very high degree without comparison, the superlative adverb may be used in an absolute manner, in which case it is introduced by **aufs (auf das)** and ends in –**ste.**

> Sie behandelten mich aufs freundlichste.
> They treated me very (*or* most) cordially.

18.9 Among the very common adverbs which form their comparative and superlative forms from other stems are: **bald (eher, am ehesten), gern (lieber, am liebsten),** and **wohl (besser, am besten).**

Ich trinke Kaffee lieber.   I like (to drink) coffee better. I prefer coffee.

(c) *PHRASES OF COMPARISON*

18.10 The phrases used in comparisons in German are: **so . . . wie** (*as . . . as*) and **nicht so . . . wie** (*not so . . . as*) with the positive; **als** (*than*) after a comparative; and **je . . . je** (or **desto,** or **umso**) (*the . . . the*) to correlate two comparatives.

Er ist so alt wie ich.	He is as old as I.
Er ist nicht so groß wie ich.	He is not so tall as I.

[5] Preceded by **immer,** the comparative renders the English double comparative. **Die Tage werden immer länger.** *The days are becoming longer and longer.*
[6] Note that *the largest* implies *city* and means **die größte,** that is, **Stadt.**

Sie ist jünger als ich.	She is younger than I.
Je mehr er hat, desto mehr	The more he has, the more
braucht er.[7]	he needs.
Er hat weniger als ich.	He has less than I.

BASIC PATTERNS

Als Ursula Ries aus dem Fleischerladen trat, dämmerte es schon leicht, und ein Nebel ließ die Umrisse von Menschen und Gegenständen noch undeutlicher erscheinen. Plötzlich fühlte sich Ursula verfolgt. Tatsächlich
5 ging ein Mann hinter ihr her. Er trug einen schwarzen Mantel mit hochgeschlagenem Kragen und folgte ihr. Nein, kein Zweifel, er verfolgte sie tatsächlich.

Wie unheimlich. Unglücklicherweise wohnte Ursula draußen am Stadtrand, wo die Straßenbeleuchtung spär-
10 lich ist. Sie ging daher schneller. Sie fühlte, daß ihr die Angst zu Herz kroch. Ein Blick zurück verriet, daß sie den Schatten immer noch nicht verloren hatte. Ihr Puls hämmerte. Sie ging schneller und schneller und doch war ihr, als käme sie keinen Schritt voran. Wenn der Mensch
15 sie jetzt überfiele? Keine Seele weit und breit! Niemand würde ihren Schrei hören. Grauenhafter Gedanke! Warum hatte sie ihren Mann nicht gebeten, ihr entgegenzukommen? Nie wieder würde sie abends allein durch die menschenleeren Straßen gehen!
20 Sollte sie in ein x-beliebiges Haus eintreten ... Aber wenn der Fremde schneller wäre? Ein dunkler, unbekannter Hausflur ... Nein, da wäre sie völlig ausgeliefert. Ihr Herz schlug ihr bis zum Halse, als sie endlich das Zweifamilienhaus, in dem sie wohnte, vor
25 sich auftauchen sah.

Ursula blickte sich um. Der Mann gestikulierte offenbar mit einem Stock heftig in der Luft herum und rief etwas, was wie „Stehenbleiben" klang. Sie dachte nicht daran und hetzte weiter. Die Vorgartentür schlug
30 dem Fremden fast ins Gesicht. Sie stürzte im Dunkeln

---

[7] Note the word order in the second clause.

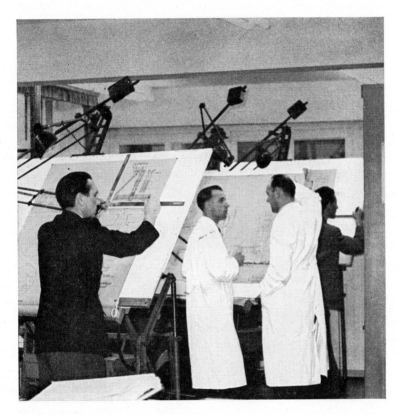

Ingenieure am Reißbrett.

die Treppe hinauf und klingelte wild. Ihr Mann kam
glücklicherweise sofort zur Tür. „Wo brennt's denn?"
fragte er. Ursula drückte die Tür zu und lehnte sich
aufatmend dagegen. „Peter, ein Mann," gab sie ihm
5 nach Atem ringend zur Antwort. „Ein Mann war hinter
mir her. Ja, er hat mich bis hierher verfolgt. Ich bin
doch so gerannt!"
    Peter lehnte sich weit aus dem Fenster. Weit und
breit war nichts zu sehen. „Liebling," sagte er, „vielleicht
10 hast du geträumt. Der Nebel..." In dem Augenblick
klingelte es. „O Peter, was habe ich gesagt. Der Fremde!
Geh ja nicht zur Tür. Um alles in der Welt! Vielleicht
ist er ein Dieb oder... ein Mörder?" Sie hielt ihren
Mann fest. „Aber das ist doch dumm," beschwichtigte
15 er sie. „Einbrecher, die klingeln..."
    Peter ging öffnen. An der Tür stand ein Mann,
schwarzgekleidet und völlig außer Atem. „Der Schirm,"
stieß er hervor. „Die Dame ließ den Schirm im Fleischerladen stehen... Ich lief ihr nach... Hier ist er."

Questions

1. Wann trat Ursula Ries aus dem Fleischerladen? 2. Wen bemerkte sie im Nebel hinter sich? 3. Wie sah der Mann aus? 4. Warum
hatte sie so große Angst? 5. Wie war die Straßenbeleuchtung am Stadtrand? 6. Was rief ihr der Fremde nach? 7. Warum trat Ursula nicht
in ein x-beliebiges Haus? 8. Was erzählte sie ihrem Mann? 9. Was
erklärte er ihr? 10. Weshalb war der Fremde ihr nachgelaufen?

Idiomatic Expressions

es ist mir, als (ob)	I feel as if
weit und breit	far and wide
wo brennt's	where's the fire
nach Atem ringen	to struggle for breath
zur Antwort geben	to reply (*in answer*)
hinter einem her sein	to be after a person
sich aus dem Fenster lehnen	to lean out the window
x-beliebig	just any, any given
außer Atem	out of breath

ihr Herz schlug bis zum Halse	her heart was in her mouth
um alles in der Welt	by all that is dear to you
nicht um alles in der Welt	not for anything in the world

EXERCISES

A. Complete the idiomatic patterns and change the tense to the perfect.

1. Es ist mir, als ob... 2. Es war weit und... 3. Sie rang nach... 4. Er gab ihm kein Wort zur... 5. Es war niemand hinter... 6. Er lehnte sich weit aus... 7. Das Kind war außer... 8. Das Herz schlug ihm...

B. (1) Include a modal auxiliary in each sentence. (2) Change the tense to the perfect. EXAMPLE: Ursula tritt in den Laden. Ursula will in den Laden treten. Ursula hat in den Laden treten wollen.

1. Ein Mann ging tatsächlich hinter ihr. 2. Er trug einen Mantel. 3. Ursula hat einen Schirm. 4. Sie wohnte am Stadtrand. 5. Sie ging allein. 6. Sie bat erst ihren Mann. 7. Dann blickte sie sich um. 8. Jemand stürzte die Treppe hinauf. 9. Ursula drückte die Tür zu. 10. Die Dame ließ den Schirm im Laden stehen.

C. Add an adjective or an adverb in the comparative or superlative to each sentence in B. EXAMPLE: Ursula tritt in den Laden. Ursula tritt schneller (*or* am schnellsten) in den Laden. Ursula tritt schneller (*or* am schnellsten) in den größeren (*or* größten) Laden. Die schnellere Ursula tritt zuerst in den Laden.

D. Supply the proper form of the adjective or adverb in parentheses.

1. Die Dämmerung ließ alles undeutlich erscheinen, aber der Nebel machte alles noch (undeutlich). 2. Der Mann ging schnell, doch Ursula ging (schnell). 3. Je schneller sie ging, desto (schnell) ging er. 4. Am Stadtrand ist die Beleuchtung spärlicher. Auf dem Lande ist sie (spärlich). 5. Kennen Sie den (alt) von ihren drei Brüdern? 6. Ursula war (hoch) erschrocken. 7. Peter hatte (wenig) Angst als Ursula. 8. Peter hatte nicht so (viel) Geld wie Ursula. 9. Er wohnt in dem (schön) Viertel der Stadt. 10. Sie wird immer (alt).

✓**E.** Change one of the paired sentences into (1) a relative clause, and (2) an adjectival modifier. EXAMPLE: Sie sieht einen Mann. Der Mann geht schnell. Sie sieht den Mann, der (*or* welcher) schnell geht. Sie sieht den schnell gehenden Mann.

1. Ursula wohnt am Stadtrand. Der Stadtrand ist spärlich beleuchtet. 2. Sie kam keinen Schritt durch den Nebel voran. Der Nebel wurde dicht. 3. Ein Mädchen hörte ihren Schrei. Das Mädchen lehnte sich aus dem kleinen Fenster. 4. Der Mann gestikulierte. Er hatte einen Stock in der rechten Hand. 5. Die Tür schlug ihm ins Gesicht. Der Mann klingelte.

Composition

1. Ursula was on her way home. 2. She was walking fast, because she lived at the edge of town and it was getting dark. 3. Suddenly she felt that someone was following her. 4. She now began to walk even faster. 5. Her heart was in her mouth when she looked back. 6. Behind her was a man in a black coat with [a] turned up collar. 7. He gesticulated violently and seemed to shout something which sounded like "stop." 8. Instead she began to run. 9. When she reached the two-family house in which she lived, she dashed up the stairs and rang the bell wildly. 10. When her husband let her in, she threw the door shut, leaned against it, and heaved a deep sigh of relief. 11. "Peter," she finally said, gasping for breath, "a man!— 12. A man was after me." 13. But when Peter leaned out the window, there was not a soul to be seen. 14. Just then, however, the doorbell rang. 15. At the door stood a man dressed in black, all out of breath. 16. "The lady left the umbrella in the butcher shop," he said. 17. "I ran after her. 18. Here it is."

Variations

Match and arrange in their proper order the portions of the familiar sayings listed in the two columns and explain their meaning in German.

viele wissen viel	keine Tat
Zeit bringt Rosen	hat nichts zu fürchten
alle Morgen	wird morgen etwas haben

alles vergeht	muß früh aufstehen
wer weit will gehen	Tugend besteht
wer heute spart	neue Sorgen
ohne Rat	aber auch Dornen
wer recht hat	niemand weiß alles

Conversation — Eine Verabredung

Fritz Werner:	Sind Sie morgen nachmittag frei?
Marie Kraue:	Nein, ich bin um drei zum Zahnarzt bestellt.
Fritz Werner:	Wie wär's übermorgen?
Marie Kraue:	Am Freitag habe ich nichts Besonderes vor.
Fritz Werner:	Dürfte ich Sie dann zu einem kleinen Ausflug einladen?
Marie Kraue:	Wohin denn?
Fritz Werner:	Aufs Land.
Marie Kraue:	Kommt sonst jemand mit?
Fritz Werner:	Fritz Müller und Lotte Groh.
Marie Kraue:	Die Lotte kenne ich aber nicht.
Fritz Werner:	Doch. Ich habe sie Ihnen in der Bücherei vorgestellt.
Marie Kraue:	Hat sie blondes Haar?
Fritz Werner:	Ja, und sie studiert Medizin.
Marie Kraue:	Jetzt entsinne ich mich.
Fritz Werner:	Dann machen Sie mit?
Marie Kraue:	Aber nur, wenn das Wetter gut ist.
Fritz Werner:	Schön. Ich hole Sie Punkt eins zu Hause ab.
Marie Kraue:	Sind wir um sechs wieder zurück?
Fritz Werner:	Noch vor sechs, denn Lotte geht nachher ins Theater.
Marie Kraue:	Also bis Freitag.
Fritz Werner:	Auf Wiedersehen.

CHAPTER NINETEEN

Coordinating and Subordinating Conjunctions

As in English, there are basically two types of conjunctions in German: (a) coordinating conjunctions and (b) subordinating conjunctions.

(a) *COORDINATING CONJUNCTIONS*

19.1 Coordinating conjunctions connect two words, phrases, or independent clauses, and do not affect the word order in English or in German. The most common coordinating conjunctions and their meanings in German [1] are:

aber		**und**	and
sondern	but	**oder**	or
allein		**denn**	for, because

Karl und Fritz warteten, aber Marie kam nicht.
Karl and Fritz waited, but Marie did not come.

19.2 In pairs coordinating conjunctions are called correlatives. The most common are:

entweder . . . oder	either . . . or
weder . . . noch	neither . . . nor

Weder er noch ich waren [2] anwesend.	Neither he nor I was [2] present.
Er ist weder dumm noch faul.	He is neither stupid nor lazy.
Entweder du kommst mit, oder ich bleibe zu Hause.	Either you come along, or I stay home.

(b) *SUBORDINATING CONJUNCTIONS*

19.3 Subordinating conjunctions do not affect the word order in English, but they do in German. In the latter they introduce dependent clauses, always set off by commas, in which the finite or inflected verb is at the end. The most common subordinating conjunctions in German and their meanings [1] are:

als	when	**bevor**	before
wenn	when, if, whenever	**ehe**	before

[1] See "Similarities and Differences" in section (c) p. 135 for some related and conflicting meanings and uses. [2] Note the differences in the usage of the verb form in English and in German.

da	since, (inasmuch) as	**bis**	until
indem	as	**daß**	that
seit(dem)	(ever) since	**damit**	in order that
obgleich		**nachdem**	after (having)
obwohl	although	**während**	while
obzwar		**weil**	because

Es geschah, während ich schlief. It happened while I slept.

19.4 In indirect questions and after verbs, such as **hören, sehen, wissen,** the interrogatives also serve as subordinating conjunctions. The most common are:

wann	when	**wieviel**	how much
warum	why	**ob**	whether
was	what	**wo**	where
wer	who	**woher**	whence, from where
wie	how	**wohin**	where (to)

Er fragte, wieviel es kostete. He asked how much it cost.

(c) SIMILARITIES AND DIFFERENCES

19.5 Of the coordinating conjunctions listed above, **aber** and **allein** are identical in meaning and usage, except that **aber** is used more commonly than **allein.**

Ich rief ihn, allein (*or* aber) sie kam. I called him, but she came.

19.6 **Sondern,** meaning *but* or *on the contrary*, is used only after a negative clause to indicate contrast.

Nicht ich, sondern er nahm es. Not I but he took it.

19.7 **Denn** and **weil** are identical in meaning, but **denn** is a coordinating and **weil** a subordinating conjunction.

Er blieb zu Hause, denn es regnete gestern. He stayed at home because
Er blieb zu Hause, weil es gestern regnete. it rained yesterday.

19.8 The subordinating conjunction **als** also means *as* or *than* (in comparisons); **da** also serves as an adverb, meaning *here* or *there*.

Als Knabe war er stärker. As a boy he was stronger.
Jetzt bin ich stärker als er (es ist). Now I am stronger than he (is).
Da er wartete, stieg ich sofort ein. Since he was waiting, I got in immediately.
Da stand er. There he stood.

135

19.9 The subordinating conjunctions **bis** (meaning *until, up to, as far as*), **seit** (meaning *since*), and **während** (meaning *during*) respectively, also serve as prepositions.

Es dauerte von Montag bis Freitag.	It lasted from Monday until Friday.
Er wartete, bis ich kam.	He waited until I came.
Ich kenne ihn, seit er hier wohnt.	I have known him, ever since he has lived here.
Er wartet seit gestern.	He has been waiting since yesterday.

19.10 The subordinating conjunctions **als, wenn,** and the interrogative adverb **wann** may all mean *when.* Yet they are not interchangeable. **Wann** refers only to time in questions, **wenn** is used in conditions, and **als** in all remaining instances to report a single event in the past.

Als er kam, fragte er, wann du hier gewesen warst.	When he came, he asked, when you had been here.
Wenn er nochmal fragt, werde ich es ihm sagen.	When he asks again, I will tell him.

BASIC PATTERNS

Papa grollte wie ein Vulkan unmittelbar vor dem Ausbruch und schlug mit der Faust auf den Tisch, daß das Geschirr hüpfte. Mama bekam Schüttelfrost vor Aufregung, und ihre Hände begannen zu zittern. Julia,
5 ihre Tochter, kämpfte mit den Tränen.
„Wir lieben uns!" schluchzte sie. „Einen Mann mit roten Haaren!" schrie Papa. „Niemals!" entsetzte sich Mama und schnappte nach Luft. „Schließlich haben deine Eltern auch noch ein Wörtchen mitzureden, wen du heira-
10 test!" warf Papa ein. „Ein anderer Mann kommt nicht in Frage," sagte Julia trotzig. Sie schien sich als erste gefaßt zu haben. Sie erhob sich rasch, warf den Kopf in den Nacken, daß die schwarzen Locken nur so herumwirbelten, warf die Serviette zu Boden und die Tür zu
15 ihrem Zimmer ins Schloß.
Empört blickten sich Papa und Mama groß an. „Deine Tochter!" sagte er. „Unsere Tochter!" ver-

besserte sie. „Ausgerechnet einen rothaarigen Schwiegersohn!" stöhnte Papa. „Das überlebe ich nicht!" meinte
Mama. „Ich werde mit dem Kind mal alles in Ruhe
besprechen," sagte Papa. Er stand auf und ging zu seiner
Tochter ins Zimmer. 5
Als er eintrat, legte Julia schnell den Hörer auf das
Telefon. „Ich habe dem Fritz eben gesagt, daß ihr ihn
nicht leiden könnt, weil er rote Haare habe!" erklärte sie
erregt. „Das ist ja unerhört!" rief Papa ärgerlich. „Wie
taktlos! Du blamierst uns ja," ergänzte Mama, die 10
inzwischen dazugetreten war. „Das muß ich gleich in
Ordnung bringen!" bestimmte die Mutter und stellte
eine neue Verbindung mit Fritz her. Sie bat ihn, am
Nachmittag zum Tee zu kommen, um das angebliche
Mißverständnis aufzuklären. Julia war indessen schon 15
an der Tür. „Wenn ich ihn nicht heiraten darf, gehe ich
ins Wasser," rief sie beim Hinausgehen.
Der Nachmittag verging. Minute auf Minute,
Stunde auf Stunde verrann. Papa begann, des öftern
auf die Uhr zu sehen. Unruhig ging er im Zimmer auf 20
und ab. „Das habe ich geahnt!" sagte Mama in weiner-
lichem Ton. „Das arme Kind! Vielleicht tut sie sich
wirklich was an." „Unsinn!" entgegnete Papa, „sie
spaziert wahrscheinlich durch die frische Luft. Das ist
sehr gesund." 25
Es war völlig dunkel, als es endlich klingelte. Vor
der Tür stand ein schwarzhaariger Fritz und drehte verlegen den Hut in den Händen. „Ich war beim Frisör,"
entschuldigte er seine Verspätung. Jetzt trat auch Julia
zur Tür herein. Sie erbleichte, als sie Fritzens schwarzes 30
Haar entdeckte. Und als er wissen wollte, wo sie denn
gewesen wäre, nahm sie fassungslos ihr Kopftuch ab.
Dabei fielen ihr ihre nun feuerroten Locken über Stirn
und Nacken, bei deren Anblick Mama ihrem zukünftigen
Schwiegersohn ohnmächtig in die Arme sank. 35

Questions

1. Mit wem saß Julia zu Tisch? 2. Warum waren ihre Eltern so erregt? 3. Weshalb wollte sie Fritz heiraten? 4. Was sagte sie ihm am Telefon? 5. Wie wollte die Mutter das Mißverständnis aufklären? 6. Was rief Julia noch beim Hinausgehen? 7. Was taten die Eltern den ganzen Nachmittag? 8. Wie entschuldigte Fritz seine Verspätung? 9. Warum war Fritz beim Frisör gewesen? 10. Was entdeckte Julia an der Tür? 11. Wie gefielen Julias rote Locken der Mutter?

Idiomatic Expressions

auf den Tisch schlagen	to pound the table
(den) Schüttelfrost bekommen	to get the shivers
vor Aufregung	in (or with or out of) excitement
nach Luft schnappen	to gasp for air
ein Wort mitzureden haben	to have something to say
in Frage kommen	to be in question
den Kopf in den Nacken werfen	to throw one's head back
die Tür ins Schloß werfen	to slam the door shut
den Hörer auf das Telefon legen	to put down the receiver
in Ordnung bringen	to straighten out
zum Tee bitten	to ask to tea
ins Wasser gehen	to jump in the river (or lake, etc.)
Minute auf Minute	minute after minute
sich etwas antun	to do oneself some harm

EXERCISES

A. Form sentences with the components of the idiomatic expressions above. EXAMPLE: Er schlägt mit der Faust auf den Tisch. Er legt das Buch auf den Tisch. Er schlägt das Kind.

B. Use each sentence in A as a main or a dependent clause of a compound or a complex sentence. EXAMPLE: Es ärgert sie, daß er mit der Faust auf den Tisch schlägt. Sie nahm das Buch, nachdem er es auf den Tisch gelegt hatte. Sie schreit, weil er das Kind schlägt.

✓C. Make two sentences out of one. EXAMPLE: Er schlug mit der Faust auf den Tisch, daß das Geschirr klirrte. Er schlug mit der Faust auf den Tisch. Das Geschirr klirrte.

1. Sie bekam Schüttelfrost, und ihre Hände zitterten. 2. Der Vater entsetzte sich, doch die Mutter schnappte nach Luft.

138

3. Sie schmiß die Serviette zu Boden, weil er ins Zimmer trat.
4. Als er eintrat, legte sie den Hörer auf das Telefon. 5. Leider kann ich ihn nicht leiden, weil er rote Haare hat. 6. Sie bat ihn zum Tee, um das Mißverständnis aufzuklären. 7. Wenn ich ihn nicht heiraten darf, gehe ich ins Wasser. 8. Es war völlig dunkel, als es endlich klingelte. 9. Fritz stand vor der Tür, aber er drehte verlegen den Hut. 10. Als er es wissen wollte, nahm sie fassungslos das Kopftuch ab.

D. Connect each pair of sentences by means of the coordinating and subordinating conjunctions in parentheses.

1. Die Tochter blickte die Mutter an. Sie sank ohnmächtig zu Boden. (als, jedoch) 2. Julia kämpfte mit den Tränen. Sie liebte Fritz. (denn, weil) 3. Die Mutter freute sich. Sie mochte keinen Schwiegersohn mit roten Haaren. (obzwar, aber) 4. Das Mädchen faßte sich zuerst. Sie wollte keinen anderen. (trotzdem, allein) 5. Sie ging auf ihr Zimmer. Der Vater erhob sich rasch. (während, und)

E. Add one or two of the following descriptive adjectives to each sentence in D: *erregt, unglücklich, trotzig, rothaarig, weinerlich, gesund, klein, ärgerlich.* EXAMPLE: Die unglückliche Tochter blickte die erregte Mutter an.

F. (1) Supply a dependent clause. (2) Change the past tense to the perfect.

1. Der Vater mußte mit der Faust auf den Tisch schlagen, weil . . . 2. Die Mutter wollte mit der Tochter reden, obzwar . . . 3. Das Mädchen konnte nicht antworten, da . . . 4. Der junge Mann möchte Julias schwarze Haare, weil . . . 5. Julia durfte nichts sagen, während . . .

Composition

1. Papa rumbled like a volcano about to erupt, Mama trembled with excitement, and their daughter, Julia, could not hold back her tears. 2. Julia wanted to marry Fritz, but Fritz had red hair, and her parents could not abide a red-headed son-in-law. 3. "If I cannot marry him," Julia finally said, "I'll drown myself." 4. Then she got up quickly, tossed her head defiantly in the air, and stormed out of the room. 5. "Of all

139

things, a red-headed son-in-law," groaned Julia's father. 6. "It will͜be͜the͜death͜of͜me," wailed her mother. 7. "Meanwhile, however, I must call Fritz to set͜things͜straight. 8. I'll invite him over for tea this afternoon." 9. But the afternoon passed without Fritz or Julia. 10. It was almost dark when the doorbell rang at͜last. 11. At the door now stood a black-haired Fritz and twisted his hat in his hands. 12. "I was at the barber's," he explained somewhat embarrassed. 13. At that moment Julia appeared. 14. She grew͜pale at the sight of Fritz' black hair. 15. But her mother fainted in the arms of her future son-in-law when she saw Julia's fiery͜red curls.

Variations

A. In addition to several basic meanings, some German words have a flavor of their own that is not readily reproduced. At times, they are therefore referred to as Füllwörter or Färbewörter and are best understood in their German context. Suggested English equivalents are often mere approximations.

denn

Among the basic meanings of *denn* are: "for" or "because," and "than" following a comparative. Ich kann nicht kommen, denn (because) ich muß arbeiten. Jetzt mehr denn (than) je. Almost as common a meaning is "then." Nimm es denn! Nun gut denn! *Es sei denn* corresponds to "lest" or "unless." Ich habe es nicht hier; es sei denn in meinem Zimmer. Very often *denn* is used for emphasis: Ist denn so etwas möglich? Weiß ich's denn?

nur

In a narrow sense *nur* means "only," "merely," "just," and "possibly." Er war nur (only) drei Tage bei uns. Ich habe nur (merely) gefragt. Reg dich nur (just) nicht auf. Er arbeitet so schnell wie er nur (possibly) kann. It corresponds to "I wonder" in „Wo hat er das nur her?" and „Wo hab' ich nur meine Uhr hingelegt?"

B. Simplify the Basic Patterns and, in the appropriate places, include variants of *denn, einmal, nur* and *der Teller, außer sich* (dat.) *sein, rufen, wollen, aufstehen, stürmen aus* (dat.), *treten, mögen, beschämen, einladen, immer wieder.*

Conversation — Im Konfektionsgeschäft

Verkäufer:	(Kommt auf Herrn Ebert zu.) Werden Sie schon bedient?
Herr Ebert:	Noch nicht! Ich möchte einen Sommeranzug.
Verkäufer:	Fertig oder nach Maß, bitte?
Herr Ebert:	Fertig (von der Stange).
Verkäufer:	Welche Größe tragen Sie?
Herr Ebert:	Ich trage zweiundfünfzig.
Verkäufer:	(Weist auf ein paar helle Anzüge.) Wie gefallen Ihnen diese Farben und Muster?
Herr Ebert:	Aus was für Stoff ist der gestreifte Anzug?
Verkäufer:	Der Stoff ist hundert Prozent Wolle und trägt sich sehr gut.
Herr Ebert:	Dann probiere ich ihn an.
Verkäufer:	Er sitzt wie angegossen.
Herr Ebert:	Aber die Ärmel müssen etwas gekürzt werden.
Verkäufer:	Ja, die Ärmel sind etwas zu lang.
Herr Ebert:	Wieviel kostet der Anzug?
Verkäufer:	Vierundachtzig Mark.
Herr Ebert:	Gut. (Bezahlt.) Dann lassen Sie ihn mir ins Haus schicken.
Verkäufer:	Danke, der Herr.

CHAPTER TWENTY

Separable and Inseparable Prefixes

As in English, simple verbs in German may be combined with certain prefixes to form new (compound) verbs. In German, however, some of these prefixes, called separable prefixes (referred to as adverbs in English), separate again in some instances, while others, called inseparable prefixes, do not.

(a) *SEPARABLE PREFIXES*

20.1   Although nouns, adjectives, verbs, adverbs, and prepositions frequently serve as separable prefixes in German (cf. **teilnehmen, gutmachen, kennenlernen, dastehen, mitmachen**), adverbs and prepositions are most common.[1] They always bear the main accent or stress, and they separate in the imperative and in the present and past tenses (in main clauses), where they stand at the end of the clause.

Der Zug kommt um acht Uhr an.	The train arrives at eight o'clock.
Der Zug kam um acht Uhr an.	The train arrived at eight o'clock.
Kommen Sie um acht Uhr an!	Arrive at eight o'clock.

20.2   The so-called separable prefixes do not separate in clauses in which the verb itself is at the end, that is, in dependent clauses and in main clauses in the present perfect, past perfect, future, and future perfect.

Der Zug ist um acht Uhr angekommen.	The train arrived at eight o'clock.
Der Zug war um acht Uhr angekommen.	The train had arrived at eight o'clock.
Der Zug wird um acht Uhr ankommen.	The train will arrive at eight o'clock.
Der Zug wird um acht Uhr angekommen sein.	The train will have arrived at eight o'clock.
Er sagt, daß der Zug um acht Uhr ankommt.	He says that the train arrives at eight o'clock.

20.3   As the regular **ge**-prefix of the past participle links the separable prefix and the verb (cf. **angekommen** above), so **zu** links the separable prefix and the infinitive.

> Um früh anzukommen, ist er vor fünf aufgestanden.
> To arrive early, he got up before five.

20.4   The literal meaning of compound verbs with separable prefixes is often a composite of the meanings of the prefix and the simple verb.   The figurative meaning varies in each case.

Kommen Sie mit?	Are you coming along?
Da komme ich nicht mit.	I don't follow you there.

[1] The most common are: **ab, an, auf, aus, ein, fort, her, hin, los, mit, nieder, um, unter, von, vorbei, weg, weiter, wieder, zu, zurück.**

(b) *INSEPARABLE PREFIXES*

20.5   The most common of the inseparable prefixes are: **be–, emp–, ent–, er–, ge–, ver–, zer–,** as in **bekommen, empfangen, entstehen, erzählen, gestehen, verstehen, zerfallen,** and **miß–** and **wider–,** as in **mißverstehen** and **widerstehen.** They have no independent meaning, never bear the main stress, never separate from the verb proper, which forms its past participle without the prefix **ge–.**

Wir erhielten Ihren Brief.	We (have) received your letter.
Wir haben Ihren Brief erhalten.	

20.6   Without the main stress and without a distinctly independent meaning **voll** ist also often used as an inseparable prefix.

> Das vollbringe ich einfach nicht allein.
> I am simply not able to accomplish that alone.

(c) *VARIABLE PREFIXES*

20.7   A few adverbs and prepositions, called variable prefixes, are sometimes used as separable prefixes and sometimes as inseparable prefixes. The most common are: **durch, hinter, über, um, unter,** and **wieder.** They bear the main stress and are separable when used in a literal sense.

Er setzte uns vor sechs über.	He ferried us across before six.
Ich hole ihn gerne wieder.	I'll be glad to fetch him back.

20.8   They do not bear the main stress and are not separated when used in a figurative sense.

Er übersetzte den deutschen Satz.	He translated the German sentence.
Wiederholen Sie den Satz!	Repeat the sentence!

Vatter wiederholt die Fragen
" hat die Fragen wiederholt
" hofft " " zu wiederholen

BASIC PATTERNS

Die Fabian-Werke waren ein modernes Unternehmen.   Moderne Unternehmen haben einen Betriebs-Psychologen.   Der Seelendoktor der Fabian-Werke hieß Dr. Plex.   Das ließ sich leicht behalten, wenn man an Komplex dachte.   Dr. Plexens Aufgabe war es vor allem, 5 bei Neuanstellungen und Beförderungen die Bewerber

anerkennen
Die U.S. erkennen C. an
Die U.S haben C. anerkannt
Die U.S hoffen nie, C. anzuerkennen

143

Fußball ist der beliebteste Sport in Deutschland.

auf ihre Tauglichkeit zu prüfen. Er tat es mit Leidenschaft und unter Verwendung zahlreicher Teste.

Eines Morgens klingelte bei ihm das Telefon. Direktor Klinger war am Apparat. „Mein lieber Plex," sagte er. „Ich werde Ihnen gleich einen Mann zuschicken. 5 Nehmen Sie ihn genau unter die Lupe. Wir haben vor, ihn zum Abteilungsleiter zu machen. Wenn Sie als Psychologe dazu ja sagen, wird er es." Zehn Minuten später war der Mann auch da. Einfach gekleidet, sehr höflich, kluge Augen unter einer hohen Stirn. „Nehmen Sie 10 Platz," sagte Dr. Plex. „Wir wollen uns ein wenig unterhalten. Zigarette?" „Sehr freundlich," sagte der Mann, nahm die Zigarette und reichte dem Psychologen Feuer.

„Gewiß werden Ihnen meine Fragen etwas seltsam vorkommen," sagte Dr. Plex. „Zerbrechen Sie sich aber 15 darüber nicht den Kopf. Antworten Sie frei von der Leber weg, kurz, genau, ohne Umschweife. Nehmen wir nun an, Sie hätten zu Haus ein Telefon. Was tun Sie, wenn es klingelt?" „Ich hebe den Hörer ab und melde mich!" Dr. Plex nickte. Seine Rechte notierte: „Absolute 20 Fähigkeit, logisch zu denken." Dann fragte er weiter: „Wie stehen Sie zu Goethes ‚Faust'?" „Positiv!" sagte der Mann. Auf Dr. Plexens Bewertungszettel erschienen die Worte: „Klar im Urteil. Starke geistige Interessen." „Noch zwei Fragen, mein Lieber. Nehmen wir an, dieser 25 Fall ist selbstverständlich krasse Theorie, ein Ochse stände mit den Vorderbeinen auf einer deutschen Wiese, mit den Hinterbeinen auf einer französischen. Wem stände, wenn wir einmal alle zolltechnischen Gesichtspunkte außer Betracht lassen, nach dem gesunden Men- 30 schenverstande die Milch zu?" „Ein Ochse," sagte der Mann einfach, „gibt keine Milch!" Dr. Plex pfiff durch die Zähne. Sein Bleistift fuhr über das Papier. „Überdurchschnittliche Allgemeinbildung," vermerkte er. „Und nun noch ein Letztes. Sind Sie verheiratet?" Der 35 Mann verneinte. Dazu schrieb Dr. Plex: „Keine Abenteuernatur."

145

Dann stand er auf und ging um den Schreibtisch herum. „Ich glaube," sagte er, „daß ich Ihnen als erster, wenn auch noch inoffiziell und ganz unter uns, zum Abteilungsleiter gratulieren darf!" Der Mann lächelte. „Nee,"
5 sagte er, „nun ist aber Schluß mit den Witzen. Bei Ihren komischen Fragen habe ich ja noch mitgemacht. Aber einmal muß jeder Spaß ein Ende haben." „Aber lieber Freund," sagte Dr. Plex, „nun, verstellen Sie sich doch nicht. Sie wissen doch ganz genau, warum Sie von der
10 Direktion zu mir geschickt worden sind."
„Von der Direktion geschickt?" sagte der Mann. „Schön wär's ja! Nee, nee, mich hat der Pförtner 'raufgeschickt, den ich gut kenne. Ich wollte Sie mal fragen, Herr Doktor, ob Sie nicht Rasierklingen gebrauchen
15 können oder 'ne Dose Schuhkrem?"

Questions

1. Was für Unternehmen haben Betriebs-Psychologen? 2. Welche Aufgabe hat ein Betriebs-Psychologe? 3. Wen sollte Dr. Plex eines Morgens prüfen? 4. Wie sah der Mann aus, der zu ihm ins Büro trat? 5. Was für Fragen stellte Dr. Plex dem Mann? 6. Wie sollte der Mann die Fragen beantworten? 7. Was hielt Dr. Plex von dem Mann? 8. Warum war der Mann zuletzt erstaunt? 9. Was wollte er in Wirklichkeit?

Idiomatic Expressions

leicht behalten	to retain (or remember) easily
prüfen auf (acc.)	to test for
bei mir klingelt das Telefon	my telephone is ringing
unter die Lupe nehmen	to give a careful going over
Platz nehmen	to be seated
es kommt mir vor	it seems to me
sich den Kopf zerbrechen	to rack one's brains
frei von der Leber weg sprechen	to speak one's mind
außer Betracht lassen	to disregard
ganz unter uns	strictly between ourselves

EXERCISES

A. Use the idiomatic expressions above to complete the sentences.

1. Da er mir etwas fremd vorkam, nahm . . . 2. Dr. Plexens Aufgabe war es, jeden Bewerber auf . . . 3. Er bat mich sofort, Platz . . . 4. Als ich jung war, konnte ich . . . 5. Ich glaubte den Mann zu erkennen, aber ihm kam . . . 6. Ich war unter der Brause, als das Telefon bei . . . 7. Über Sachen, die mich nicht betreffen, zerbreche . . . 8. Daß er Psychologe ist, dürfen wir nicht ganz außer . . . 9. Was halten Sie von ihm, so ganz . . . 10. Da wir ganz unter uns waren, sprach . . .

B. Substitute the verbs in parentheses.

1. Moderne Unternehmen haben einen Betriebs-Psychologen. (betätigen, anstellen) 2. Dr. Plex prüfte alle Bewerber. (befragen, willkommen heißen) 3. Der Psychologe verwendete zahlreiche Teste. (gebrauchen, einsehen) 4. Der Direktor sandte ihm einen Mann. (zuschicken, empfehlen) 5. Die Fragen scheinen mir etwas seltsam. (vorkommen, klingen) 6. Wem schmeckt die Milch? (gehören, zustehen) 7. Er notierte es mit einem Bleistift. (vermerken, aufschreiben) 8. Dann sprang der Mann auf. (sich erheben, aufstehen) 9. Bei der Arbeit habe ich zugesehen. (sich beteiligen, mitmachen) 10. Bitte, fragen Sie nicht. (sich verstellen, nachgeben)

C. Was ist *ein Unternehmen, ein Abteilungsleiter, ein Bewertungszettel, ein Gesichtspunkt, eine Rasierklinge?*

D. Use the following adjectives in the comparative in sentences 1–9 in B: *jung, alt, erfahren, einfach, kurz, frisch, lang, erregt, leicht.*

E. Include each of the following verbs in an original sentence illustrating the use of the basic tenses in German (Chapter II): *zuschicken, unterbrechen, behalten, unterhalten, vorkommen, mitmachen.*

F. Form at least five compound verbs each of *kommen, gehen, tragen* with the following separable and inseparable prefixes and use one compound of each verb in a German sentence: *an–, auf–, ver–, mit–, um–, zer–.* EXAMPLE: *fahren — an-fahren* to start up, to bark at; *auf-fahren* to drive up, to start (*or* jump) up; *verfahren* to drive into a rut, to proceed; *mit-fahren* to drive along (with); *um-fahren* to run over; *umfahren* to skirt; *zerfahren* to ruin (by driving over). Zwei Wagen sind aufgefahren. (Two cars have driven up.) Er fuhr aus seinem tiefen Schlaf auf. (He awakened from his deep sleep with a start.)

Composition

1. Since Dr. Plex was the psychologist who tested all the applicants for new‿jobs and promotions, the manager telephoned him and told him that he was sending a man over. 2. "Look him over carefully," he said. 3. "We intend to make him a section head." 4. Ten minutes later a simply dressed man walked into Dr. Plex' office. 5. The psychologist asked him to be seated and offered him a cigarette. 6. "My questions will seem strange to you," said the psychologist. 7. "But think‿nothing‿of‿it. 8. Just speak‿your‿mind‿freely." 9. Then Dr. Plex asked the man four questions. 10. First he asked him what he would do if the phone rang. 11. Then he asked him how he felt‿about Goethe's *Faust*. 12. The third question was a‿bit more odd. 13. "To whom does the milk belong," Dr. Plex asked, "if an ox stands with his front‿legs on French soil and his hind‿legs on German soil?" 14. Lastly the psychologist wanted to know whether the man was married. 15. When the man answered all four questions quickly and correctly, Dr. Plex congratulated him. 16. But the man merely smiled. 17. "I wasn't sent‿here by the director," he said. 18. "I just wanted to ask you whether you could use [some] razor‿blades or a can of shoe‿polish."

Variations

A. In addition to several basic meanings, some German words have a flavor of their own that is not readily reproduced. At times, they are therefore referred to as Füllwörter or Färbewörter and are best understood in their German context. Suggested English equivalents are often mere approximations.

gerade

Among the more concise meanings of *gerade* are: "even," "just," "straight," "exactly." Zwei ist eine gerade (even) Zahl. Ziehen Sie eine gerade (straight) Linie, jene ist krumm. Sitz gerade (straight)! Das ist gerade (just) so gut. Du kommst gerade (just) recht. Das war nicht gerade (exactly) nett von dir. Meine Wohnung liegt der Post gerade (right) gegenüber. Other shades are more elusive. Gerade von ihm hätte ich das nicht erwartet. (He is the last person of whom I would have expected it.) Das hat mir gerade noch gefehlt. (That is all I needed.) Nun tue ich's gerade nicht. (Now I'll never do it.)

sonst

In some instances *sonst* connotes "otherwise," "else," "or (else)," "usually." Was würden Sie sonst (otherwise) tun? Was kann ich sonst (else) tun? Lauf, sonst (or) kommst du zu spät! Du bist doch sonst (usually) nicht so empfindlich. But it cannot be translated that way in other instances. Wenn es sonst nichts ist! (If that's all there is to it!) *Sonst noch etwas* and *sonst (noch) jemand* mean respectively "anything else" and "anybody else." Wünschen Sie sonst noch etwas? Ist sonst noch jemand hier? Another combination is *wie sonst*, "as usual." Es war alles wie sonst.

eigentlich

Eigentlich has several basic meanings: (1) "real" *or* "actual;" (2) "actually," "exactly," "just;" (3) "as a matter of fact," "indeed;" (4) "sort of;" (5) "by rights." Der eigentliche (actual) Grund war ein ganz anderer. Was heißt das eigentlich (just)? Da haben Sie eigentlich (as a matter of fact) recht. Ich bin eigentlich (sort of) froh. Eigentlich (by rights) gehört das ihm.

B. Simplify the Basic Patterns and, in the appropriate places, include variants of *gerade, sonst, eigentlich,* and *gebrauchen, ich sehe ihn mir an, beabsichtigen, befremden, sich Sorgen machen über (acc.), voraussetzen, der Fernsprecher, sich stellen zu, gehören, nachfragen.*

Conversation — Beim Schuster

Herr Jahn:	(Tritt mit einem Paar Schuhe in der Hand in eine Schusterwerkstatt.) Guten Tag.
Schuhmacher:	Guten Tag! Was wünscht der Herr?
Herr Jahn:	(Hält die Schuhe hoch.) Ich möchte diese Schuhe besohlen lassen.
Schuhmacher:	(Besieht sich die Schuhe.) Halbe oder ganze Sohlen?
Herr Jahn:	Mit halben ist mir auch gedient.
Schuhmacher:	Möchten Sie die Sohlen genäht oder genagelt haben?
Herr Jahn:	Genäht, bitte.
Schuhmacher:	Und die Absätze?
Herr Jahn:	Die können Sie auch machen.
Schuhmacher:	Sollen es Gummiabsätze sein?
Herr Jahn:	Nein, ich habe lieber Leder.

149

Schuhmacher:	Das kostet dann 8 Mark 50 Pfennig.
Herr Jahn:	Gut. Und wann sind die Schuhe fertig?
Schuhmacher:	Sie können sie sich schon am Mittwoch holen.
Herr Jahn:	Schön. Also Mittwoch nachmittag.
Schuhmacher:	Auf Wiedersehen.

CHAPTER TWENTY-ONE

Reflexive Verbs and Pronouns

As in English, there are reflexive verbs and reflexive pronouns in German.

(a) *REFLEXIVE VERBS*

21.1 In a reflexive construction in English and in German the subject and the (direct and indirect) pronoun object are one and the same.

Ich wasche mich jeden Tag.	I wash myself every day.
Ich kaufte mir ein Buch.	I bought myself a book.

21.2 Often, moreover, the corresponding verbs, as *wash* — **waschen** and *buy* — **kaufen,** may be reflexive in both languages.

21.3 But there are a number of German verbs which do not have reflexive equivalents in English.

Fürchten Sie sich nicht!	Do not be afraid!
Verlassen Sie sich auf mich!	Rely on me!

21.4 Some of the more common reflexive verbs which require a direct (accusative) pronoun object are:

sich anziehen	to dress	**sich bedienen**	to use
sich ärgern	to be an-noyed	**sich beeilen**	to hurry
		sich befinden	to be, to feel
sich ausruhen	to rest up	**sich begnügen**	to content
sich ausziehen	to undress		oneself

150

sich beklagen	to complain	**sich freuen**	to be glad
sich bemühen	to make an	**sich fürchten**	to be afraid
	effort	**sich interessieren**	to be interested
sich besinnen	to reflect	**sich irren**	to be mistaken
sich betragen	to behave	**sich kümmern**	to be concerned
sich entscheiden	to decide	**sich nähern**	to approach
sich entschließen	to resolve	**sich schämen**	to be ashamed
sich erbarmen	to take pity	**sich setzen**	to sit down
sich erholen	to recover	**sich verlassen**	to rely
sich erkundigen	to inquire	**sich weigern**	to refuse
sich erinnern	to remember	**sich wundern**	to be sur-
sich erkälten	to catch cold		prised

21.5 Some of the more common reflexive verbs which require an indirect (dative) pronoun object are:

sich aneignen	to acquire	**sich vornehmen**	to resolve
sich einbilden	to imagine	**sich vorstellen**	to imagine
sich erlauben	to take the liberty	**sich weh tun**	to hurt oneself
sich helfen	to help oneself		

21.6 All reflexive verbs are regarded as transitive verbs and use the auxiliary **haben.**

Er hat sich sehr geschämt.   He was very much ashamed.

(b) *REFLEXIVE PRONOUNS*

21.7 In German the reflexive pronoun forms of the first and second person, singular and plural, which correspond to *myself, thyself* or *yourself, ourselves* and *yourselves* in English, are identical with those of the personal pronoun object, indirect and direct. The reflexive pronoun object of the third person, singular and plural, indirect (dative) and direct (accusative), is **sich.** Grouped with the subject, the reflexive pronouns are:

SUBJECT	DATIVE REFLEXIVE OBJECT	ACCUSATIVE REFLEXIVE OBJECT
ich	mir	mich
du	dir	dich
er, sie, es	sich	sich
wir	uns	uns
ihr	euch	euch
sie, Sie	sich	sich

21.8 In normal word order and in the familiar imperative the reflexive pronoun stands after the inflected verb.

Er hat sich bei mir beklagt.	He complained to me.
Wir freuen uns auf euren Besuch.	We look forward to your visit.
Setz dich, bitte.	Please, be seated.

21.9 If the subject is a pronoun, the reflexive pronoun usually stands after it in (1) inverted word order, (2) dependent word order, and (3) in the polite form of the imperative.

Gestern hat er sich geirrt.	Yesterday he made a mistake.
Da er sich gestern irrte, war er heute vorsichtig.	Since he made a mistake yesterday, he was careful today.
Setzen Sie sich, bitte.	Please, be seated.

21.10 If the subject is a noun, the reflexive pronoun usually stands before it in (1) inverted word order, and (2) dependent word order.

Gestern hat sich der Vater geirrt.	Yesterday the father made a mistake.
Da sich der Vater gestern irrte, war er heute vorsichtig.	Since the father made a mistake yesterday, he was careful today.

21.11 In German the reflexive pronoun must not be confused with the intensive pronoun or the reciprocal pronoun.

21.12 The intensive pronoun, **selbst** or **selber,** is used in German to intensify the subject, and is indeclineable.

Ich holte es selbst (*or* selber).	I fetched it myself.
Ich selbst sah es.	I myself saw it.

21.13 As *myself* in English, **selbst** or **selber** usually stands after the subject or word it emphasizes. When **selbst** (never **selber**) precedes the subject it means *even*.

Selbst ich mußte lachen.	Even I had to laugh.

21.14 The reciprocal pronoun is **einander,** meaning *each other* or *one another*. The reflexive pronoun **sich** is used in its place only when the meaning is clear.

Sie lieben einander (*or* sich).	They love each other.
Sie reden immer von einander.	They always talk about each other.

152

BASIC PATTERNS *

„Schmidt zu heißen hat den Vorteil der Allgemeinheit," dachte Hugo Schmidt eines Tages auf dem Wege
ins Büro. „Schmidt haben schon Hunderttausende vor
mir geheißen," sagte er zu sich. „Dichter, Philosophen,
Arbeiter, Staatsmänner, Lustmörder . . . und kleine Büro- 5
angestellte wie ich."

Er war vergnügt, als er die Straßenbahn bestieg. Er
bemerkte nicht, daß er zehn Minuten gewartet hatte,
kaum mehr einen Platz auf dem Trittbrett fand, daß er
sich an einen Mann pressen mußte, der entsetzlich nach 10
Knoblauch roch, daß heute erst der Zwanzigste war und
er keinen Pfennig mehr in der Tasche hatte, daß die
Zeitungen in Schlagzeilen einen neuen Krieg vorbereiteten.
Er vergaß, daß er noch vom letzten eine klappernde Prothese trug, daß ihm Lilly aus dem Vorzimmer des Direk- 15
tors wahrscheinlich deshalb einen Korb gegeben hatte,
daß er in einem kleinen Zimmer wohnte, in das es regnete,
und daß ihn in verschiedenen Zeitabständen eine tiefe
Traurigkeit anfiel. Das alles vergaß er.

Er stieg aus und atmete tief. Das war bei ihm ein 20
Zeichen von Zufriedenheit. Die Luft roch noch immer
nach feuchter Erde. Schmidt pfiff, er pfiff das Lied des
guten Menschen, oder zumindest derer, die mit dem
Wochenlohn nicht auskommen, denen es hereinregnet,
die Prothesen tragen und deshalb bei Mädchen kein Glück 25
haben, mit denen herumgeschrien wird.

Schmidt bog um die Ecke, und da zeigte es sich, daß
ein Glück selten allein kommt, genau so wie ein Unglück.
Zwei neue Fünfmarkstücke lagen blank und leuchtend auf
dem Gehsteig. Schmidt geriet in eine merkwürdige Erre- 30
gung. Plötzlich wurden seltsame Kräfte in ihm frei. Sie
paßten nicht zu seinen abgetretenen Schuhen, auch nicht
zu der wundersamen Luft dieses Morgens. Sie waren

---

* Nach Hans M. Loews „Ungenutzte Chance" aus *Stimmen der Gegenwart*, Buch-
Kunst-Zeitungsdruckerei „Albrecht Dürer," Wien, 1953.

dunkel und stiegen aus einer geheimnisvollen, uner-
gründlichen Tiefe.

Sollte sich das Blatt wenden? Er blieb vor einer
nahen Lotterie stehen und drehte die Münzen zwischen
5 den Fingern. Er las die Gewinne, und es begann ihm
warm zu werden. Jetzt krampfte sich die Faust um die
Münzen, vielleicht hatte er es in der Hand . . .

Ein Strom wirrer, phantastischer Gedanken riß ihn
unwiderstehlich mit sich fort. „Man müßte das Geld
10 arbeiten lassen, es vermehren," ging es ihm durch den
Kopf. „Es müßte mich groß machen, unendlich groß,
mächtig, einflußreich. Lilly würde einwilligen, selbstverständlich, aber sie allein würde nicht mehr genügen. Ein
Cadillac, Zentralheizung in der Villa, Weltreisen."
15 Schmidt stieß mit dem Fuß auf den Asphalt und atmete
hastig und tief. „Ich würde Untergebene haben," sagte
er sich. „Diener, Personal, Angestellte. Die müßten
sich ducken! Ich . . . befehlen!" Der kleine Schmidt
stand vor der Lotterie des Lebens. Er hatte seine große
20 Chance. Doch er bekam einen roten Kopf. Eine Frau
sah ihn verwundert an. Jemand lachte.

Die Metallstücke zwischen seinen bloßen Fingern
begannen teuflisch zu brennen. Die Luft war noch immer
kühl und voll Duft. Aber er bemerkte es nicht mehr.
25 Da wandte er sich entschlossen um, ging zur nächsten
Straßenecke und warf die blanken Münzen, die Münzen
seiner Möglichkeit, in die Kappe eines Bettlers. Dann
klapperte er erleichtert weiter mit seiner Prothese, eins,
zwei, eins, zwei, außerordentlich zufrieden darüber,
30 Schmidt zu heißen. Ein Gefühl der Verantwortung stieg
in ihm hoch, das Gefühl, einen Namen zu besitzen, mit
dem man noch ein guter Mensch sein konnte.

Questions

1. Warum war Hugo froh, Schmidt zu heißen? 2. Weshalb hätte
er Grund, unglücklich zu sein? 3. Was fand er auf dem Wege ins Büro?
4. Wie wollte er die Münzen vermehren? 5. Was müßte das Geld ihm

machen? 6. Wem könnte er dann Befehle geben? 7. Warum geriet Schmidt aber in eine merkwürdige Aufregung? 8. Was wurde aus seiner großen Chance? 9. Was tat er schließlich mit den Geldstücken? 10. Warum war er darüber zufrieden?

Idiomatic Expressions

riechen nach (*dat.*)	to smell of
keinen Pfennig mehr	not another penny
einem einen Korb geben	to turn (a suitor) down
es fällt mich an	I am overcome with
auskommen mit (*dat.*)	to get along on (*or* with)
um die Ecke biegen	to turn the corner
in Erregung geraten	to get excited
das Blatt wendet sich	(my) luck is changing
das Blatt hat sich gewendet	the tables are turned
ich habe es in der Hand	it is up to me
es geht mir durch den Kopf	it runs through my mind

EXERCISES

A. Form ten German sentences, in the first and third person singular and second person plural wherever possible, which combine one of the above idiomatic expressions with one of the following reflexive verbs: *sich sagen, sich pressen an, sich zeigen, sich wenden, mit sich fortreißen, sich ducken, sich umsehen nach, sich ärgern, sich krampfen, es sich gefallen lassen.*

B. Rewrite the Basic Patterns above with the aid of the following substitute expressions: *genannt werden, Vorzug, weithin bekannt, froh, steigen in, es entgeht mir, zu stehen kommen, sich lehnen, verkünden, nicht heiraten wollen, traurig sein, sich kaum durchschlagen, es stellt sich heraus, aufsteigen, halten, einstürmen auf, ja sagen, auskommen mit, ganz rot werden, zu Feuer werden, mit sich zufrieden sein.*

C. Rewrite each sentence with *lassen* or *sich lassen.*
EXAMPLE: Schmidt sagt nichts. Er läßt Schmidt nichts sagen. Schmidt läßt sich nichts sagen.

1. Schmidt besteigt die Straßenbahn. 2. Sie merkte nichts. 3. Er hatte zehn Minuten gewartet. 4. Man preßte ihn an eine Wand. 5. Der Mann las die Zeitung vor. 6. Er fragt sie. 7. Sie

gibt ihm eine Antwort.   8. Dann steigt er aus.   9. Er pfeift ein
Lied.   10. Aber sie fährt um die Ecke.

D. Use each of the verbs in a German sentence.

zeigen	sich zeigen
legen	sich legen
stellen	sich stellen
wenden	sich wenden
werfen	sich werfen

E. Introduce each sentence with an "anticipatory" *es.*
EXAMPLE: Schmidt zu heißen, hat den Vorteil der Allgemeinheit.
Es hat den Vorteil der Allgemeinheit, Schmidt zu heißen.

1. Schmidt haben schon viele vor mir geheißen.   2. Auf
dem Trittbrett war kaum mehr Platz.   3. Eine Traurigkeit fällt
ihn in verschiedenen Zeitabständen an.   4. Ein Glück kommt
selten allein.   5. Seltsame Kräfte wurden in ihm frei.   6. Das
Blatt sollte sich wenden.   7. Jetzt krampfte sich die Faust um
die Münze.   8. Ein Strom riß ihn mit sich fort.   9. Eine Frau
sah ihn verwundert an.   10. Ein Gefühl der Verantwortung stieg
in ihm dann auf.

F. Complete each sentence.

1. Hugo Schmidt dachte, . . .   2. Als er die Straßenbahn
bestieg, . . .   3. Daß der Mann nach Knoblauch roch, . . .   4. Obwohl er zehn Minuten gewartet hatte, . . .   5. Er vergaß, . . .
6. Er atmete tief, . . .   7. Sobald er um die Ecke bog, . . .   8. Vor
der Lotterie begann er, . . .   9. Beim Lesen der Gewinne begann
es, . . .   10. Er atmete erst auf, . . .

Composition

1. Hugo Schmidt was a clerk who barely got along on his
weekly salary.   2. But he was a modest and contented man.
3. At times a deep sadness came over him, but he hardly ever
complained.   4. He was on his way to the office one day, when it
happened.   5. As he turned the corner, two shiny silver coins
lay gleaming on the sidewalk.   6. And suddenly strange forces
welled up in him.   7. "Is my luck really going to change?" he
asked himself.   8. He stopped in front of the nearest lottery
and rolled the coins between his fingers.   9. "They'll make me

156

rich," he said to himself. 10. "Then I'll have employees and they'll have to cringe. 11. I'll have a country house with central heating." 12. Now his thoughts became confused. 13. He grew warm and the coins between his fingers began to burn. 14. Resolved, he rushed to the next street corner and tossed them into a beggar's cap. 15. With a sigh of relief he then continued on his way to the office, one, two, one, two, extremely satisfied to be called Hugo Schmidt.

Variations

A. In addition to several basic meanings, some German words have a flavor of their own that is not readily reproduced. At times, they are therefore referred to as Füllwörter or Färbewörter and are best understood in their German context. Suggested English equivalents are often mere approximations.

gleich

Gleich may mean "equal" or "alike," "same," "equally," "right," "right away." Die beiden sind gleich (equal, alike). Wir sind im gleichen (same) Alter. Sie sind gleich (equally) gut. Wir gehen gleich (right) nach dem Essen. Das habe ich gleich (right away) gedacht. But its idiomatic functions differ. Mir ist alles gleich. (It's all the same to me.) Gleich und gleich gesellt sich gern. (Birds of a feather flock together.) Wie war doch gleich Ihr Name? (What did you say your name was?)

ja

The adverbial aspects of the affirmative particle almost preclude analysis. Da sind Sie ja (so). Es ist ja (really) nicht sehr weit. Kommen Sie ja (be sure to) morgen. Sie sehen's ja (can . . . for) selbst. Sie wissen ja (but), daß ich nicht gehen kann. Tun Sie es ja (dare) nicht.

wohl

Semantically *wohl* is one of the most elusive adverbs in German. Note: Ob er es wohl (I wonder) weiß? Das weiß er wohl (full well). Ich fühle mich heute nicht wohl (well). Ihm ist heute wohl zu Mute (. . . in good spirits). Bei ihm fühle ich mich wohl (at home). Es ist wohl (all right *or* to be sure) fertig, aber wie? Nun sind Sie wohl (I suppose) zufrieden.

B. Simplify the Basic Patterns and, in the appropriate places, include variants of *gleich, ja, wohl,* and *guten Mutes, sich drücken gegen* (acc.), *zeigen, aufschreien, erregt werden, sich ändern, einem durch den Kopf schwirren, verwirrt werden, sich umdrehen.*

157

Conversation — Im Gasthaus

	(Im Gasthaus tritt ein Kellner zur Mittagszeit an Herrn Müller heran, reicht ihm die Speisekarte und fragt:)
Kellner:	Wünschen der Herr unser Tagesgericht oder nach der Karte zu speisen?
Herr Müller:	Was haben Sie heute als Tagesgericht?
Kellner:	Erbsensuppe, Schweinebraten mit Salzkartoffeln und grünen Bohnen, und als Nachspeise Schokoladenpudding.
Herr Müller:	Was können Sie sonst empfehlen?
Kellner:	Die Gemüsesuppe ist sehr gut, und der Rinderbraten ist ausgezeichnet.
Herr Müller:	(Sieht von der Speisekarte auf.) Also, eine Erbsensuppe bitte, Forelle, Kalbsbraten mit gerösteten Kartoffeln und Blumenkohl.
Kellner:	Und was möchten der Herr als Nachspeise?
Herr Müller:	Ein Stück Käsekuchen und dazu eine Tasse Kaffee.
Kellner:	Wünschen der Herr sonst was zu trinken?
Herr Müller:	Ein Glas Löwenbräu (Bier), bitte.
Kellner:	Hell oder dunkel?
Herr Müller:	Ein Glas Helles und zum Kaffee einen kleinen Benediktiner.
Kellner:	Jawohl. (Bringt alles.)
Herr Müller:	(Eine halbe Stunde später winkt Herr Müller den Kellner herbei und sagt:) Herr Ober, zahlen.
Kellner:	(Rechnet, reicht Herrn Müller die Rechnung und sagt:) Acht Mark vierzig, einschließlich (Bedienung), wenn ich bitten darf.
Herr Müller:	(Gibt dem Kellner das Geld und erhebt sich.) Das Essen war ausgezeichnet. Auf Wiedersehen!
Kellner:	Auf Wiedersehen, der Herr.

CHAPTER TWENTY-TWO

The Passive Voice

In English and in German, the active voice (cf. Appendices IX–XIV) represents the subject as acting, while the passive voice (cf. Appendix XV) represents it as being acted upon.[1]

(a) *FORMATION OF THE PASSIVE*

22.1　The passive voice is formed in both languages by combining the inflected forms of an auxiliary (*to be* in English, **werden** [2] in German) with the past participle of the acting verb.

Ich werde von dem Mann gesehen.	I am (being) [3] seen by the man.
Du wurdest von dem Mann gesehen.	You were (being) seen by the man.
Er ist von dem Mann gesehen worden.[4]	He has been seen by the man.
Wir waren von dem Mann gesehen worden.[4]	We had been seen by the man.
Ihr werdet von dem Mann gesehen werden.	You will be seen by the man.
Sie werden von dem Mann gesehen worden [4] sein.[5]	They will have been seen by the man.

Note, however, that in German only a direct (accusative) object can become the subject of a passive verb. Passive constructions, such as *He was given the book*, are not possible in German. Since the indirect object of an active construction must remain an indirect object in the corresponding passive construction in German, some verbs, including those requiring the dative (cf. 7.3, 7.4), are therefore made passive with an impersonal subject (**es**). These impersonal constructions can be rendered in English only when the **es** is omitted in inverted order.

---

[1] Compare *I → see the man* (**Ich → sehe den Mann**) with *I ← am (being) seen by the man* (**Ich ← werde von dem Mann gesehen.**) [2] All told, **werden** has three functions: (a) it serves as a verb meaning *to become, to turn, to grow*, etc., as in **Er wird alt;** (b) it is used as an auxiliary verb to form the future tense (cf. Chapters XIV, XV, XVI), as in **Er wird gehen;** and (c) it is used as an auxiliary verb to form the passive voice, as indicated above. [3] English is ambiguous without the progressive form. Cf. "True and False Passives" below. [4] In the present perfect, past perfect, and future perfect the prefix **ge–** of the past participle of **werden** is dropped, leaving **worden.** [5] **Sein** is the auxiliary of **werden.**

ACTIVE

Man gab ihm ein Buch.	They gave him a book.
Er riet mir.	He advised me.

PASSIVE

Es wurde ihm ein Buch gegeben.
Es wurde ihm geraten.

Ihm wurde das Buch gegeben.	He was given the book.
Ihm wurde geraten.	He was advised.

22.2   Agency and means are both generally introduced by the preposition *by* in English.   In German, agency is indicated by the preposition **von** (with the dative); means, usually by the preposition **durch** (with the accusative).

Sie wurde von ihm gerufen.	She was called by him.
Das Haus ist durch Feuer zerstört worden.	The house was destroyed by fire.

(b) *SUBSTITUTE CONSTRUCTIONS*

22.3   The passive voice is used less frequently in German than in English.   There are, however, various substitutes in German. The most common are:

(1) an impersonal construction, as	Hier tut man das nicht.
	That isn't done here.
(2) a reflexive construction, as	Das versteht sich.
	That is understood.
(3) an active infinitive with **sich lassen,** as	Das läßt sich nicht leicht erklären.
	That is not easily explained.
(4) an active infinitive with **sein** and **zu,** as	Sie war nirgends zu finden.
	She was nowhere to be found.

(c) *TRUE AND FALSE PASSIVES*

22.4   In English some constructions seem to be in the passive voice and yet are active.   They are sometimes called false or apparent passives.   These are easily identified by the insertion of *being* after the verb.   If *being* fits the context, the construction is in the passive voice.   If it does not, it is in the active voice.

160

Das Haus wurde weiß angestrichen.	The house was (being) painted white.
Das Haus war weiß angestrichen.	The house was (already) painted white.
Im Sommer werden die Türen um fünf geschlossen.	In summer the doors are (being) closed at five.
Im Sommer sind die Türen um fünf geschlossen.	In summer the doors are (already) closed at five.

BASIC PATTERNS

Es war Mitternacht. Auf der Straße sah man keinen Menschen. Nur ein Ventilator surrte noch. Die letzten Gäste waren gegangen, und Mutter Michels saß allein in ihrem armseligen Gasthaus dicht am Hafen. Über die offene Registrierkasse gebeugt, zählte sie Scheine und 5 Silbergeld. „Achtzig Mark fünfzig," murmelte sie. „Hundert Mark dreißig, hundertdreißig Mark zehn . . ." „Gib's her," ertönte da plötzlich eine Stimme hinter ihr.

Als Mutter Michels aufsah, blickte sie in die Mündung eines Revolvers. Zwei Männer standen vor ihr. 10 Die hatten sich irgendwie eingeschlichen, ohne von jemandem gesehen worden zu sein. Die Hutkrempen warfen dunkle Schatten über ihre fremden Gesichter, harte Gesichter mit bösen Augen. Mutter Michels sah auch, daß sie jung waren, so alt etwa wie ihre Söhne jetzt 15 wären. „Wird's bald?" schnarrte der Ältere. Die Hände der alten Frau zitterten. Es wurde ihr fast übel. Doch sie raffte die Scheine zusammen und gab sie ihm. Als sie nach dem Silbergeld griff, fielen ein paar Münzen herunter und rollten über den Boden. „Die kannst du behalten 20 für 'ne doppelte Portion Buletten mit Bratkartoffeln," erklärte er.

„Die Küche ist geschlossen," sagte darauf die Alte ärgerlich. „Dann mach sie wieder auf," befahl jetzt der Jüngere und grinste. Er hatte schöne, weiße Zähne wie 25 Rolf, ihr Jüngster.

„Los," sagte der andere, „beeil dich," und machte eine ungeduldige Bewegung mit dem Revolver. Da ging

Oberammergau und sein Passionsspiel.

die Mutter Michels hinter die Theke. Die Heizplatte
wurde angestellt und die Kaffeemaschine. Dann holte
sie Gehacktes aus dem Eisschrank und schnitt Kartoffeln
in die Pfanne. Die zwei hatten sich indessen am nächsten
Tisch hingelümmelt. Eine Zigarette nach der anderen 5
wurde geraucht, kein Auge von ihr gelassen.

„Das ist nun das Ende eines Tages," dachte Mutter
Michels. „Zwölf Stunden Bedienen, Hitze, Kochen,
Braten, Tellerwaschen, und wenn man die paar Mark
zusammen hat fürs Leben, fürs Licht und die Miete, dann 10
kommen die." Wut stieg in ihr hoch wie eine heiße
Welle und drohte sie zu ersticken, wenn sie sich nicht
Luft machte.

„Schämen solltet ihr euch!" schrie sie endlich auf
und drehte die zischenden Bratkartoffeln um. „Schämen 15
solltet ihr euch," wiederholte sie, „einer alten Frau, die
zwölf Stunden schuftet, um das bißchen Leben zu verdienen, das Brot aus dem Munde zu reißen. Das Geld
wird euch nie bekommen. Ich hatte auch zwei Söhne,
so alt wie ihr wären sie jetzt. Aber das waren gute Jungen, 20
anständige Jungen, arbeiteten von früh bis spät. Nun
sind sie jedoch tot, gefallen in Rußland, und dann kommt
ihr. Jung, lebendig, und raubt alte Frauen aus. Eure
Mutter könnte ich sein." Dabei drehte sie das Fleisch
auf die andere Seite, daß es zischte und köstlich duftete. 25
„Schämen solltet ihr euch, schämen!" schrie sie ihnen in
die grinsenden Gesichter.

Mutter Michels scheltende Stimme drang wie durch
Nebel zu ihnen, und das Grinsen erstarb allmählich. Die
Stimme und die Augen, die jetzt im Zorn flammten, 30
schienen auf einmal wie die Stimme und die Augen einer
alten Frau, die auch für sie einst geschuftet und gesorgt,
gebetet und geschimpft hatte. Es wurde ihnen immer
ungemütlicher zu Mute. Der Revolver wurde eingesteckt.
Wortlos stand nun der Ältere auf und warf die zerknitter- 35
ten Scheine und das Silbergeld auf den Tisch. Dann
gingen beide zur Tür, die Hüte ins Gesicht gedrückt.

163

Das Fleisch duftete und brutzelte. Die Kartoffeln waren goldbraun und knusperig geworden. Da schrie Mutter Michels den beiden mütterlich nach: „Sofort setzt ihr euch hin! Das Essen ist fertig, und ihr habt doch
5 gesagt, daß ihr hungrig seid."

Questions

1. Was tat Mutter Michels um Mitternacht? 2. Von wem wurde sie dabei überrascht? 3. Wie sahen die zwei Jungen aus? 4. Was verlangten sie außer dem Geld? 5. Woraus machte Mutter Michels ihnen die Buletten? 6. Wo lümmelten sich die Männer indessen hin? 7. Was dachte nun Mutter Michels? 8. Wie machte sie sich Luft? 9. Warum schien Mutter Michels den Jungen jetzt wie ihre eigene Mutter? 10. Wie zeigten sie es? 11. Was rief Mutter Michels den Jungen an der Tür zu?

Idiomatic Expressions

gib's her	hand it over
wird's bald	(will you) make it snappy
greifen nach (*dat.*)	to reach for
mir ist übel	I feel nauseous
kein Auge lassen von (*dat.*)	not to take one's eyes off
sich Luft machen	to give vent to one's feelings
das Brot aus dem Munde reißen	to take the bread right out of a person's mouth
einem ins Gesicht schreien	to scream right at someone
es bekommt mir	I enjoy it, it agrees with me
von früh bis spät	from dawn to dusk
es ist mir ungemütlich zu Mute	I am ill at ease

EXERCISES

A. Use four of the above idiomatic expressions in sentences in the passive voice. EXAMPLE: Gib's her. Ich gebe nichts her. Hier wird nichts hergegeben. (Note the intermediate step.)

B. Use substitute impersonal active constructions for each of the following passives.

1. Die Gäste wurden hinausgeschickt. 2. Die jungen Männer sind nirgends gesehen worden. 3. Die Scheine waren

schnell zusammengerafft worden. 4. Dann wurde die Heizplatte angestellt. 5. Die alten Frauen wurden ausgeraubt. 6. Nun wurden die Hüte tiefer ins Gesicht gedrückt.

C. Use passive substitutes or change the active voice to the passive voice.

1. Man konnte die beiden Jungen nicht sehen. 2. So etwas sagt man hier nicht. 3. Plötzlich öffnete sich die Tür. 4. Niemand achtete auf die scheltende Stimme. 5. Kartoffeln können in Fett gebraten werden. 6. Nur eine Zigarette wurde von ihm zu Ende geraucht.

D. Change the tense to the future tense in each of the following sentences.

1. Der letzte Gast geht um zwölf. 2. Dann sieht man keinen Menschen. 3. Mutter Michels setzte sich an den Tisch. 4. Sie merkte nichts. 5. Zwei Männer standen hinter ihr. 6. Ihre Hutkrempen warfen dunkle Schatten über ihre Gesichter. 7. Die Hände der alten Frau haben gezittert. 8. Sie gab ihnen die Scheine und das Silbergeld.

E. Replace the English terms in parentheses.

1. Im Frühling (*are getting*) die Tage länger. 2. Es war ihm so kalt, daß er blau (*turned*). 3. Wir (*grow*) jeden Tag älter. 4. Was wird aus ihm (*become*)? 5. Dann (*fell*) er plötzlich still.

F. Use each verb in the left-hand column in a sentence in the passive voice and its reflexive in the right-hand column in a sentence in the active voice.

merken	sich merken
zusammenraffen	sich zusammenraffen
stellen	sich stellen
umdrehen	sich umdrehen
werfen	sich werfen

G. Verify the following statements.

1. Mutter Michels schlief um zwölf Uhr ein. 2. Auch der Ventilator stand still. 3. Die jungen Männer zählten das Geld. 4. Mutter Michels hatte keinen Revolver. 5. Der Ältere hatte keinen Hut auf. 6. Der Jüngere bestellte Wein. 7. Das Ge-

hackte war im Ofen. 8. Mutter Michels hatte zwei Töchter gehabt. 9. Den Jungen wurde übel. 10. Die alte Frau wurde
hungrig.

H. Complete the following statements.

1. Das Gasthaus lag ... 2. Das Geld lag ... 3. Das
Fleisch lag ... 4. Rolf lag ... 5. Daran lag ...

Composition

1. It was almost midnight. 2. The streets were empty and
Mother Michels sat alone in her little restaurant. 3. She was
tired and glad that the day was over. 4. After twelve hours of
cooking, roasting, serving, and dishwashing each day, she scarcely
had enough money for (the) light and (the) rent and for her meager
existence. 5. But as she counted her money, she suddenly heard
a voice say: "Hand it over!" 6. When she looked‿up, she saw
two young men, (the) hats pulled‿down‿over‿their‿eyes. 7. One
had a revolver. 8. Mother Michels' hands trembled, as she handed
the money to the man with the revolver. 9. She did not grow furious until he motioned impatiently with his revolver and ordered a
plate of meat‿balls with home‿fried‿potatoes. 10. "You ought
to be ashamed to rob old women," she finally cried. 11. "My
boys were decent boys who worked from‿dawn‿to‿dusk.
12. But they were killed‿in‿the‿war in Russia and you ..."
13. Suddenly her voice and her eyes reminded the two young men
of their own mother who had also starved and worried and prayed.
14. Without saying a word the older one threw the crumpled bills
on the table and both walked out the door.

Variations

A. Match and arrange in their proper order the portions of
the familiar sayings listed in the two columns and explain their
meaning in German.

wer viel redet	wenig Werke
wenig Korn	alter Bettler
so wird die Kälte strenger	viel Stroh
wie der Wirt	fauler Mann
junger Spieler	so der Gast
voller Mann	werden die Tage länger

viel Worte   muß auch Feuer sein
wo Rauch ist   lügt viel

B. Derive three or four simple or compound nouns, verbs, adjectives, or adverbs from the words in each proverb and use each in a German sentence. EXAMPLES: *viel—vielmals, vielfach, vielleicht, vervielfältigen, der Vielfraß; reden — redlich, zureden, mitreden, der Redner, die Redeweise; wenig — wenigstens, nichtsdestoweniger, die Wenigkeit; Werk — werktätig, werken, das Werkzeug, der Werktag.*

Conversation — Auf der Zimmersuche

Hugo Schmidt:	Guten Tag. Verzeihen Sie, haben Sie ein Zimmer zu vermieten?
Frau Ball:	Ja, bitte treten Sie ein.
Hugo Schmidt:	Darf ich mich vorstellen? Ich heiße Hugo Schmidt und studiere Medizin.
Frau Ball:	Sehr angenehm. (Es) freut mich sehr, Herr Schmidt. Bitte, hier links ist das Zimmer.
Hugo Schmidt:	(Besieht es sich.) Etwas klein ist es schon.
Frau Ball:	Aber das Bad ist nebenan, und das Fenster geht auf den Garten hinaus.
Hugo Schmidt:	Wie teuer ist das Zimmer?
Frau Ball:	100 Mark den Monat mit Frühstück, Licht und Bedienung.
Hugo Schmidt:	Was geben Sie zum Frühstück?
Frau Ball:	Kaffee oder Milch, frische Brötchen mit Butter und Marmelade und ein Ei.
Hugo Schmidt:	Ist die Universität weit von hier?
Frau Ball:	Etwa 10 Minuten zu Fuß. Mit der Straßenbahn ist es nur ein Sprung.
Hugo Schmidt:	(Überlegt.) Gut, ich nehme das Zimmer.
Frau Ball:	Wann möchten Sie einziehen?
Hugo Schmidt:	Morgen früh, wenn es Ihnen paßt.
Frau Ball:	Dann melden Sie sich gleich bei der Polizei an.[6]
Hugo Schmidt:	Ja, schön. Hier ist die Miete.
Frau Ball:	(Zählt nach.) Stimmt. Danke.
Hugo Schmidt:	Bis morgen um neun. Auf Wiedersehen.

[6] In most European countries residents and transients register with the police.

CHAPTER
TWENTY-THREE

The Subjunctive. Its Formation. Indirect Discourse

As in the instances remaining in English,[1] the subjunctive in German is the mood of the probable, the desirable, the uncertain.

(a) FORMATION OF THE SUBJUNCTIVE

23.1 In German the subjunctive is formed by adding the personal endings –**e,** –**est,** –**e,** –**en,** –**et,** –**en** [2] to the present and past tense stems of weak and strong verbs (Appendices IX–XVI). Past tense stems of strong verbs also add an umlaut to the stem vowel, whenever possible. (Weak verbs do not modify the vowel.)

er sag –e   er sagt –e   er sing –e   er säng –e

23.2 Some common exceptions are:

(1) the first and third person singular present [3] subjunctive of **sein:**

ich sei   I be   **er sei**   he be

(2) the past [3] subjunctive of a number of strong verbs with special vowel change, as **ich hülfe, du hülfest, er hülfe,** etc.

INDICATIVE		SUBJUNCTIVE	
half	helped	**hülfe**	were helping
starb	died	**stürbe**	were dying
warf	threw	**würfe**	were throwing

---

[1] Only vestiges of the subjunctive remain in English. But they are still widely used. Cf. *Long live the king! So be it! If only it were true! I suggested that he do it over again.* [2] Cf. Chapter XIV (b), "The Conjugation of the Present and Past Tenses" of weak verbs. As a result the past indicative and the past subjunctive of weak verbs are identical. [3] In the subjunctive the terms "present" and "past" refer to form rather than tense or time. The present, present perfect, and future forms of the subjunctive are often referred to as Type 1. The past, past perfect forms, and the forms of **würde** plus the infinitive as Type 2.

(3) the past subjunctive of several irregular weak verbs, as **ich brennte, du brenntest, er brennte,** etc.

INDICATIVE		SUBJUNCTIVE	
brannte	burned	**brennte**	were burning
kannte	knew	**kennte**	were knowing
nannte	named	**nennte**	were naming
rannte	ran	**rennte**	were running
sandte	sent	**sendete**	were sending
wandte	turned	**wendete**	were turning
brachte	brought	**brächte**	were bringing
dachte	thought	**dächte**	were thinking
wußte	knew	**wüßte**	were knowing

(4) the past subjunctive of the auxiliaries, as **ich hätte, du hättest, er hätte,** etc.

INDICATIVE		SUBJUNCTIVE	
hatte	had	**hätte**	were having
wurde	became	**würde**	were becoming

(5) the past subjunctive of four of the modals, as **ich dürfte, du dürftest, er dürfte,** etc.

INDICATIVE		SUBJUNCTIVE	
durfte	was permitted	**dürfte**	were permitted
konnte	was able	**könnte**	were able
mochte	liked	**möchte**	were liking
mußte	had to	**müßte**	were having to

(b) *INDIRECT DISCOURSE*

23.3 In indirect discourse in German, the subjunctive is used to report rather than quote a statement, question, or command of another.[4]

---

[4] The indicative is used in indirect discourse: (1) after verbs expressing certainty, as **sehen, wissen: Er weiß, daß er kommt** (*He knows that he is coming*); (2) to report established facts: **Er sagt, Goethe wurde 1749 geboren** (*He says Goethe was born in 1749*); (3) after verbs in the first person singular: **Ich sage, er ist krank** (*I say he is sick*); (4) to vouch for or concur in a reported statement: **Er hat mir gesagt, daß er dort war** (*He told me that he was there*); **Unser Arzt sagt, ich bin abgearbeitet** (*Our doctor says I am run down*).

23.4 A statement in the present indicative, for example, is reported indirectly in the present or past subjunctive.[5]

Er sagt: ,,Ich bin hier.''	He says: "I am here."
Er sagt, er sei (wäre) hier.[6]	He says he is here.
Er sagte: ,,Ich bin hier.''	He said: "I am here."
Er sagte, er wäre (sei) hier.	He said he was here.

23.5 A question in the present indicative is reported indirectly in the present or past subjunctive.

Er fragt: ,,Gehst du?''	He asks: "Are you going?"
Er fragt, ob er gehe (ginge).[7]	He asks whether he is going.
Er fragte: ,,Gehst du?''	He asked: "Are you going?"
Er fragte, ob er ginge (gehe).[8]	He asked whether he were going.

23.6 A command in the present indicative is reported indirectly in the present or past subjunctive (of **sollen**) and the infinitive (of the verb).[9]

Er sagt: ,,Komm!''	He says: "Come!"
Er sagt, er soll(t)e kommen.	He says he should come.
Er sagte, er soll(t)e kommen.	He said he should come.

23.7 Statements and questions in the past (and present and past perfect) are reported indirectly in the present or past perfect subjunctive.

Er sagt: ,,Ich war dort.''	He says: "I was there."
Er sagt, er sei (wäre) dort gewesen.	He says he has been there.
Er sagte, er wäre (sei) dort gewesen.	He said he had been there.

23.8 Statements and questions in the future indicative are reported indirectly in the present or past subjunctive of **werden** and the infinitive.

Er sagt: ,,Ich werde gehen.''	He says: "I will go."
Er sagt, er werde (würde) gehen.	He says he will go.
Er sagte, er würde (werde) gehen.	He said he would go.

[5] Rhythm and a desire to avoid forms which resemble the indicative, rather than a supposed difference in the degree of reality between Type 1 and Type 2, generally determine the choice of the tense. [6] The introductory verb and the verb in the reported clause need not be in the same tense in German, but the sequence is properly maintained in English: **sagt ... sei** or **sagte ... sei** and **sagt ... wäre** or **sagte ... wäre** but *says ... is* and *said....was*. [7] **Ob** introduces indirect questions in German, *whether* introduces indirect questions in English. Both function as subordinating conjunctions. [8] Note the proper use of the subjunctive *were*. [9] The present or past subjunctive of **sollen** (sometimes **mögen**) is used in indirect commands in German; only *should* is used in English.

BASIC PATTERNS *

Der zivilisierte Mensch, sagt man, habe keine Zeit. Statt dessen habe er nur eine Uhr. In der Tat hat er nicht nur eine Uhr. Er lebt sozusagen zwischen den Uhren, mit den Uhren, gegen die Uhren. Er hat sie an der Hand, in der Hand. Er hat sie auf dem Schreibtisch, 5 auf der Straße, im Auto, auf dem Nachttisch. Er hat sie überall.

Und wozu ihm die Uhr diene? Sie schneidet ihm die Zeit in Scheiben, recht viele und recht dünne, wie man es bei der Wurst macht, wenn sie lange reichen soll. 10 Doch wie die dünnen Blättchen nicht schmecken, denn in eine Wurst muß man hineinbeißen können, so ist es ihm auch mit der Zeit. Dazu sind alle Uhren noch grausam. Das, sagt man, wäre ihr Beruf. Die Normaluhr zeigt dem ungeduldigen Menschen, wie lange er 15 vergeblich auf den anderen gewartet hat. Die Turmuhr zieht ihm die schlaflosen Nächte unendlich in die Länge, während der Wecker ihm den Schlaf unbarmherzig zerreißt, gerade wenn er am schönsten ist. An der Bahnhofsuhr sieht der Mensch, wieviel Minuten er zu spät 20 gekommen ist, an der Taschenuhr die Stunden, die er verschwendet hat.

Umso merkwürdiger ist es daher, daß der Mensch seine Präzisionsuhr oft absichtlich verstellt. Manchmal um zehn Minuten zurück. Dann soll die Uhr als Ent- 25 schuldigung dienen, beim Chef, bei der Gattin. Manchmal auch eine Viertelstunde vor. Damit will man sich zur Pünktlichkeit zwingen. Aber da man Bescheid weiß, zieht man eine Viertelstunde in Gedanken ab — und alles bleibt beim alten. Ist die Uhr inzwischen von un- 30 berufener Seite richtiggestellt worden, so führt das zu allerlei Ärgerlichkeiten.

Über das Wesen der Zeit streiten die Philosophen schon lange. Bei ihnen ist von objektiver und subjektiver

* Nach Heinrich Spoerl „Zeit ohne Zeit" aus *Der Lachende Lesering*, 1959. Verlag Bertelsmann, G.m.b.H., Gütersloh.

Zeit die Rede. Jene, sagen sie, messe man an den Himmelskörpern, diese hänge von Erlebnissen ab. Denn wer von Deutschland nach Frankreich fährt, muß seine Uhr zurückstellen. Dabei gewinnt er eine Stunde. Fährt er
5 nach New York weiter, so hat er bereits fünf Stunden gewonnen, in Frisko acht. Wer rund um die Welt fährt, gewinnt daher einen ganzen Tag. Daraus könnte der Mensch natürlich Nutzen ziehen. Er könnte sich in ein Düsenflugzeug setzen und mittags abfliegen. In vier-
10 undzwanzig Stunden wäre er dann um die Erde. Überall bliebe ewiger Mittag. Die Zeit stände still. Er würde nicht älter und sähe einer ewigen Jugend entgegen.

Doch umkehrbar ist die Zeit nicht. Das wissen die Philosophen genau. Deshalb geht es der Menschheit wie
15 dem Menschen. Man träumt vom Jugendland und wird unerbittlich älter. Man kann sich kurze Hosen anziehen und mit Bleisoldaten spielen, Märchenbücher lesen und Schaukelpferd reiten: man wird dadurch kein Kind. Kein Sehnen bringt die guten alten Zeiten zurück. Die
20 Zeiten sind eben vorbei, und ein Vorwärts kann kein Rückwärts sein.

Der Mensch, der heutzutage keine Uhr braucht, ist fast wie ein Kind einer anderen Zeit. Er hat irgendwie die Zeit, sich nach dem Rhythmus der Umwelt zu richten.
25 Wenn zum Beispiel der Bäckerjunge morgens im Hof nebenan die leeren Marmeladeneimer kegelt, weil er arbeiten muß, während die anderen noch schlafen, dann weiß dieser sonderbare Mensch, daß es sechs Uhr ist. Klingelt es bei ihm zweimal, ist es die Post und ein Viertel
30 nach acht. Wenn seine Zeitung kommt, so weiß er, daß es halb elf ist. Wenn die Beamten das große Gebäude verlassen, das seinem Hause gegenüberliegt, ist es zwölf Uhr neunundfünfzig. Erheben die Zeitungsmänner ihr Wettgebrüll an der Ecke, so ist es bestimmt halb fünf. Wenn er
35 Durst bekommt, ist es neun. Und wenn er müde wird, geht er zu Bett. Er weiß auch ohne Uhr, wieviel es geschlagen hat.

Questions

1. Was für Uhren hat der zivilisierte Mensch? 2. Wozu dienen ihm die Uhren? 3. Warum sind Uhren oft grausam? 4. Wie wollen sich manche Menschen zur Pünktlichkeit zwingen? 5. Von was für Zeit ist bei den Philosophen die Rede? 6. Wie kann man im Flugzeug einen ganzen Tag gewinnen? 7. Was für ein Mensch braucht heutzutage keine Uhr? 8. Wonach richtet sich ein solcher Mensch? 9. Wie weiß er, daß es in Deutschland halb elf ist? 10. Woran erkennt man einen solchen Menschen?

Idiomatic Expressions

in der Tat	as a matter of fact, indeed
lange reichen	to go far (*or* a long way)
Bescheid wissen	to know the facts
in Gedanken	mentally, in (one's) thoughts
beim alten bleiben	to remain as it was
bei mir ist die Rede von (*dat.*)	I talk about
messen an (*dat.*)	to measure by
Nutzen ziehen aus (*dat.*)	to profit from
sich richten nach (*dat.*)	to be guided by
Durst bekommen	to get thirsty

EXERCISES

A. Use each of the above expressions in (1) an indirect statement introduced with *Er sagt*, and (2) an indirect question introduced with *Er fragt.*

B. Change the direct commands into indirect commands.

1. Schneid die Wurst in Scheiben! 2. Beißt in sie hinein! 3. Warten Sie auf mich! 4. Weck ihn um zehn! 5. Stellen Sie die Uhr zehn Minuten vor!

C. Introduce each of the following statements with *Er wußte* and *Ich glaube.*

1. Es ist fünf Uhr. 2. Es ist spät. 3. Er hat keine Taschenuhr. 4. Sie zieht die Geschichte absichtlich in die Länge. 5. Sie wollen dich sehen.

173

D. Complete the clause on the left with any of the suitable phrases on the right, and add a suitable dependent clause.

Er zieht die Sache . . .	. . . gar keine Rede.
Aus seinen Erfahrungen zog ich . . .	. . . in der Tat.
Er will es . . .	. . . die guten alten Zeiten.
Man kann sie nicht zurück-sehnen . . .	. . . sehr großen Nutzen.
Gestern früh war davon . . .	. . . unendlich in die Länge.

E. Explain in one or two sentences in German: *ein moderner Mensch, die guten alten Zeiten, subjektive Zeit, allerlei Uhren, der Rhythmus der Umwelt.*

F. Expand upon each of the following statements.

1. Er hat keine Uhr, sondern Zeit. 2. An Uhren mangelt es ihm sehr, aber noch mehr an Zeit. 3. Er hat mehr Zeit als Uhren. 4. Mit der Uhr an der Hand wird man älter mit der Zeit. 5. Die Zeit mißt nicht die Uhr, sondern die Uhr die Zeit.

Composition

1. They say that [the] civilized man no longer has [any] time, but that he has watches instead. 2. These are not only supposed to tell him the time, but to indicate to him how many hours he has wasted. 3. They‿are‿said‿to drag‿out his sleepless nights and to eat‿up his busy days. 4. Yet there is hardly a person who would now want to get‿along without them. 5. The person who doesn't need a watch nowadays seems like a man of another age. 6. He can still be‿guided‿by the rhythm of the‿ world‿about‿him. 7. He can still rise when the sun rises and go to bed when he is tired. 8. When his bell rings twice, he knows that it is the mail and time to‿get‿to‿work. 9. When the morning‿paper arrives, he knows that it is ten thirty. 10. And when his neighbors leave their office, he knows that it is almost one. 11. He usually gets hungry at five and thirsty at nine. 12. To him time is indeed subjective. 13. It is irretrievable. 14. He knows that the good old days cannot be wished‿back. 15. He doesn't live in a world‿of‿dreams. 16. He knows‿the‿score and makes the best of it.

Variations

A. Match and arrange in their proper order the portions of the familiar sayings listed in the two columns and explain their meanings in German.

wie einer redet	guter Rat
wer Rosen bricht	was nicht ist
prüfet alles	wer den Pfennig ehrt
so der Tanz	trifft endlich
kurzer Rat	so ist er
kann noch werden	die Finger sticht
ist den Taler wert	behaltet das Beste
wer oft schießt	wie die Pfeife

B. Derive three or four simple or compound nouns, verbs, adjectives, or adverbs from the words in each proverb and use each in a German sentence. EXAMPLES: *wie — wieso, wieviel, der Wievielte; gut — gütig, vergüten, begutachten, das Gut; Rat — ratsam, raten, der Berater.*

Conversation — Deutsche Universitäten

Peter Juergen: Im großen ganzen ähneln sich die Universitäten in allen Ländern.

Karl Schuh: Aber die deutschen Hochschulen sind im einzeln doch wohl anders.

Peter Juergen: Das schon. Erstens sind die deutschen Universitäten staatliche Einrichtungen und die Professoren Staatsbeamte.

Karl Schuh: Das gefährdet wohl die Lehr- und Forschungsfreiheit?

Peter Juergen: Mit nichten. Seit Anfang des neunzehnten Jahrhunderts haben die deutschen Universitäten völlige Selbstverwaltung.

Karl Schuh: Wer beruft denn die Professoren?

Peter Juergen: Die Fakultät beruft die Professoren und entscheidet alle anderen einschlägigen Fragen.

Karl Schuh: Setzt der Staat den Rektor und die Dekane ein?

Peter Juergen:	Nein. Sie werden jedes Jahr aus dem Kreise der Professoren gewählt.
Karl Schuh:	Und wie werden die Studenten zum Studium zugelassen?
Peter Juergen:	Sie kommen gewöhnlich mit 19 oder 20 Jahren nach Abschluß des Abiturs auf die Universität, d. h. nach einer Endprüfung an der höheren Schule.
Karl Schuh:	Steht es den deutschen Studenten frei, sich Vorlesungen und Professoren selbst auszuwählen?
Peter Juergen:	Ja. Das ist ein wesentlicher Teil der deutschen akademischen Freiheit.
Karl Schuh:	Und wieviel Semester studiert ein deutscher Student?
Peter Juergen:	Meistens 8 oder 10 Semester.
Karl Schuh:	Gibt es auf deutschen Universitäten wirklich keine Zwischenexamen?
Peter Juergen:	In manchen Fakultäten schon. Aber in der Mehrzahl der Fächer gibt es jetzt Zwischenexamen und Endprüfungen.
Karl Schuh:	Zu welchen Titeln führen die Prüfungen?
Peter Juergen:	Hauptsächlich zum Doktor.
Karl Schuh:	Nächstes Mal müssen Sie mir noch einiges über die deutschen Universitäten erzählen.
Peter Juergen:	Gerne. (Verabschiedet sich von Karl.)

CHAPTER TWENTY-FOUR

The Subjunctive in Conditions

As in English, a condition in German may be "real" (plausible) or "unreal" (contrary to fact). In other words, it may suggest a considerable degree or a remote degree of reality or probability of fulfillment. Its realization may hinge on a single *if* or a compound set of conjectures.

(a) *REAL CONDITIONS*

24.1 Real conditions, which hinge on a simple *if*, are expressed by the indicative in both English and German. A present real condition is rendered by the present indicative, a past real condition by the past indicative, a future real condition by the future indicative, and so forth. Examples are:

Wenn es stark regnet, bleibt sie immer zu Hause.	If it rains hard, she always stays at home.
Wenn es stark regnete, blieb sie zu Hause.[1]	If it rained hard, she stayed at home.

24.2 Note that the conclusion may precede the *if*-clause in all real conditions in English and in German. However, when the *if*-clause stands first in German, the conjunction **wenn** may be omitted, in which case the finite verb occupies first place, and the conclusion is generally introduced by **so** or **dann**, neither of which further affects the word order.

Sie bleibt zu Hause, wenn es stark regnet.	She stays at home, if it rains hard.
Regnet es stark, so bleibt sie zu Hause.	If it rains hard, she stays at home.

(b) *UNREAL CONDITIONS*

24.3 Unreal conditions suggest only a remote degree of promise of fulfillment. They are expressed by the subjunctive in English and in German, as suggested by the following pattern:

REAL CONDITIONS	UNREAL CONDITIONS
wenn ich . . . bin	wenn ich . . . wäre
if I am	if I were
wenn ich . . . war	wenn ich . . . gewesen wäre
if I was	if I had been
wenn ich . . . sein werde	wenn ich . . . sein würde
if I shall be	if I were to be

[1] Compare the meanings of the following three clauses introduced by **wenn** (*if, whenever*) and **als** (*when*):

Wenn es stark regnete, . . .	If it did rain hard, . . .
Wenn es stark regnete, . . .	If it were to rain hard, . . .
Als es stark regnete, . . .	When it rained hard, . . .

24.4 Specifically in both languages, the *if*-clause of a condition relating to the present is expressed by the past subjunctive.

> Wenn ich hungrig wäre, ...   If I were hungry, ...

24.5 The conclusion of an unreal condition relating to the present may be expressed by the so-called present conditional in English and in German, that is, by *would* and the infinitive of the verb in English, and by the past subjunctive of **werden** and the infinitive of the verb in German.

> ... würde ich essen.   ... I would eat.

24.6 In German the conclusion of an unreal condition relating to the present may also be expressed by the past subjunctive of the verb.

> ... äße ich.   ... I would eat.

24.7 The *if*-clause of a condition relating to the past is expressed by the past perfect (indicative in English, subjunctive in German).

> Wenn ich hungrig gewesen   If I had been hungry, ...
> wäre, ...

24.8 The conclusion of an unreal condition relating to the past may be expressed by the so-called past conditional in English and in German, that is, by *would*, the past participle of the verb, and the infinitive of its auxiliary in English, and by the past subjunctive of **werden,** the past participle of the verb, and the infinitive of its auxiliary in German.

> ... würde ich gegessen haben.   ... I would have eaten.

24.9 In German the conclusion of an unreal condition relating to the past may also be expressed by the past perfect subjunctive of the verb.[2]

> ... hätte ich gegessen.   ... I would have eaten.

---

[2] As a result, a condition in the past subjunctive is usually followed by a conclusion in the past subjunctive (or the present conditional), a condition in the past perfect subjunctive is followed by a conclusion in the past perfect subjunctive. Because of a time differential between the condition and the conclusion, however, a condition in the past perfect subjunctive may be followed by a conclusion in the past subjunctive.

Wenn es gestern nicht so stark geregnet hätte, wäre alles heute nicht so naß.
If it hadn't rained so hard yesterday, everything would not be so wet today.

24.10 In all unreal conditions the conclusion may precede the *if*-clause in English and in German. However, when the *if*-clause stands first, the conjunction (*if* — **wenn**) may be omitted, in which case the finite verb occupies first place, and the conclusion is generally introduced by **so** or **dann.**

Ich würde essen, wenn ich hungrig wäre.	I would eat, if I were hungry.
Wäre ich hungrig, so würde ich essen.	Were I hungry, I would eat.

24.11 **Als ob** [3] (*as if* or *as though*) and **als wenn** [3] (*as if* or *as though*) introduce so-called variations of unreal conditions. An example is:

Er tut, als ob er hungrig wäre.	He acts as if he were hungry.

(c) *PARTIAL CONDITIONS*

24.12 The *if*-clause of an unreal condition in English and in German is frequently also used independently to express a wish. It is then called an optative.[4] **Nur** or **doch** is generally added to such a wish in German.

Wenn ich nur so gut singen könnte!	If only I could sing that well!
Wenn sie doch gewartet hätte!	If only she had waited!

24.13 The conclusion of an unreal condition is frequently also used in both languages as a concessive or potential subjunctive.

Das wäre möglich.	That might (would) be possible.
Das wäre hier nie möglich gewesen.	That would never have been possible here.

BASIC PATTERNS *

„Wenn die Haifische Menschen wären," fragte Herrn Keuner die kleine Tochter seiner Wirtin, „wären sie dann netter zu den kleinen Fischen?" „Sicher," sagte er.

---

[3] **Ob** or **wenn** may be omitted. Whenever either is omitted, the order is inverted.

Er tut, als wäre er hungrig.   He acts as if he were hungry.

[4] Wishes possible of fulfillment are expressed by the present subjunctive.

So sei es.   So be it.
Dein Wille geschehe.   Thy will be done.

* Nach Bertold Brecht „Wenn die Haifische Menschen wären" aus den „Geschichten von Herrn Keuner" in den *Kalendergeschichten*, Gebrüder Weiss Verlag, Berlin-Schöneberg, 1959.

Der Oberkirchner Kinderchor ("Angels in Pigtails")
vor seiner dritten Reise nach Amerika.

„Wenn die Haifische Menschen wären, würden sie für die Fischlein sorgen. Sie würden im Meer für sie gewaltige Kästen bauen lassen mit allerhand Nahrung drin. Sie würden zusehen, daß die Kästen immer frisches Wasser hätten, und überhaupt allerhand sanitäre Maßnahmen 5 treffen. Damit die Fischlein nicht trübsinnig würden, gäbe es natürlich ab und zu große Wasserfeste. Es gäbe bestimmt auch Schulen in den großen Kästen. In diesen Schulen würden die Fischlein lernen, wie man in den Rachen der Haifische schwimmt. Dazu würden 10 sie auch Geographie brauchen, damit sie die großen Haifische, die gerne faul herumliegen, leicht finden könnten. Die Hauptsache wäre jedoch die moralische Ausbildung der kleinen Fische. Sie würden unterrichtet 15 werden, daß es das Größte und das Schönste sei, an die Haifische zu glauben und sich für sie freudig aufzuopfern. Vor allen niedrigen, materialistischen Neigungen müßten sich die Fischlein hüten und sofort den Haifischen melden, wenn eines von ihnen solche Neigungen verriete. 20

Wenn die Haifische Menschen wären, würden sie natürlich auch untereinander Kriege führen, besonders um fremde Fischkästen und fremde Fischlein zu erobern. Die Kriege würden sie von ihren eigenen Fischlein führen lassen. Sie würden die Fischlein lehren, daß zwischen 25 ihnen und den Fischlein der anderen Haifische ein riesiger Unterschied bestehe. Die Fischlein, würden sie verkünden, sind bekanntlich stumm. Da sie aber ebenso bekanntlich in ganz verschiedenen Sprachen schweigen, können sie einander unmöglich verstehen. Jedem Fisch- 30 lein, das im Krieg ein paar andere Fischlein, d. h. feindliche, in anderer Sprache schweigende, tötete, würden sie einen kleinen Orden aus Seetang anheften und den Titel Held verleihen.

Wenn die Haifische Menschen wären, gäbe es bei 35 ihnen natürlich auch Kunst. Es gäbe schöne Bilder, auf denen die Zähne der Haifische in prächtigen Farben

181

gemalt wären, und deren Rachen als reine Lustgärten dargestellt wären, in denen es sich herrlich tummeln läßt. Die Theater auf dem Meeresgrunde würden zeigen, wie heldenmütige Fischlein begeistert in die Haifischrachen schwimmen. Die Musik wäre auch so schön, daß die Fischlein unter ihren Klängen, die Kapelle voran, träumerisch, und in allerangenehmste Gedanken gehüllt, in die Haifischrachen strömten.

Übrigens würde es auch aufhören, wenn die Haifische Menschen wären, daß alle Fischlein, wie es jetzt ist, gleich sein würden. Einige von ihnen würden Ämter bekommen und über die anderen gesetzt werden. Die ein wenig größeren dürften dann sogar die kleineren auffressen. Das wäre für die Haifische nur angenehm, da sie dadurch selber öfter größere Brocken zu fressen bekämen. Die größeren Fischlein würden natürlich für die Ordnung unter den Fischlein sorgen. Sie würden Lehrer, Offiziere, Ingenieure im Kastenbau usw. werden. Kurz, es gäbe überhaupt erst eine Kultur im Meer, wenn die Haifische Menschen wären," versicherte Herr Keuner der kleinen Tochter seiner Wirtin.

Questions

1. Wie kam Herr Keuner auf Haifische zu sprechen? 2. Was wollte die Tochter der Wirtin von Haifischen wissen? 3. Weshalb, meinte Herr Keuner, würden die Haifische Kästen im Meer bauen? 4. Was würden die Fischlein in den Kästen tun? 5. Was würden die kleinen Fischlein in den Schulen lernen? 6. Worin würde ihre moralische Ausbildung bestehen? 7. Wie würden die Haifische die Fischlein für den Krieg begeistern? 8. Wozu gäbe es bei den Fischlein Kunst? 9. Warum dürfte keine Gleichheit zwischen ihnen bestehen? 10. Wann gäbe es bei den Fischlein erst eine Kultur, meinte Herr Keuner?

Idiomatic Expressions

nett sein zu (*dat.*)	to be nice to
sorgen für (*acc.*)	to care for
zusehen	to see to it
Maßnahmen treffen	to take steps

ab und zu	now and then
glauben an (*acc.*)	to believe in
sich hüten vor (*dat.*)	to guard against
sich aufopfern für (*acc.*)	to sacrifice one's life for
für die Ordnung sorgen	to (be responsible for) maintain(ing) order
Krieg führen	to wage war

EXERCISES

A. Use each of the above idiomatic expressions in an "if" clause. EXAMPLE: Wenn er ab und zu nachfragen würde, wäre ich ihm dankbar.

B. Separate the real from the unreal conditions.

1. Wenn ich ein Haifisch wäre, sorgte ich nicht für kleine Fische. 2. Bin ich ein Ingenieur, baue ich Kästen. 3. Wäre ich ein Fischlein, so würde ich schwimmen. 4. In diese Schulen würden sie gehen, wenn sie lernen wollten. 5. Wenn die Haifische Menschen gewesen wären, hätten die Kriege aufgehört. 6. Wenn sie die Musik hören werden, werden sie begeistert in die Rachen der Haifische schwimmen. 7. Es wäre für die Haifische angenehm, wenn die größeren Fischlein die kleinen auffressen würden. 8. Wenn Sie wollen, warte ich. 9. Gehe ich, so geht er. 10. Die Fischlein würden trübsinnig, wenn sie nicht schwimmen dürften.

C. Report indirectly. EXAMPLE: Er fragte mich: „Wer bist du?" Er fragte mich, wer ich wäre.

1. Wer bist du? 2. Ich bin froh. 3. Dazu brauchten sie keine Geographie. 4. Die Hauptsache ist die moralische Ausbildung. 5. Geben Sie ihm einen Orden! 6. Zeig mir das Theater! 7. Warum werden die Fischlein für die Ordnung sorgen? 8. Die Haifische aßen Fischlein. 9. Wie steht es bei den Fischen mit der Kunst? 10. Ich werde schön zusehen.

D. Separate the optatives from the concessives and change the time from the present to the present perfect.

1. Das wäre möglich. 2. Wenn sie nur aufhörte. 3. Könnte ich nur so gut singen. 4. Gäbe er es doch zu. 5. Das ließe sich machen. 6. Wenn es ihm nur gefiele.

183

E. Complete the following:

1. Es lebe . . .   2. So sei . . .   3. Gott gebe . . .   4. Es geschehe . . .   5. Er habe . . .

F. Complete in the past tense:

1. Die Haifische (lassen) . . .   2. Die Fische (schwimmen) . . . 3. Die Schulen (lehren) . . .   4. Kriege (führen) . . .   5. Unterschiede (bestehen) . . .   6. In verschiedenen Sprachen (schweigen) . . .   7. Die Theater (zeigen) . . .   8. Die Offiziere (sorgen) . . . 9. Die Maßnahmen (treffen) . . .   10. In die Haifischrachen (strömen) . . .

Composition

1. "If sharks were humans," said Mr. Keuner to the little girl beside him, "they would indeed be very kind to the little fish in the sea.   2. They would build large boxes for them and equip these boxes with food and fresh water.   3. They would also build schools for the little fish.   4. In these schools the little fish would learn how kind sharks are and how wonderful it is to die for them. 5. Beautiful paintings would portray the jaws of the sharks as lovely gardens in which one could romp about merrily.   6. The theaters at the bottom of the sea would show how little fish swam enthusiastically into the jaws of the sharks.   7. Yes, if sharks were humans they would bring culture to the sea.   8. Each shark would take care of his little fish.   9. Since fish cannot speak, he would point out to his own little fish how different they were from other little fish in their silence.   10. He would let them wage his wars against the little fish of the other sharks and reward the heroes with decorations of seaweed.   11. Some of them would then be placed in charge of the other little fish and be allowed to eat the smaller [ones].   12. He himself would then eat the larger [ones] who were not kind to the little fish in the sea. 13. In short, there is no doubt, my child," said Mr. Keuner to the girl beside him, "if sharks were humans, they would indeed be very kind to the little fish in the sea."

Variations

A. Match and arrange in their proper order the portions of the familiar sayings listed in the two columns and explain their meaning in German.

je länger man lebt	wer gut gesattelt
reitet gut	muß bezahlen
geht nicht ins Wasser	je älter man wird
wer schuldig ist	halten schwer
vom ersten Streiche	wer nicht schwimmen kann
Glück und Glas	fällt keine Eiche
versprechen ist leicht	wie leicht bricht das
da geht nichts aus	wo nichts innen ist

B. Derive three or four simple or compound nouns, verbs, adjectives, or adverbs from the words in each proverb and use each in a German sentence. EXAMPLES: *lang — entlang, langsam, längst, verlängern, die Verlängerung; leben — lebendig, lebenslänglich, beleben, der Lebemann; satteln — sattelfest, umsatteln, der Sattel, der Sattler.*

Conversation — Goethe und Faust

Fräulein Werner: Sind Goethe und Faust wirklich eng miteinander in Verbindung zu bringen?

Cand. Phil. Born: Gewiß. Man kann sagen, Goethes Liebesschicksale, sein Hoffen, Kämpfen, Zweifeln und letzter Glaube schließen sich alle zusammen im Faust.

Fräulein Werner: Was brachte Goethe überhaupt auf den Gedanken, einen *Faust* zu schreiben?

Cand. Phil. Born: Es war wohl das Hauptzugstück des Puppenspiels, das schon den Knaben Goethe fesselte.

Fräulein Werner: Kannte der junge Goethe Marlowes *Faust* (1595)?

Cand. Phil. Born: Nein. In den Frankfurter Jahren kannte er sicherlich das *Faustbuch des Christlich Meynenden* (aus dem Jahre 1725). Das Pfizerische Volksbuch (1674) und Marlowes Drama las er erst viele Jahre später.

Fräulein Werner: In keiner von diesen Quellen ist aber die Rede von Erlösung.

185

Cand. Phil. Born: Ob Klopstock und Lessing ihn auf diese brach-
ten? Denn der *Messias* (1748) fängt an: „Sing,
unsterbliche Seele, der sündigen Menschheit
Erlösung," und Lessing hatte schon 1759 bei
der Veröffentlichung seiner Faustszene den völlig neuen Gedanken der Rettung Fausts gehegt.

Fräulein Werner: Verdient Faust auch, erlöst zu werden?

Cand. Phil. Born: Im engeren Sinne kaum. Doch ...

Fräulein Werner: Ich weiß schon. Sie zitieren jetzt aus dem
Prolog im Himmel. „Es irrt der Mensch, so
lang er strebt," und „Ein guter Mensch in
seinem dunklen Drange ist sich des rechten
Weges wohl bewußt."

Cand. Phil. Born: Ja, deshalb singen auch die Engel, die Faustens
Unsterbliches forttragen, „Wer immer stre-
bend sich bemüht, den können wir erlösen."

Fräulein Werner: Ich gebe zu, Faust hat sich immer bemüht.
Aber wie erklären Sie den Pakt mit Mephisto?

Cand. Phil. Born: Sehr einfach. Die Wette lautet:

„Werd' ich beruhigt je mich auf ein Faul-
bett legen,
So sei es gleich um mich getan!
. . . .
Werd' ich zum Augenblicke sagen:
Verweile doch, du bist so schön!
Dann magst du mich in Fesseln schlagen,
Dann will ich gern zu Grunde gehn!"

Fräulein Werner: Aber Faust sagt ja zuletzt zu dem Augenblick:
„Verweile doch, du bist so schön!"

Cand. Phil. Born: Merken Sie jedoch genau, wie er es sagt:

„(Könnt' ich)
Auf freiem Grund mit freien Menschen
stehn.
Zum Augenblicke dürft' ich sagen:
Verweile doch, du bist so schön!"

Fräulein Werner: Jetzt verstehe ich's. Vielen Dank.

Cand. Phil. Born: Bitte, es hat mir viel Spaß gemacht.

186

Appendix

Appendix

I. *The Definite Article and **der**-Words**

CASE	Masculine	Feminine	Neuter	All Genders
		SINGULAR		PLURAL
Nom.	der	die	das	die
	dieser	diese	dieses	diese
Gen.	des	der	des	der
	dieses	dieser	dieses	dieser
Dat.	dem	der	dem	den
	diesem	dieser	diesem	diesen
Acc.	den	die	das	die
	diesen	diese	dieses	diese

II. *The Indefinite Article and **ein**-Words†*

CASE	Masculine	Feminine	Neuter	All Genders
		SINGULAR		PLURAL
Nom.	ein	eine	ein	
	mein	meine	mein	meine
Gen.	eines	einer	eines	
	meines	meiner	meines	meiner
Dat.	einem	einer	einem	
	meinem	meiner	meinem	meinen

* The **der**-words are: **dies–, jed–, jen–, solch–, welch–, manch–.**
† The **ein**-words are: **mein, dein, sein, ihr, sein, unser, euer, ihr, Ihr,** and **kein.**

187

| CASE | SINGULAR | | | PLURAL |
	Masculine	Feminine	Neuter	All Genders
Acc.	einen	eine	ein	
	meinen	meine	mein	meine

III. The Demonstrative Pronoun der

| CASE | SINGULAR | | | PLURAL |
	Masculine	Feminine	Neuter	All Genders
Nom.	der	die	das	die
Gen.	dessen	deren	dessen	deren
Dat.	dem	der	dem	denen
Acc.	den	die	das	die

IV. The Demonstratives derjenige and derselbe

| CASE | SINGULAR | | | PLURAL |
	Masculine	Feminine	Neuter	All Genders
Nom.	derjenige	diejenige	dasjenige	diejenigen
	derselbe	dieselbe	dasselbe	dieselben
Gen.	desjenigen	derjenigen	desjenigen	derjenigen
	desselben	derselben	desselben	derselben
Dat.	demjenigen	derjenigen	demjenigen	denjenigen
	demselben	derselben	demselben	denselben
Acc.	denjenigen	diejenige	dasjenige	diejenigen
	denselben	dieselbe	dasselbe	dieselben

V. The Relative Pronouns der and welcher

| CASE | SINGULAR | | | PLURAL |
	Masculine	Feminine	Neuter	All Genders
Nom.	der	die	das	die
	welcher	welche	welches	welche
Gen.	dessen	deren	dessen	deren
Dat.	dem	der	dem	denen
	welchem	welcher	welchem	welchen
Acc.	den	die	das	die
	welchen	welche	welches	welche

VI. *The Personal Pronoun*

SINGULAR

	1st Person	*2nd Person*		*3rd Person*		
Nom.	ich	Sie	du	er	sie	es
Gen.	(meiner)	(Ihrer)	(deiner)	(seiner)	(ihrer)	(seiner)
Dat.	mir	Ihnen	dir	ihm	ihr	ihm
Acc.	mich	Sie	dich	ihn	sie	es

PLURAL

Nom.	wir	Sie	ihr	sie
Gen.	(unser)	(Ihrer)	(euer)	(ihrer)
Dat.	uns	Ihnen	euch	ihnen
Acc.	uns	Sie	euch	sie

VII. *The Declension of Nouns*

A. The Declension of Nouns in Class I

SINGULAR

CASE	*Masculine*	*Feminine*	*Neuter*
Nom.	der Apfel	die Mutter	das Mädchen
Gen.	des Apfels	der Mutter	des Mädchens
Dat.	dem Apfel	der Mutter	dem Mädchen
Acc.	den Apfel	die Mutter	das Mädchen

PLURAL

Nom.	die Äpfel	die Mütter	die Mädchen
Gen.	der Äpfel	der Mütter	der Mädchen
Dat.	den Äpfeln	den Müttern	den Mädchen
Acc.	die Äpfel	die Mütter	die Mädchen

B. The Declension of Nouns in Class II

SINGULAR

CASE	*Masculine*	*Feminine*	*Neuter*
Nom.	der Sohn	die Hand	das Gas
Gen.	des Sohnes	der Hand	des Gases
Dat.	dem Sohn	der Hand	dem Gas(e)
Acc.	den Sohn	die Hand	das Gas

PLURAL

CASE	*Masculine*	*Feminine*	*Neuter*
Nom.	die Söhne	die Hände	die Gase
Gen.	der Söhne	der Hände	der Gase
Dat.	den Söhnen	den Händen	den Gasen
Acc.	die Söhne	die Hände	die Gase

C. The Declension of Nouns in Class III

SINGULAR

CASE	*Masculine*	*Feminine*	*Neuter*
Nom.	der Mann		das Haus
Gen.	des Mannes	None	des Hauses
Dat.	dem Mann		dem Haus(e)
Acc.	den Mann		das Haus

PLURAL

Nom.	die Männer		die Häuser
Gen.	der Männer		der Häuser
Dat.	den Männern		den Häusern
Acc.	die Männer		die Häuser

D. The Declension of Nouns in Class IV

SINGULAR

CASE	*Masculine*	*Feminine*	*Neuter*
Nom.	der Student	die Frau	
Gen.	des Studenten	der Frau	None
Dat.	dem Studenten	der Frau	
Acc.	den Studenten	die Frau	

PLURAL

Nom.	die Studenten	die Frauen	
Gen.	der Studenten	der Frauen	
Dat.	den Studenten	den Frauen	
Acc.	die Studenten	die Frauen	

E. The Declension of "Mixed" Nouns

SINGULAR

CASE	Masculine	Feminine	Neuter
Nom.	der Professor		das Bett
Gen.	des Professors	None	des Bettes
Dat.	dem Professor		dem Bett
Acc.	den Professor		das Bett

PLURAL

CASE	Masculine	Feminine	Neuter
Nom.	die Professoren		die Betten
Gen.	der Professoren		der Betten
Dat.	den Professoren		den Betten
Acc.	die Professoren		die Betten

F. The Declension of "Irregular" Nouns

SINGULAR

CASE	Masculine	Feminine	Neuter
Nom.	der Name		das Herz
Gen.	des Namens	None	des Herzens
Dat.	dem Namen		dem Herz
Acc.	den Namen		das Herz

PLURAL

CASE	Masculine	Feminine	Neuter
Nom.	die Namen		die Herzen
Gen.	der Namen		der Herzen
Dat.	den Namen		den Herzen
Acc.	die Namen		die Herzen

VIII. The Declension of Adjectives

A. Strong Declension

(Adjectives not preceded by an inflected der-word or ein-word)

SINGULAR

CASE	Masculine	Feminine	Neuter
Nom.	treuer Freund	gute Frau	schönes Land
Gen.	treuen Freundes	guter Frau	schönen Landes
Dat.	treuem Freunde	guter Frau	schönem Lande
Acc.	treuen Freund	gute Frau	schönes Land

PLURAL

CASE	Masculine	Feminine	Neuter
Nom.	treue Freunde	gute Frauen	schöne Länder
Gen.	treuer Freunde	guter Frauen	schöner Länder
Dat.	treuen Freunden	guten Frauen	schönen Ländern
Acc.	treue Freunde	gute Frauen	schöne Länder

B. Weak Declension

(Adjectives preceded by an inflected **der**-word)

SINGULAR

CASE	Masculine	Feminine
Nom.	der treue Freund	diese gute Frau
Gen.	des treuen Freundes	dieser guten Frau
Dat.	dem treuen Freunde	dieser guten Frau
Acc.	den treuen Freund	diese gute Frau

PLURAL

Nom.	die treuen Freunde	diese guten Frauen
Gen.	der treuen Freunde	dieser guten Frauen
Dat.	den treuen Freunden	diesen guten Frauen
Acc.	die treuen Freunde	diese guten Frauen

SINGULAR

Neuter

Nom.	jenes schöne Land
Gen.	jenes schönen Landes
Dat.	jenem schönen Land
Acc.	jenes schöne Land

PLURAL

Nom.	jene schönen Länder
Gen.	jener schönen Länder
Dat.	jenen schönen Ländern
Acc.	jene schönen Länder

C. Mixed Declension

(Adjectives preceded by an inflected **ein**-word)

SINGULAR

CASE	*Masculine*	*Feminine*
Nom.	kein treuer Freund	meine gute Frau
Gen.	keines treuen Freundes	meiner guten Frau
Dat.	keinem treuen Freunde	meiner guten Frau
Acc.	keinen treuen Freund	meine gute Frau

PLURAL

Nom.	keine treuen Freunde	meine guten Frauen
Gen.	keiner treuen Freunde	meiner guten Frauen
Dat.	keinen treuen Freunden	meinen guten Frauen
Acc.	keine treuen Freunde	meine guten Frauen

SINGULAR

Neuter

Nom.	sein kleines Land
Gen.	seines kleinen Landes
Dat.	seinem kleinen Land
Acc.	sein kleines Land

PLURAL

Nom.	seine kleinen Länder
Gen.	seiner kleinen Länder
Dat.	seinen kleinen Ländern
Acc.	seine kleinen Länder

IX. *The Conjugation of* **sein**

Indicative	Subjunctive
PRESENT	PRESENT
ich bin	sei
du bist	seiest
er ist	sei
wir sind	seien
ihr seid	seiet
sie sind	seien

Indicative	Subjunctive
PAST	PAST
ich war	wäre
du warst	wärest
er war	wäre
wir waren	wären
ihr wart	wäret
sie waren	wären

PRESENT PERFECT	PRESENT PERFECT
ich bin gewesen	sei gewesen
PAST PERFECT	PAST PERFECT
ich war gewesen	wäre gewesen
FUTURE	FUTURE
ich werde sein	werde sein
du wirst sein	werdest sein
FUTURE PERFECT	FUTURE PERFECT
ich werde gewesen sein	werde gewesen sein
du wirst gewesen sein	werdest gewesen sein
PRESENT CONDITIONAL*	PRESENT CONDITIONAL*
ich würde sein	würde sein
PAST CONDITIONAL*	PAST CONDITIONAL*
ich würde gewesen sein	würde gewesen sein

Infinitive	Participle
PRESENT: sein	PRESENT: seiend
PERFECT: gewesen (zu) sein	PERFECT: gewesen

Imperative
sei, seid, seien Sie

X. The Conjugation of *haben*

Indicative	Subjunctive
PRESENT	PRESENT
ich habe	habe
du hast	habest
er hat	habe

* Notice that in the conditionals the indicative and the subjunctive are the same.

PRESENT	PRESENT
wir haben	haben
ihr habt	habet
sie haben	haben
PAST	PAST
ich hatte	hätte
du hattest	hättest
er hatte	hätte
wir hatten	hätten
ihr hattet	hättet
sie hatten	hätten
PRESENT PERFECT	PRESENT PERFECT
ich habe gehabt	habe gehabt
du hast gehabt	habest gehabt
PAST PERFECT	PAST PERFECT
ich hatte gehabt	hätte gehabt
du hattest gehabt	hättest gehabt
FUTURE	FUTURE
ich werde haben	werde haben
du wirst haben	werdest haben
FUTURE PERFECT	FUTURE PERFECT
ich werde gehabt haben	werde gehabt haben
du wirst gehabt haben	werdest gehabt haben
PRESENT CONDITIONAL	PRESENT CONDITIONAL
ich würde haben	ich würde haben
PAST CONDITIONAL	PAST CONDITIONAL
ich würde gehabt haben	ich würde gehabt haben

Infinitive	**Participle**
PRESENT: haben	PRESENT: habend
PERFECT: gehabt (zu) haben	PERFECT: gehabt

Imperative

hab(e), habt, haben Sie

XI. *The Conjugation of* **werden**

Indicative	Subjunctive
PRESENT	PRESENT
ich werde	werde
du wirst	werdest
er wird	werde
wir werden	werden
ihr werdet	werdet
sie werden	werden
PAST	PAST
ich wurde	würde
du wurdest	würdest
er wurde	würde
wir wurden	würden
ihr wurdet	würdet
sie wurden	würden
PRESENT PERFECT	PRESENT PERFECT
ich bin geworden	sei geworden
PAST PERFECT	PAST PERFECT
ich war geworden	wäre geworden
FUTURE	FUTURE
ich werde werden	werde werden
du wirst werden	werdest werden
FUTURE PERFECT	FUTURE PERFECT
ich werde geworden sein	werde geworden sein
du wirst geworden sein	werdest geworden sein
PRESENT CONDITIONAL	PRESENT CONDITIONAL
ich würde werden	würde werden
PAST CONDITIONAL	PAST CONDITIONAL
ich würde geworden sein	würde geworden sein

Infinitive	Participle
PRESENT: werden	PRESENT: werdend
PERFECT: geworden (zu) sein	PERFECT: geworden

Imperative
werde, werdet, werden Sie

XII. *The Conjugation of Weak Verbs*

Indicative	**Subjunctive**
PRESENT	PRESENT
ich frage	frage
du fragst	fragest
er fragt	frage
wir fragen	fragen
ihr fragt	fraget
sie fragen	fragen
PAST	PAST
ich fragte	fragte
du fragtest	fragtest
er fragte	fragte
wir fragten	fragten
ihr fragtet	fragten
sie fragten	fragtet
PRESENT PERFECT	PRESENT PERFECT
ich habe gefragt	habe gefragt
du hast gefragt	habest gefragt
PAST PERFECT	PAST PERFECT
ich hatte gefragt	hätte gefragt
du hattest gefragt	hättest gefragt
FUTURE	FUTURE
ich werde fragen	werde fragen
du wirst fragen	werdest fragen
FUTURE PEPFECT	FUTURE PERFECT
ich werde gefragt haben	werde gefragt haben
du wirst gefragt haben	werdest gefragt haben
PRESENT CONDITIONAL	PRESENT CONDITIONAL
ich würde fragen	würde fragen
PAST CONDITIONAL	PAST CONDITIONAL
ich würde gefragt haben	würde gefragt haben

Infinitive	**Participle**
PRESENT: fragen	PRESENT: fragend
PERFECT: gefragt (zu) haben	PERFECT: gefragt

Imperative
frag(e), fragt, fragen Sie

XIII. The Conjugation of the Strong Verbs

Indicative	Subjunctive
PRESENT	PRESENT
ich gebe	gebe
du gibst	gebest
er gibt	gebe
wir geben	geben
ihr gebt	gebet
sie geben	geben
PAST	PAST
ich gab	gäbe
du gabst	gäbest
er gab	gäbe
wir gaben	gäben
ihr gabt	gäbet
sie gaben	gäben
PRESENT PERFECT	PRESENT PERFECT
ich habe gegeben	habe gegeben
du hast gegeben	habest gegeben
PAST PERFECT	PAST PERFECT
ich hatte gegeben	hätte gegeben
du hattest gegeben	hättest gegeben
FUTURE	FUTURE
ich werde geben	werde geben
du wirst geben	werdest geben
FUTURE PERFECT	FUTURE PERFECT
ich werde gegeben haben	werde gegeben haben
du wirst gegeben haben	werdest gegeben haben
PRESENT CONDITIONAL	PRESENT CONDITIONAL
ich würde geben	würde geben
PAST CONDITIONAL	PAST CONDITIONAL
ich würde gegeben haben	würde gegeben haben
Infinitive	**Participle**
PRESENT: geben	PRESENT: gebend
PERFECT: gegeben (zu) haben	PERFECT: gegeben

Imperative

gib, gebt, geben Sie

XIV. *The Conjugation of dürfen, können, mögen, müssen, sollen, wollen*

A. Indicative

PRESENT

ich	darf	kann	mag	muß	soll	will
du	darfst	kannst	magst	mußt	sollst	willst
er	darf	kann	mag	muß	soll	will
wir	dürfen	können	mögen	müssen	sollen	wollen
ihr	dürft	könnt	mögt	müßt	sollt	wollt
sie	dürfen	können	mögen	müssen	sollen	wollen

PAST

ich	durfte	konnte	mochte	mußte	sollte	wollte

PRESENT PERFECT
ich habe gedurft (gekonnt, gemocht, gemußt, gesollt, gewollt)
BUT   ich habe sagen dürfen (können, *etc.*)

PAST PERFECT
ich hatte gedurft (gekonnt, *etc.*)
BUT   ich hatte sagen dürfen (können, *etc.*)

FUTURE
ich werde dürfen (können, *etc.*)

FUTURE PERFECT
ich werde gedurft (gekonnt, *etc.*) haben
BUT   ich werde haben sagen dürfen (können, *etc.*)

CONDITIONAL
ich würde dürfen (können, *etc.*)

PAST CONDITIONAL
ich würde gedurft (gekonnt, *etc.*) haben
BUT   ich würde haben sagen dürfen (können, *etc.*)

199

B. Subjunctive

PRESENT

ich	dürfe	könne	möge	müsse	solle	wolle
du	dürfest	könnest	mögest	müssest	sollest	wollest
er	dürfe	könne	möge	müsse	solle	wolle
wir	dürfen	können	mögen	müssen	sollen	wollen
ihr	dürfet	könnet	möget	müsset	sollet	wollet
sie	dürfen	können	mögen	müssen	sollen	wollen

PAST

ich	dürfte	könnte	möchte	müßte	sollte	wollte

PRESENT PERFECT

ich habe gedurft (gekonnt, *etc.*)
du habest gedurft (gekonnt, *etc.*)
BUT ich habe sagen dürfen (können, *etc.*)
du habest sagen dürfen (können, *etc.*)

PAST PERFECT

ich hätte gedurft (gekonnt, *etc.*)
BUT ich hätte sagen dürfen (können, *etc.*)

FUTURE

ich werde dürfen (können, *etc.*)
du werdest dürfen (können, *etc.*)

FUTURE PERFECT

ich werde gedurft (gekonnt, *etc.*) haben
du werdest gedurft (gekonnt, *etc.*) haben
BUT ich werde haben sagen dürfen (können, *etc.*)
du werdest haben sagen dürfen (können, *etc.*)

CONDITIONAL

ich würde dürfen (können, *etc.*)

PAST CONDITIONAL

ich würde gedurft (gekonnt, *etc.*) haben
BUT ich würde haben sagen dürfen (können, *etc.*)

Infinitives

PRESENT:	dürfen	können	mögen	müssen	sollen	wollen
PERFECT:	gedurft haben	gekonnt haben	gemocht haben	gemußt haben	gesollt haben	gewollt haben

Participles

PRESENT: dürfend   könnend   mögend   müssend   sollend   wollend
PERFECT: gedurft   gekonnt   gemocht   gemußt   gesollt   gewollt

XV. *The Passive Voice*

Indicative	Subjunctive
PRESENT	**PRESENT**
ich werde gefragt du wirst gefragt	ich werde gefragt du werdest gefragt
PAST	**PAST**
ich wurde gefragt	ich würde gefragt
PRESENT PERFECT	**PRESENT PERFECT**
ich bin gefragt worden	ich sei gefragt worden
PAST PERFECT	**PAST PERFECT**
ich war gefragt worden	ich wäre gefragt worden
FUTURE	**FUTURE**
ich werde gefragt werden du wirst gefragt werden	ich werde gefragt werden du werdest gefragt werden
FUTURE PERFECT	**FUTURE PERFECT**
ich werde gefragt worden sein du wirst gefragt worden sein	ich werde gefragt worden sein du werdest gefragt worden sein
PRESENT CONDITIONAL	**PRESENT CONDITIONAL**
ich würde gefragt werden	ich würde gefragt werden
PAST CONDITIONAL	**PAST CONDITIONAL**
ich würde gefragt worden sein	ich würde gefragt worden sein

Infinitive	Participle
PRESENT: gefragt (zu) werden	PRESENT: —
PERFECT: gefragt worden (zu) sein	PERFECT: gefragt worden

Imperative
werde gefragt, werdet gefragt, werden Sie gefragt

XVI. *Forms of Strong and Irregular Verbs*

Infinitive	Present Indicative	Past Indicative	Past Participle
to bake backen	bäckt	backte (*or* buk)	gebacken
to command befehlen	befiehlt	befahl	befohlen
to begin beginnen	beginnt	begann	begonnen
to bite beißen	beißt	biß	gebissen
To save bergen	birgt	barg	geborgen
to move bewegen	bewegt	bewog	bewogen
To bend biegen	biegt	bog	gebogen
To offer bieten	bietet	bot	geboten
to tie binden	bindet	band	gebunden
to beg bitten	bittet	bat	gebeten
to blow blasen	bläst	blies	geblasen
To remain bleiben	bleibt	blieb	geblieben (ist)
to fry braten	brät	briet	gebraten
to break brechen	bricht	brach	gebrochen
to burn brennen	brennt	brannte	gebrannt
to bring bringen	bringt	brachte	gebracht
to think denken	denkt	dachte	gedacht
to penetrate dringen	dringt	drang	gedrungen (ist)
to be permitted dürfen	darf	durfte	gedurft
to recommend empfehlen	empfiehlt	empfahl	empfohlen
to grow pale erbleichen	erbleicht	erblich	erblichen (ist)
to die out erlöschen	erlischt	erlosch	erloschen (ist)
to frighten erschrecken	erschrickt	erschrak	erschrocken (ist)
to eat essen	ißt	aß	gegessen
to drive fahren	fährt	fuhr	gefahren (ist)[1]
to fall fallen	fällt	fiel	gefallen (ist)
to catch fangen	fängt	fing	gefangen
to find finden	findet	fand	gefunden
to fly fliegen	fliegt	flog	geflogen (ist)
to flee fliehen	flieht	floh	geflohen (ist)
to flow fließen	fließt	floß	geflossen (ist)
to eat fressen	frißt	fraß	gefressen
to be born gebären	gebiert	gebar	geboren
to give geben	gibt	gab	gegeben

[1] Fahren *to drive* (a car, etc.) is transitive.

Infinitive	Present Indicative	Past Indicative	Past Participle	
gehen	geht	ging	gegangen (ist)	*to go*
gelingen	gelingt	gelang	gelungen (ist)	*to succeed*
gelten	gilt	galt	gegolten	*to apply, to be valid*
genießen	genießt	genoß	genossen	*to enjoy*
geschehen	geschieht	geschah	geschehen (ist)	*to happen*
gewinnen	gewinnt	gewann	gewonnen	*to win*
gleiten	gleitet	glitt	geglitten (ist)	*to slide*
graben	gräbt	grub	gegraben	*to dig*
greifen	greift	griff	gegriffen	*to reach*
haben	hat	hatte	gehabt	*to have*
halten	hält	hielt	gehalten	*to hold*
hängen	hängt	hing	gehangen	*to hang* / *to lift, to heighten*
heben	hebt	hob	gehoben	
heißen	heißt	hieß	geheißen	*to call*
helfen	hilft	half	geholfen	*to help*
kennen	kennt	kannte	gekannt	*to know*
klingen	klingt	klang	geklungen	*to ring*
kommen	kommt	kam	gekommen (ist)	*to come*
können	kann	konnte	gekonnt	*to be able*
kriechen	kriecht	kroch	gekrochen (ist)	*to creep*
laden	lädt	lud	geladen	*to load*
lassen	läßt	ließ	gelassen	*to let*
laufen	läuft	lief	gelaufen (ist)	*to run*
leiden	leidet	litt	gelitten	*to bear, to endure*
leihen	leiht	lieh	geliehen	*to lend*
lesen	liest	las	gelesen	*to read*
liegen	liegt	lag	gelegen	*to lie, to be situated*
meiden	meidet	mied	gemieden	*to avoid*
messen	mißt	maß	gemessen	*to measure*
mißlingen	mißlingt	mißlang	mißlungen (ist)	
mögen	mag	mochte	gemocht	*to like*
müssen	muß	mußte	gemußt	*to have to*
nehmen	nimmt	nahm	genommen	*to take*
nennen	nennt	nannte	genannt	*to name*
pfeifen	pfeift	pfiff	gepfiffen	*to whistle*
raten	rät	riet	geraten	*to advise*
reißen	reißt	riß	gerissen	*to tear*
reiten	reitet	ritt	geritten (ist)	*to ride*
rennen	rennt	rannte	gerannt (ist)	*to run*
riechen	riecht	roch	gerochen	*to smell*

203

Infinitive	Present Indicative	Past Indicative	Past Participle
to struggle ringen	ringt	rang	gerungen
to call rufen	ruft	rief	gerufen
to manage schaffen	schafft	schuf	geschaffen
to part/leave scheiden	scheidet	schied	geschieden
to seem to shine scheinen	scheint	schien	geschienen
to reproach schelten	schilt	schalt	gescholten
to shave scheren	schert	schor	geschoren
to sleep schlafen	schläft	schlief	geschlafen
to strike schlagen	schlägt	schlug	geschlagen
to conclude schließen	schließt	schloß	geschlossen
to intwine schlingen	schlingt	schlang	geschlungen
to cut schneiden	schneidet	schnitt	geschnitten
to write schreiben	schreibt	schrieb	geschrieben
to cry out schreien	schreit	schrie	geschrien
to stride schreiten	schreitet	schritt	geschritten (ist)
to be silent schweigen	schweigt	schwieg	geschwiegen
to swim schwimmen	schwimmt	schwamm	geschwommen (ist)
to disappear schwinden	schwindet	schwand	geschwunden (ist)
to sway schwingen	schwingt	schwang	geschwungen
to swear schwören	schwört	schwor	geschworen
to see sehen	sieht	sah	gesehen
to be sein	ist	war	gewesen (ist)
to send senden	sendet	sandte	gesandt
to sing singen	singt	sang	gesungen
to sink sinken	sinkt	sank	gesunken (ist)
to muse sinnen	sinnt	sann	gesonnen
to sit sitzen	sitzt	saß	gesessen
to be suppose to sollen	soll	sollte	gesollt
to speak sprechen	spricht	sprach	gesprochen
to jump springen	springt	sprang	gesprungen (ist)
to pierce stechen	sticht	stach	gestochen
to stand stehen	steht	stand	gestanden
to steal stehlen	stiehlt	stahl	gestohlen
to climb steigen	steigt	stieg	gestiegen (ist)
to die sterben	stirbt	starb	gestorben (ist)
to push stoßen	stößt	stieß	gestoßen
to quarrel streiten	streitet	stritt	gestritten
to carry tragen	trägt	trug	getragen
to hit treffen	trifft	traf	getroffen
to drive treiben	treibt	trieb	getrieben
to step treten	tritt	trat	getreten (ist, hat)

204

Infinitive	Present Indicative	Past Indicative	Past Participle	
trinken	trinkt	trank	getrunken	*to drink*
tun	tut	tat	getan	*to do*
vergessen	vergißt	vergaß	vergessen	*to forget*
verlieren	verliert	verlor	verloren	*to lose*
verzeihen	verzeiht	verzieh	verziehen	*to pardon forgive*
wachsen	wächst	wuchs	gewacnsen (ist)	*to grow*
waschen	wäscht	wusch	gewaschen	*to wash*
weichen	weicht	wich	gewichen (ist)	*to yield*
weisen	weist	wies	gewiesen	*to point*
wenden	wendet	wandte	gewandt	*to turn*
werben	wirbt	warb	geworben	*to inlist*
werden	wird	wurde	geworden (ist)	*to become*
werfen	wirft	warf	geworfen	*to throw*
winden	windet	wand	gewunden	
wissen	weiß	wußte	gewußt	*to know*
wollen	will	wollte	gewollt	*to want to*
ziehen	zieht	zog	gezogen	*to draw*
zwingen	zwingt	zwang	gezwungen	*to force*

XVII. *Numerals*

Cardinal

Ordinal [1]

Cardinal		Ordinal [1]
Null	0	
eins	1	erst-
zwei [2]	2	zweit-
drei	3	dritt-
vier	4	viert-
fünf	5	fünft-
sechs	6	sechst-
sieben	7	sieb(en)t-
acht	8	acht-
neun	9	neunt-
zehn	10	zehnt-
elf	11	elft-
zwölf	12	zwölft-

[1] Friedrich II. = Friedrich der Zweite.   [2] On the telephone **zwo** is used for clarity.

Cardinal		Ordinal
dreizehn	13	dreizehnt-
vierzehn	14	vierzehnt-
fünfzehn	15	fünfzehnt-
sechzehn	16	sechzehnt-
siebzehn	17	siebzehnt-
achtzehn	18	achtzehnt-
neunzehn	19	neunzehnt-
zwanzig	20	zwanzigst-
einundzwanzig	21	einundzwanzigst-
dreißig	30	dreißigst-
vierzig	40	vierzigst-
fünfzig	50	fünfzigst-
sechzig	60	sechzigst-
siebzig	70	siebzigst-
achtzig	80	achtzigst-
neunzig	90	neunzigst-
hundert; einhundert	100	(ein)hunderst-
hundertundeins	101	hundertunderst-
tausend; eintausend	1 000	(ein)tausendst-
tausendundeins	1 001	tausendunderst-
hunderttausend- undeins	100 001	hunderttausendunderst-
eine Million	1 000 000	(ein)millionst-

XVIII. *Decimals*

The English decimal point, i.e. 0.1, is replaced by a comma in German, 0,1.

XIX. *Fractions*

In English the ordinal numbers also serve as fractions, i.e. fourth, twentieth. In German -**el** is added to the ordinal, which is often still capitalized, i.e. (das) Viertel, (das) Zwanzigstel.

XX. *Arithmetical Expressions*

addieren (zusammenzählen)
drei + (und *or* plus) eins = (ist) vier

subtrahieren (abziehen)
drei − (weniger *or* minus) eins = (ist) zwei

multiplizieren (vervielfachen)
drei · (mal) drei = neun

dividieren (teilen)
sechs : (geteilt durch *or* dividiert durch) zwei = (ist) drei

potenzieren (zur Potenz erheben)
2^2 = zwei hoch zwei (*or* 2 zum Quadrat) = vier
2^3 = zwei hoch drei (*or* 2 zur dritten Potenz) = acht

wurzelziehen
$\sqrt{4}$ = die Quadratwurzel aus (*or* von) vier = zwei
$\sqrt[3]{9}$ = die Kubikwurzel (*or* die kubische Wurzel)
aus (*or* von) neun = drei

XXI. *Time Expressions*

As in English, the twelve-hour and the twenty-four-hour clock are used in German. Time is generally counted toward the approaching hour, but variations are not uncommon.

3:15	Es ist Viertel vier.
	Es ist drei Uhr fünfzehn.
	Es ist Viertel nach drei.
3:30	Es ist halb vier.
	Es ist drei Uhr dreißig.
3:45	Es ist drei Viertel vier.
	Es ist Viertel vor vier.

letztes (voriges) Jahr	heute	morgen
vor einem Jahr	heute morgen*	morgen früh
vor vierzehn Tagen	heute früh	morgen abend
vor einer Woche	heute vormittag	übermorgen
vor acht Tagen	heute mittag	heute über acht Tage
vorvorgestern	heute nachmittag	in acht Tagen
vorgestern	heute abend	in vierzehn Tagen
gestern	heute nacht	nächstes Jahr

* In connection with an expression of time (heute, morgen, etc.) the following noun is not capitalized.

XXII. *Punctuation*

On the whole, punctuation in German closely parallels that in English. The most important differences can be classified under four headings.

Comma

In German the comma is *not* used to set off adverbial clauses. Example: In die Schule geht sie heute nicht. It is used to set off *all* subordinate or dependent clauses, including relative clauses, as well as infinitive phrases containing modifiers, since the latter can be said to be "contracted dependent clauses." Example: Der junge Mann, der dort in der Ecke steht, sagte mir gestern, daß er darauf brennt, dich bald kennenzulernen.

Exclamation Point

In German the exclamation point is used more frequently than in English, i.e., after *all* imperative sentences and in the heading of letters where a colon is used in English: Geehrter Herr Schmidt! Kommen Sie doch!

Apostrophe

As in English, the apostrophe in German denotes omission of one or more letters. Example: Wie geht's, *i.e.*, Wie geht es. Unlike English, it is used only in the genitive of those proper names in German which end in an s-sound. Note: Karls Bruder, but Voß' Luise.

Quotation Marks

In German the first of each pair of quotation marks is placed at the bottom. Example: Er sagt: „Warte!"

XXIII. *Accent*

The vast majority of all German words of more than one syllable are accented on the first syllable. That is true of simple words, as **Apfel, gehen, langsam, unten, dieser.** It is also true of compounds with (the separable prefixes) **ab–, an–, aus–, bei–, ein–, nach–, vor–,** etc., as **abfahren, Ankunft, Beistand.** Compounds with (the inseparable prefixes) **be–, emp–, ent–, er–, ge–, ver–, zer–,** etc. are accented on the root, i.e. first syllable of the (underlying) verb form, as **Besuch, erklären, Verstand.**

Compound verbs with **durch–, über–, um–, unter–, wieder–,** etc. are usually accented on the first syllable when the meaning is literal, as **wiederholen** (to fetch back) and on the root syllable of the simple verb when the meaning is figurative, as **unterziehen** (to subject). Compound nouns with these prefixes are accented on the first syllable, **Umgang, Unterricht.** Compounds of prepositions or conjunctions and adverbs, as **dabei, vorher, herbei,** are usually accented on the first syllable when emphasized. As prefixes they are usually accented on the second syllable.

Nouns ending in –**ei** and –**ie** are usually accented on the last syllable, as **Brauerei.** Verbs ending in –**ieren** and their derivatives are always accented on the **ie, spazieren, Spaziergang.**

Loan words frequently retain the original pattern of stress.

Vocabulary

Vocabulary

With the exception of the words for numerals and time units (days, months), the possessives and personal pronouns (listed in the Appendix), the vocabulary includes all the words used in the Basic Patterns and the Exercises.

The nouns are given in the nominative singular and plural: **das Buch, ⸗er = das Buch, die Bücher.** The genitive singular is indicated only when the noun is weak or irregular: **das Herz (–ens), –en = das Herz, des Herzens, die Herzen.**

The principal parts of simple strong (ablaut) and irregular verbs are given either in full or by indicating the vowel change. Irregularities which occur in the second and third persons singular of the present tense are added in parentheses, e.g., **geben, a, e (i) = geben, er gab, er hat gegeben, er gibt.** Unless especially indicated by **ist** or (*s*), the verbs are conjugated with **haben.** Compound verbs having separable prefixes are hyphenated and marked with an asterisk if strong or irregular. In the English-German Vocabulary all strong verbs are identified only by means of an asterisk. Their parts may be found in the Appendix.

Deviations from the usual pattern of stress (cf. Appendix XXIII) are indicated by means of subscript accent marks, as ạ or iẹ.

Abbreviations

acc.	accusative	*decl.*	declension	*pers.*	person
adj.	adjective	*gen.*	genitive	*pl.*	plural
conj.	conjunction	*h*	haben	*s*	sein
coord.	coordinating	*intrans.*	intransitive	*trans.*	transitive
dat.	dative				

211

Pronunciation

Simplified German equivalent spellings are given in parenthesis after loanwords which retain all or some of their original pronunciation, as **Chef** (*schef*). When necessary, other parallels, as **garage** (g as in *garage*), are suggested. Minor deviations, as **Familie** (*familje*), are not noted.

German–English

A

ab off; — **und zu** now and then
ab-biegen* (s) to turn the corner
der **Abend, -e** evening; **zu — essen*** to eat supper
das **Abendbrot, -e** supper
abends evenings, in the evening
die **Abenteuernatur, -en** adventurous type
aber but; however; certainly; — **ja** of course
ab-fahren* (s) to depart; to leave; **Abfahren!** Anchors aweigh!
die **Abfahrt, -en** departure
ab-fliegen* (s) to take off (by plane)
ab-geben* to deliver
abgefallen dropped
abgemacht agreed
abgetreten worn down
ab-hängen* **von** (*dat.*) to depend on
ab-heben* to lift off
ab-holen to call for
ab-horchen to listen to
das **Abitur, -e** (final) comprehensive (state) examination (in high school)
ab-legen to lay off; to take off
ab-lehnen to decline
ab-nehmen* to take off; to remove
ab-reisen (s) to depart, to leave
der **Absatz, ⁻e** heel
der **Abschied, -e** leave, farewell, parting; **beim —** in parting
ab-schließen* to conclude, to make
der **Abschluß (-sses), ⁻sse** completion, passing

die **Abschmiervorrichtung, -en** grease gun
absichtlich intentional
absolut absolute, complete
das **Abteil, -e** compartment
der **Abteilungsleiter, —** section chief
sich ab-trocknen to dry oneself
die **Abwechslung, -en** change, variety; **zur —,** for a change
ab-ziehen* to take out, to remove, to subtract
ach oh; **Weh und Ach** groaning and moaning
die **Achselhöhle, -n** armpit
achten auf (*acc.*) to pay attention to
ächzen to groan
sich ähneln to resemble one another
ahnen to surmise; to have a premonition
akademisch academic
der **Alkohol, -e** alcohol
all– all
alle all, everybody; — **Hände voll zu tun haben*** to have all one can do to take care of it; — **Morgen** every morning; — **Mühe** a great deal of effort; — **sechs Stunden** every six hours; —**s** all, everything; **vor** —**m** above all else
allein alone; however, but
allerangenehmst most pleasant
allerhand all kinds of
allerhöchst highest
allerlei all sorts of (things)
die **Allgemeinbildung** broad (*or* general) education
die **Allgemeinheit** universality
allmählich gradually
als when; as; than; — **erste** the first one

212

also thus, hence; well; therefore
alt old; **beim —en bleiben** to remain as it was
die **Alte** (*adj. decl.*) old woman
das **Alter,** — age
der **Ältere** (*adj. decl.*) older (person)
ältlich elderly
am = an dem; — hellen Tage in broad daylight; **— Hute** in his hat
(das) **Amerika** America
der **Amerikaner** (*adj. decl.*) American (*person*)
amerikanisch American
die **Ampel, –n** (street) light; signal
das **Amt, ⁺er** office; position; (official) post
amtlich official
das **Amtsgericht, –e** city (*or* district) court
an on; next to, at; near, about; **— Bord** aboard; **— den Gesichtern** by their faces; **— meiner Seite** by my side; **— sich selbst** by (*or* in) itself; **Sie sind — der Reihe** it is your turn
der **Anblick, –e** glimpse; appearance; sight
an-blicken to look at; **sich groß —,** to look at each other in amazement
ander– other
sich ändern to change
anders different
sich an-eignen to acquire
an-fahren * (*s*) (*intrans.*) to start (up); (*h*) (*trans.*) to bark at
an-fallen * to attack; **es fällt mich an** I am overcome
der **Anfang, ⁺e** beginning
an-fangen, i, a (ä) to begin
an-geben * to indicate
angeblich supposed
das **Angebot, –e** offer
angegossen: wie —, (fit) like a glove
der **Angeklagte** (*adj. decl.*) accused, defendant
angenehm pleasant; (**es ist mir**) **sehr —,** (I am) charmed, delighted
der **Angestellte** (*adj. decl.*) employee

angezogen dressed
die **Angst, ⁺e** fear
ängstlich fearful; frightened
an-haben * to wear
an-halten * to stop
der **Anhänger,** — trailer
an-heften to pin on
an-hören to tell by listening to
die **Anklage, –n** accusation; **die — erheben** * to make (*or* level) the charge
an-kommen * (*s*) to arrive
die **Ankunft, ⁺e** arrival
an-lächeln to smile at
an-legen to open (an account)
(**sich**) **an-melden** to register
die **Anmeldung, –en** registration
an-merken to note; **es einem —,** to tell by looking at a person
an-nehmen * to accept; to assume; **Haltung —,** to straighten up
an-probieren to try on
an-rufen * to call up; to appeal to
ans = an das
an-sehen * to look at; **ich sehe ihn mir an** I look at him; **sehen wir ihn uns an** let's look at him
anständig decent, respectable
anstatt instead (of)
an-stellen to employ; to turn on
an-treten * (*s*) to start
sich etwas an-tun * to do oneself harm
die **Antwort, –en** answer; **zur — geben** * to answer in reply
antworten (*dat.*) to answer
der **Anwalt, ⁺e** attorney
an-ziehen * to dress; to put on; to tighten; **sich —,** to dress
der **Anzug, ⁺e** suit
der **Apfel, ⁺** apple
der **Apfelsinensaft, ⁺e** orange juice
die **Apotheke, –n** pharmacy
der **Apparat, –e** apparatus; radio; telephone; **am —,** on the phone
der **Appetit, –e** appetite
die **Arbeit, –en** work, task
arbeiten to work
der **Arbeiter,** — worker
arbeitslos unemployed, out of

213

work; — **werden*** (*s*) to be laid off

das **Arbeitsverfahren,** — working process

der **Ärger** annoyance; **vor** —, in (his) anger

ärgerlich annoyed; annoying

die **Ärgerlichkeit,** –en annoyance

ärgern to annoy; **sich** —, to be annoyed

arm poor

der **Arm,** –e arm; **einem in die** —**e sinken*** (*s*) to sink into someone's arms

der **Ärmel,** — sleeve

armselig paltry, dingy

die **Art,** –en way, manner; method

der **Arzt,** ⸚e physician

der **Asphalt** asphalt

der **Atem** breath; **außer** —, out of breath; **nach** — **ringen*** to gasp for breath

atemlos breathless

atmen to breathe

auch also, too; in addition; actually; — **nicht** neither; — **noch** in addition; to boot

auf up(on); at; — **einmal** at once, suddenly; — **dem Lande** in the country; — **der Straße** in(to) the street; — **der Straße stehen*** to be without a roof over one's head; — **das richtige Tempo kommen*** (*s*) to attain the right speed, to hit on all four; — **und ab** to and fro; up and down; — **welche Weise** in what way; — **Wiedersehen** good-by, so long; — **zwei Wochen** for two weeks; **tätig sein** — (*dat.*) to work in; **sie ging** — **ihr Zimmer** she went to her room

auf-atmen to breathe a sigh of relief

aufatmend breathing a sigh of relief

auf-brechen* (*s*) to start out; leave (for home)

der **Aufenthalt,** –e stopover; — **haben*** to stop (over)

auf-fahren* (*s*) to drive up; to jump up

auf-fallen* (*s*) to draw attention;

es fällt mir auf I notice it; it strikes me

auf-flammen (*s*) to flare up

auf-fressen* to devour

auf-füllen to fill (up)

die **Aufgabe,** –n lesson, task

auf-geben* to send (*by wire*); to mail

aufgeregt excited

auf-haben* to have on, to wear

sich auf-halten* to stay on, to tarry

auf-hören to stop

auf-klären to clear up; to explain; to enlighten

auf-machen to open; **ganz** —, to open wide

aufmerksam machen auf (*acc.*) to call attention to

auf-nehmen*: es — **mit** (*dat.*) to cope (*or* compete) with

sich auf-opfern für (*acc.*) to give one's life for

auf-passen to be careful; **besser** —, to be more careful

auf-probieren to try on

aufrecht erect

sich auf-regen to get excited

die **Aufregung,** –en excitement; **vor** —, in his (*or* her) *or* with excitement

sich auf-richten to sit up; to straighten up

aufs = **auf das;** — **Land** to the country

auf-sammeln to gather up

auf-schreiben* to write down

auf-schreien* to cry out

auf-sehen* to look up

auf-sein* (*s*) to be up

auf-springen* (*s*) to jump up; to snap open

auf-stehen* (*s*) to get up

auf-steigen* (*s*) to rise up; to climb aboard

auf-tauchen (*s*) to bob up; to appear (*suddenly*)

sich auf-türmen to loom up

das **Auge,** –n eye; **kein** — **zu-tun*** not to sleep a wink

der **Augenblick,** –e moment, instant

aus out (of); from; — **dem Weg**

214

fahren* (*s*) to get (*or* move) out of the way; **was wurde — ihm?** what became of him?

die **Ausbildung** training, development

aus-bleiben* (*s*) to be lacking

der **Ausbruch,** ⁀e eruption

aus-dehnen to expand

die **Ausfallstraße,** –n main thoroughfare, open road

der **Ausflug,** ⁀e excursion

aus-füllen to fill out

aus-gehen* (*s*) to go out; **leer —,** to go empty-handed

ausgeliefert (*dat.*) at the mercy of

ausgerechnet of all things

ausgezeichnet excellent

aus-gleiten* (*s*) to slip

aus-helfen* (*dat.*) to help out

die **Aushilfe,** –n help(ing out)

die **Aushilfssekretärin,** –nen temporary secretary

sich **aus-kennen*** to know one's way around

aus-kommen* (*s*) **mit** (*dat.*) to get along on (*or* with)

die **Auskunft,** ⁀e information; **— ein-holen** to make inquiries

die **Auskunftei,** –en information office

das **Auskunftsbüro,** –s information office

aus-rauben to rob

aus-rufen* to exclaim

aus-rutschen (*s*) to slip

aus-schalten to turn off

aus-schimpfen to scold, to give a scolding

aus-sehen* to look like, to appear

außer besides; **— Atem** out of breath

außerdem moreover

außerordentlich extremely, unusually, extraordinary

aus-setzen to suspend; **— an** (*dat.*) to find fault with

aussichtslos hopeless

aus-sprechen* to pronounce; to utter

aus-steigen* (*s*) to get out (*or* off)

aus-tragen* to deliver

ausverkauft sold out

die **Auswahl,** –en selection, choice

(sich) **aus-wählen** to select

aus-weichen* (*s*) (*dat.*) to get out of one's way

das **Auto,** –s auto(mobile)

der **Autobus** (–sses), –sse bus

das **Autofahren** driving

B

backen, backte *or* **buk, gebacken** (**bäckt**) to bake

der **Bäcker,** — baker

der **Bäckerjunge** (–n), –n bakery boy

das **Bad,** ⁀er bath

der **Badestrand,** –e beach

der **Bahnbeamte** (*adj. decl.*) railroad clerk

der **Bahnhof,** ⁀e railroad station

die **Bahnhofsuhr,** –en station clock

bald soon; **wird's —,** (will you) make it snappy

der **Ball,** ⁀e ball

das **Band,** ⁀er ribbon

die **Bank,** ⁀e bench

die **Bank,** –en bank

der **Bankbeamte** (*adj. decl.*) bank clerk

der **Barbierstuhl,** ⁀e barber chair

das **Barometer,** — barometer

die **Batterie,** –n battery

bauen to build

die **Bäuerin,** –nen peasant woman

der **Baum,** ⁀e tree

die **Baumwolle,** –n cotton

beabsichtigen to intend to do

beachten to observe

der **Beamte** (*adj. decl.*) clerk, official

beantragen to propose; to recommend

der **Bedacht** care, caution

der **Bedarf** need; demand

bedenken* to consider

bedeuten to mean

bedienen to operate; to wait on; to service; **sich —,** to make use of, to help oneself

das **Bedienen** waiting on, serving

die **Bedienung** (maid) service

sich **beeilen** to hurry up
der **Befehl, -e** command
befehlen, a, o (ie) to command
sich befinden* to be (located)
die **Beförderung, -en** promotion
befragen to question
befremden to estrange; to seem strange
begegnen (s) (dat.) to meet
begeistern to enthuse, to inspire
begeistert enthusiastic
beginnen, a, o to begin
begleiten to accompany
die **Begleitung** accompaniment; company
der **Begriff, -e** concept; **im —e** on the point of, about to
begrüßen to greet
begutachten to evaluate, to give an expert opinion on
behaglich comfortable
behalten* to keep; to keep in mind, to remember
behandeln to treat
behaupten to maintain; to say
bei with; at; at the home of; by; among; **— Bonn** near Bonn; **— einem Glas Bier** over a glass of beer; **— mir klingelt das Telefon** my phone is ringing; **— Schmidt** at Schmidt's; **— weitem** by far; **—m alten** as it was
beide both; **die —n** the two
beim = bei dem
das **Bein, -e** leg
beinah(e) almost
beirren to confuse; **sich nicht — lassen*** not to be deterred
beiseite aside; **—-legen** to put aside
das **Beispiel, -e** example
die **Bekämpfung** control
bekannt known; **— (dat.)** known to
der **Bekannte** (adj. decl.) acquaintance
bekanntlich as is known; **ebenso —,** as is equally well known
bekommen* to get; to receive; to be becoming; **das Geld wird euch nie —,** you will never get any joy out of the money; **einen**

roten Kopf —, to turn red in the face; **Mut —,** to take courage
beleben to revive
belebt busy; lively
belegt coated
die **Beleuchtung, -en** illumination, lighting
beliebig any given; **x-—,** any given
beliebt popular
die **Belohnung, -en** reward
bemerken to observe; to notice; to note
bemessen* to allot; **spärlich —,** a tight fit
bemühen to trouble; **sich —,** to take the trouble, to make an effort
benachbart neighboring
der **Benediktiner, —** Benedictine (liqueur)
beneiden to envy
benutzen to use
das **Benzin, -e** gasoline
die **Benzinleitung, -en** fuel line
die **Benzinuhr, -en** gasoline gauge
beobachten to observe
der **Berater, —** adviser
die **Beratung, -en** consultation
bereit ready
bereiten to prepare
bereits already
bereuen to regret
der **Bericht, -e** report
der **Berliner, —** Berliner
der **Beruf, -e** trade; calling; occupation; **(freier) —,** profession; **von —,** by trade; **die Berufsschule, -n** vocational (trade) school; **der Berufsschüler, —** vocational (trade) school student
berufen* to appoint
beruhigt content; calmed .
berühmt famous
berühren to touch
sich beschäftigen mit to be engaged in
beschäftigt sein* (s) to be employed
beschämen to (put to) shame

216

Bescheid wissen* to know the facts (*or* one's way around)

beschließen* to decide

beschwichtigen to calm

besehen* to examine, to look at; **sich —,** to examine *or* look at; **ich besehe es mir** I look at it

sich besinnen, a, o to reflect

besitzen* to own

der **Besitzer, —** owner

besohlen to put on soles

das **Besondere** (*adj. decl.*) special (thing)

besonders especially

besorgen to take care of; to attend to; **sich —,** to get (for oneself), to procure

besprechen* to discuss

besser better

die **Besserung** improvement; **gute —!** Get well!

best– best; **mach das Beste daraus** make the best of it

bestehen* to exist; to be; to last; to abide; **— auf** (*acc.*) to insist on; **— aus** (*dat.*) to consist of; **— in** (*dat.*) to consist of; **die Prüfung —,** to pass the test

besteigen* to get aboard (*or* on); to climb aboard (*or* into); to mount

bestellen to order; **ich bin auf vier bestellt** I have been asked to come at four; **ich bin zum Zahnarzt bestellt** I have an appointment with the dentist

bestens most kindly

bestimmen to decide; to determine

bestimmt definite; certain; definitely

bestrafen to punish; to convict

der **Besuch, -e** visit; **zu —,** for a visit

besuchen to visit; to attend

betätigen to employ; to use

sich beteiligen to participate

beten to pray

der **Betracht** consideration; **außer — lassen*** to disregard

sich betragen* to behave

betreffen* to concern

betreten* to enter in

der **Betrieb, -e** plant

der **Betrug** deception

das **Bett, -en** bed; **das — hüten** to stay in bed; **zu —,** in bed; **zu — gehen*** (*s*) to go to bed

sich betten to make one's bed

der **Bettler, —** beggar

sich beugen über (*acc.*) to bend over

beunruhigt disquieted, disturbed

bevor before

die **Bewährung** probation

sich bewegen to move

die **Bewegung, -en** movement; motion; **in — kommen*** (*s*) to start moving; **sich in — setzen** to start to move

beweisen* (*dat.*) to demonstrate (to), to show (to)

der **Bewerber, —** candidate, applicant

der **Bewertungszettel, —** evaluation slip

bewirken to cause, to bring about

bewußt aware; **sich — sein*** (*gen.*) to be aware of

bezahlen to pay

bezeigen to show

die **Bibliothek, -en** library

biegen, o, o (*h*) (*trans.*) to bend; **— (*s*) (*intrans.*) to turn

das **Bier, -e** beer

bieten, o, o to offer

das **Bild, -er** picture

billig cheap

binden, a, u to tie

der **Bindfaden, ⸚** string; **es regnet Bindfäden** it is raining cats and dogs

die **Birne, -n** bulb

bis until; up to; **— hierher** (up to) here, thus far

bisher thus far, up to now

bißchen little; **ein — Leben** a bit of an existence

bitte (*in making a request*) please; (*in acknowledging an expression of thanks*) not at all; **— (schön)** (*in meeting a request*) here you are

die **Bitte, -n** request

bitten, bat, gebeten to beg; to ask; to request; **— um** (*acc.*) to ask for; **zum Tee —,** to ask to

217

tea; **wenn ich — darf** may I, if you please

blamieren to put to shame, to embarrass

blank shiny

das **Blatt,** ⸚**er** sheet; leaf; **das — hat sich gewendet** the tables are turned; **das — wendet sich** my luck is changing

das **Blättchen,** — slice; slab

blättern to leaf through

blau blue; **ich bin —,** I am tipsy; **— sein*** (s) to be stewed

bleiben, ie, ie (s) to remain, to stay

bleich pale

der **Bleisoldat** (**-en**), **-en** lead soldier

der **Bleistift, -e** pencil

der **Blick, -e** glance; **auf den ersten —,** at a glance

blicken to gaze; to look; **— auf** (acc.) to glance at; **an sich herab-—** to glance down at oneself

blind blind

blond blonde

bloß bare

die **Blume, -n** flower

der **Blumenkohl** cauliflower

der **Boden,** ⸚ soil, ground; floor; **zu — sinken*** (s) to drop to the floor; **zu — werfen*** to throw on the floor

die **Bohne, -n** bean

Bord: an —, on board

böse angry; **—** (dat.) angry with

braten, ie, a (**ä**) to fry, to roast

das **Braten** roasting, frying

die **Bratkartoffel, -n** fried potato

brauchen to use; to need

braun brown

die **Brause, -n** shower

brechen, a, o (**i**) to break

breit wide; **sich — machen** to spread oneself out; **weit und —,** far and wide

die **Bremse, -n** brake

brennen, brannte, gebrannt to burn; **wo brennt's denn?** where's the fire?

das **Brett, -er** board

der **Brief, -e** letter

das **Brieftelegramm, -e** night letter

der **Briefträger,** — letter carrier

die **Brillantine** (briljan–), **-n** brilliantine

die **Brille, -n** glasses

bringen, brachte, gebracht to bring; **es zu etwas —,** to get somewhere; **in Ordnung —,** to straighten out; **in Verbindung —,** to associate; **auf den Gedanken —,** to give the idea; **ich lasse Ihre Koffer auf Ihr Zimmer —,** I'll have your bags taken to your room

der **Brocken,** — morsel

das **Brot, -e** bread

das **Brötchen,** — roll

der **Bruder,** ⸚ brother

brüllen to roar

die **Brust,** ⸚**e** chest

brutzeln to sizzle

das **Buch,** ⸚**er** book

die **Bücherei, -en** library

die **Bulette, -n** meatball

das **Büro, -s** office

der **Büroangestellte** (adj. decl.) office employee

die **Butter** butter

C

die **Chance** (schanße (with **an** as "en" in English "ensemble"), **-n** chance

der **Charakter, -ere** character

der **Chef** (schef), **-s** boss

der **Chemiker,** — chemist

christlich Christian

D

da there; since; then; here; over there; therefore; otherwise

dabei at the same time; at that (point)

das **Dach,** ⸚**er** roof

dadurch through that, by means of that, as a result of that, thereby

dafür for it

dagegen on the other hand; opposed; against it

sich dagegen-lehnen to lean against

dagegen-sagen to counter

daher therefore

dahinten behind it; in back of it

da-liegen* to lie there

die **Dame, -n** lady; **meine —,** Madame

damit with it (or that); in order that; so that; by that

der **Damm, ⁔e** road

dämmern to get dark

die **Dämmerung** dusk

der **Dampfer, —** steamer

danach according to it

der **Dank** thanks; **besten** (or **schönen**) **—,** thank you kindly

dankbar grateful; **—** (dat.) grateful (to)

danke thanks; **— vielmals** many thanks

danken to thank; to acknowledge (greetings); **—d** gratefully; with thanks

dann then

daran of it

daran-liegen* (dat.) to be concerned about

darauf thereupon; on it; to it

daraus (out) of it; from that

darin in it

die **Darmkolik, -en** intestinal colic

dar-stellen to depict

darüber about that

daß (so) that

da-stehen* to stand there

die **Dauer** duration; period

dauern to last; to take

die **Dauerpatientin** (-tsjentin), **-nen** regular patient

davon of it

davon-fahren* (s) to drive off

davon-rasen (s) to race away

dazu in addition; (in reply) to that; with it

dazu-treten* (s) to step up, to join (the group)

das **Deck, -e** deck

dehnen to stretch, to expand

der **Dekan, -e** dean

denken, dachte, gedacht to think; **— an** (acc.) to think of; **sich —,** to imagine

denn for, because; than; then; **es sei —,** unless, lest (often not translated)

dergleichen the like

derjenige the (very) (one)

derselbe the (very) same (one)

derweil while

deshalb therefore; for that reason

des öftern frequently

desto: je ... —, the ... the

deutlich clear

(das) **Deutsch** German (language)

deutsch German

der **Deutsche** (adj. decl.) German (person)

(das) **Deutschland** Germany

d.h. = das heißt that is

dicht thick; **— an** (dat.) close by

der **Dichter, —** poet

dick thick

der **Dicke** (adj. decl.) obese (or stout) person

der **Dieb, -e** thief

der **Diebstahl, ⁔e** theft; **wegen —s bestrafen** to convict of theft

dienen to serve; **womit kann ich —?** what can I do for you? **mit halben Sohlen ist mir auch gedient** half soles will do (for me)

der **Diener, —** servant

die **Dienstvorschrift, -en** official regulation

dies this (one)

dieselbe the same

dieser this (one); the latter

diesmal this time

das **Ding, -e** thing

direkt direct

die **Direktion** (-tsjon), **-en** main office

das **Direktionsgebäude, —** main office building

der **Direktor, -oren** director, manager

doch anyhow; but; however; nevertheless; still; yet; indeed; after all; yes, you do; (often not

translated); **geh — einmal** do
go; **wenn er — da wäre** if only
he were here
der **Doktor, -ǫren** doctor('s degree); **Herr —,** Doctor
der **Dom, -e** cathedral
donnern thunder
Donnerwetter! Thunderation!
Damnation!
der **Dorn, -en** thorn
dort there
die **Dose, -n** can
Dr. med. = M.D.
das **Drama, -men** drama
der **Drang, ꞈe** urge
draußen outside
drehen to turn, to twist; **sich
(um-)—,** to turn (around)
drein inside
drin in it
dringen, a, u (*s*) to penetrate; **—
zu** (*dat.*) to reach
die **Drogerie, -n** drugstore
drohen (*dat.*) to threaten
drüben (over) there
der **Druck** pressure
drücken to press; **sich — gegen**
(*acc.*) to press against; **den Hut
ins Gesicht —,** to pull the hat
down over one's face
sich ducken to duck
der **Duft, ꞈe** fragrance
duften to smell good
dulden to endure, to bear
dumm stupid, dumb
dumpf dull
düngen to fertilize
dunkel dark; **in seinem dunklen
Drange** in his groping drive;
—braun dark brown; **—grün**
dark green
das **Dunkel** dark(ness)
dünn fine, thin
durch through, by (means of)
durch-blasen, ie, a (**ä**) to blow
out
durch-fallen* (*s*) to fail
durchfliegen* to skim through
sich durch-hungern to eke out
an existence
die **Durchreise, -n** way through;
auf der —, passing through on
the way

sich durch-schlagen* to make
one's way; to get by
der **Durchschnitt** average
dürfen, durfte, gedurft (darf)
to be permitted (may); **was
darf es sein?** what will you have,
what will it be? **wenn ich bitten
darf** if you please, may I; **wir
— nicht** we must not
der **Durst** thirst; **— bekommen***
to get thirsty
die **Düse, -n** jet injector
das **Düsenflugzeug, -e** jet plane
das **Dutzend, -e** dozen

E

eben just; about; even; flat
ebenso just as, similarly
echt genuine, real
die **Ecke, -n** corner, edge
das **Ehepaar, -e** married couple
die **Ehre, -n** honor; **zu —n** in
honor of
ehren to honor, to regard
das **Ei, -er** egg
die **Eiche, -n** oak
der **Eid, -e** oath; **einen — leisten**
to take an oath
eigen own
die **Eigenschaft, -en** property;
characteristic
eigentlich real, actual(ly), as a
matter of fact; exactly, just;
indeed; sort of; by rights
das **Eigentum, ꞈer** property
die **Eile** haste; **in der —,** in his
(*or* her) haste; **— haben*** to be
in a hurry
eilen (*s*) to hurry
der **Eilzug, ꞈe** fast train
ein one; a, an; **— wenig** somewhat; **— paar** a few; **die —en
... die anderen** some ... others; the one (kind) ... the other
(kind); **—er** someone
ein-atmen to breathe in, to inhale
der **Einbrecher, —** burglar
eindeutig clear
einfach simple
ein-fallen* (*s*) (*dat. of pers.*) to
occur to

220

einflußreich influential
ein-füllen to pump (*of gasoline*)
der **Eingang, ⸚e** entrance
ein-gehen* (*s*) to arrive
eingenommen für (*acc.*) prejudiced in favor of; partial to
eingeschickt submitted
der **Eingriff, -e** operation
die **Einheit, -en** unit
ein-holen to gather in; to catch up with; **Auskunft —,** to make inquiries
einig agreed
einige some, a few; **noch —,** a few more; **—s** something; **nach —m Zögern** after some hesitation
der **Einkauf, ⸚e** purchase; **einige Einkäufe machen** to do some shopping; to run some errands
ein-laden* to invite; **zu sich nach Amerika —,** to invite to visit one('s home) in America
ein-lassen* to let (*or* step) in
ein-lösen to cash
einmal once, one time; long ago; some time in the past (*or* the future); **noch —,** once more; **geh doch —,** do go; **es war —,** once upon a time
ein-reichen to file (*an application, etc.*); to hand in
die **Einrichtung, -en** arrangement; furniture, institution
eins: — zweiter und zurück one round trip (ticket) second (class)
ein-schalten to turn on
ein-schicken to send in
ein-schlafen* (*s*) to fall asleep
einschlägig related
sich ein-schleichen* to sneak in
einschließlich including (tips)
ein-sehen* to examine
sich ein-seifen to lather one's . . .
ein-setzen to appoint; to install; to put in
einst once
ein-stecken to pocket; to put away
ein-steigen* (*s*) to climb aboard, to get on
ein-stellen to stop; to tune in; to employ

ein-stürmen (*s*) **auf** (*acc.*) to rush at; to race through one's mind
ein-teilen to divide
ein-treten* (*s*) to enter; **— in** (*acc.*) to enter
ein-werfen* to interject
ein-willigen to agree
einzeln singly; **im —,** in detail
ein-ziehen* (*s*) to move in
einzig sole, only
die **Eisenbahn, -en** railway, train
eisern of iron; **die —e Pflicht** stern duty
der **Eisschrank, ⸚e** refrigerator
der **Elefant** (-en), -en elephant
elektrisch electrical
die **Elektrische** (*adj. decl.*) street car
(das) **Elsaß** Alsace
die **Eltern** (*pl.*) parents
empfangen, i, a (**ä**) to receive
empfehlen, a, o (**ie**) to recommend; **sich —,** to take leave, to bid adieu
empfindlich touchy
empört outraged
emsig busily
das **Ende, -n** end; **zu —,** at an end; finished; **zu — lesen*** to finish reading; **letzten —s** after all
enden to end
endlich finally, at last
die **Endprüfung, -en** final (*or* comprehensive) exam
die **Endstation** (-*tsjon*), **-en** end of the line
eng close; narrow; **im —eren Sinne** in a narrower sense
der **Engel, —** angel
(das) **Englisch** English (*language*)
entdecken to discover
entfalten to unfold
entgegen-kommen* (*s*) (*dat.*) to come forward (*or* to meet a person); to head toward
entgegen-sehen* (*dat.*) to look forward to
entgegnen to answer
entgehen* (*s*) to escape
entlang along(side of)
entlassen* to dismiss, to discharge
entlocken to elicit

sich entscheiden* to decide
sich entschließen* to decide (to do)
entschlossen. resolved
der **Entschluß** (–sses), ⸗sse decision; **den — fassen** to resolve
entschuldigen to excuse
die **Entschuldigung, –en** excuse
sich entsetzen to be up in arms; to protest
entsetzlich horrible
sich entsinnen, a, o to remember, to recall
entstehen* (s) to originate; to rise up
entweder . . . oder either . . . or
die **Entzündung, –en** inflammation
erbleichen, i, i (s) to pale; to grow pale
die **Erbsensuppe, –n** pea soup
die **Erde, –n** earth
das **Ereignis** (–sses), –sse event
erfahren* to learn
erfahren experienced
die **Erfahrung, –en** experience
die **Erfindung, –en** discovery, invention
erfreulich gratifying
erfreut elated
erfrischt refreshed
ergänzen to add, to complete
erhalten* to receive
erheben* to raise; **die Anklage —,** to make (or level) the charges; **sich —,** to rise; to get up
erhöhen to raise
erinnern to remind; **sich — an** (acc.) to remember
erkennen* to recognize, to perceive
erklären to declare, to explain
sich erkundigen to inquire; **— nach** (dat.) to inquire about
das **Erlebnis** (–sses), –sse experience
erleichtert relieved
erlernen to learn
erlösen to save
die **Erlösung** salvation
ermüden to tire
erobern to conquer
erregt excited

erreichen to reach
erscheinen* (s) to appear, to seem
erschrocken frightened
ersetzen to replace
erst first, at first; only; not until
erst– first; **im —en Stock** on the second floor
erstaunt surprised
erstenmal: zum —, (or **ersten Male**) for the first time
erstens firstly
ersterben* (s) to die out, to fade out
ersticken to suffocate
ertönen to sound, to resound
ertragen* to bear; **zum Ertragen** bearable
erwachsen grown up
erwarten to expect; **— von** (dat.) to expect of
sich erweisen* als to prove to be
erzählen to tell, to relate
erzeugen to produce
die **Erzeugung** production
erziehen* to raise
erzogen bred, educated
das **Essen, —** meal
essen, aß, gegessen (ißt) to eat
essend eating
etwa about, approximately
etwas some; somewhat; something; a bit; a while; anything
(das) **Europa** Europe
ewig eternal
die **Ewigkeit** eternity
das **Examen, —** exam; **das — machen** to pass the exam
extra extra

F

das **Fach,** ⸗**er** field
der **Facharzt,** ⸗**e** (medical) specialist
fad dull
fähig able; **—** (gen.) capable (of)
die **Fähigkeit, –en** ability
die **Fahrbahn, –en** roadway
der **Fahrdamm,** ⸗**e** roadway
fahren, u, a (ä) (s) (intrans.) to travel; to go; to ride; to jour-

ney; **der Bleistift fährt über das Papier** the pencil races over the paper; (*h*) (*trans.*) —, to drive

der **Fahrleiter,** — driving instructor

die **Fahrprüfung, -en** driver's test

das **Fahrrad,** ⸚**er** bicycle

die **Fahrt, -en** trip; journey; **die — frei geben*** to give the right of way; **während der** —, while in motion; during the trip

die **Fakultät, -en** faculty; division; college

der **Fall,** ⸚**e** case

fallen, ie, a (ä) (*s*) to fall; **sie fiel mir um den Hals** she threw her arms around me

fällen to fell

fallend falling

falsch false; wrong; **die Uhr geht wohl** —, the watch is probably wrong

die **Familie, -n** family

der **Familienname (-ns), -n** last name

famos splendid; **-er Kerl** fine fellow

die **Farbe, -n** color

färben to color; to dye

das **Färbewort,** ⸚**er** word adding flavor

fassen to seize; to grasp; to hold; to take hold of; **den Entschluß** —, to resolve; **sich** —, to compose oneself

fassungslos beside oneself

fast almost; — **zu schön** almost too good

faul lazy, idle

das **Faulbett, -en** bed of sloth

die **Faust,** ⸚**e** fist; **mit der — auf den Tisch schlagen*** to strike the table with one's fist

das **Faustbuch,** ⸚**er** Faust Book

faustgroß as big as a fist

die **Faustszene,** ⸚**n** Faust scene

die **Feder, -n** pen; feather

fehlen to lack; to (be) miss(ing); **es fehlt mir etwas (nichts)** something (nothing) is wrong with me

die **Feier, -n** party

der **Feierabend, -e** quitting time; **am** —, after work

fein fine, delicate; sheer

die **Feindin, -nen** (*female*) enemy

feindlich inimical

das **Feld, -er** field

das **Fenster,** — window

die **Ferien** (*pl.*) vacation; **in** —, on vacation

fern far, distant

das **Fernamt,** ⸚**er** long distance (office)

die **Fernamtnummer, -n** long distance number

die **Ferne, -n** distance

das **Ferngespräch, -e** long distance call

der **Fernlastwagen,** — long distance van

fertig finished, ready, done; ready-made

die **Fessel, -n** fetter; **in -n schlagen*** to cast in fetters

fesseln to captivate

fest-halten* to hold on to

fest-stellen to establish; to note

das **Fett, -e** fat

feucht damp, moist

das **Feuer,** — fire; **zu — werden*** (*s*) to turn to fire

feuerrot as red as a beet

das **Fieber** fever; — **haben*** to have a temperature

das **Finanzamt,** ⸚**er** office of the treasurer

finden, a, u to find; **in Ordnung** —, to find (to be) in order; **findest du nicht auch?** don't you think so, too?

der **Finger,** — finger

die **Firma, Firmen** firm

der **Fisch, -e** fish

der **Fischkasten,** ⸚ fish crate

das **Fischlein,** — little fish

flammen to burn, to flame

die **Flasche, -n** bottle

flehen to plead

das **Fleisch** meat

der **Fleischerladen,** ⸚ butcher shop

der **Fleiß** zeal, industry

fleißig diligent

fliegen, o, o (*s*) to fly
der **Fluchtversuch, -e** attempt to escape
flugs swiftly
das **Flugzeug, -e** airplane
der **Fluß (-sses),** ⁻**sse** river
flüstern whisper
folgen (*s*) (*dat.*) to follow
die **Forelle, -n** trout
das **Formular, -e** blank
die **Forschungsfreiheit, -en** freedom to do research
fort gone, away
fort-fahren* continue
fort-reißen* to tear along; **mit sich** —, to carry (*or* sweep) away
fort-setzen to continue; **sich** —, to continue
fort-tragen* to carry away
die **Frage, -n** question; **in** — **kommen*** (*s*) to be in question
fragen to ask; — **nach** (*dat.*) to ask about
(das) **Frankfurt** Frankfort; **-er** (*pertaining to*) Frankfort
(das) **Frankreich** France
französisch French
die **Frau, -en** woman; wife; Mrs.
das **Fräulein,** — girl; miss
frei free; **es steht mir** —, I am at liberty; — **von der Leber weg sprechen*** to speak one's mind
die **Freiheit, -en** freedom
frei-machen to free; **sich oben** —, to unbutton one's shirt
frei-stehen* to be at liberty
fremd strange; — (*dat.*) strange (to)
der **Fremde** (*adj. decl.*) stranger
fressen, fraß, gefressen (frißt) to wolf, to eat (*of animals*)
die **Freud(e), -(e)n** joy
freudig gladly
sich freuen to rejoice; to be glad; — **auf** (*acc.*) to look forward to; **es freut mich** I am glad
der **Freund, -e** friend
freundlich friendly, kind, cordial; **sehr** —, very kind
die **Freundschaft, -en** friendship

der **Friede (-ns)** peace
frisch fresh; — **machen** to refreshen
frischgebacken brand-new
der **Frisör, -e** barber
die **Frisur, -en** hair style
froh glad, happy; — (*gen.*) glad of
die **Fruchtbarkeit** fertility
früh early; — **morgens** early in the morning; **gestern** —, yesterday morning; **von** — **bis spät** from dawn to dusk
der **Frühling, -e** spring
das **Frühstück, -e** breakfast
frühstücken to breakfast
fühlen to feel; **sich verfolgt** —, to feel that one is being followed
führen to lead
füllen to fill
das **Füllwort,** ⁻**er** (word) filler
das **Fünfmarkstück, -e** five mark piece
funktionieren to function, to work
für for
furchtbar terrible
sich fürchten vor (*dat.*) to be afraid of
fürs = für das
der **Fuß,** ⁻**e** foot; **zu** —, on foot
der **Fußball** soccer
der **Fußgänger,** — pedestrian
füttern to feed
die **Futterpflanze, -n** fodder crop
der **Futterpreis, -e** food price

G

der **Gang,** ⁻**e** gait; passageway
ganz full; whole; entire; quite; — **unter uns** strictly between us; — **Ohr** all ears; — **aufmachen** to open wide; **im großen -en** on the whole, generally speaking
gar even, to boot; — **nicht** not at all
die **Garage (-g-** *as in English* "garage"**), -n** garage
der **Garten,** ⁻ garden
das **Gas, -e** gas
der **Gast,** ⁻**e** guest

die **Gastfreundschaft** hospitality
das **Gasthaus, ⸚er** inn; restaurant
die **Gattin, -nen** spouse, wife
das **Gebäude, —** building
geben, a, e (i) to give; **Kredit —**
to extend credit; **sich Mühe —**
— mit (*dat.*) to trouble with; **es**
gibt there is (*or* are); **gib's her!**
let's have it!
das **Gebet, -e** prayer
gebeugt bent
geboren born
gebrauchen to use
die **Geburt, -en** birth
der **Geburtsort, -e** place of birth
der **Geburtstag, -e** birthday, day
of birth
die **Geburtstagsfeier, -n** birthday party
der **Gedanke (-ns), -n** thought;
idea; **der — kam mir** I got the
idea; **er kam auf den —n**
he got (*or* hit upon) the idea; **in**
—n in thoughts, mentally
der **Gedankengang, ⸚e** train of
thoughts, line of reasoning
gedenken* (*gen.*) to remember
das **Gedicht, -e** poem
die **Geduld** patience
geduldig patient
die **Gefahr, -en** danger
gefährden to endanger
gefährlich dangerous
gefallen killed in battle
gefallen* (*dat. of pers.*) to please;
es gefällt mir I like it; **es**
gefällt mir an ihm I like about
him
gefälscht counterfeit
das **Gefängnis (-sses), -sse**
prison, jail; imprisonment
geflogen aflying
das **Gefühl, -e** feeling
gegen against; **so —,** around
der **Gegenstand, ⸚e** object; subject
gegenüber against; across (*the*
street) from; opposite
gegenüber-liegen* to lie *or* be
opposite *or* across (*the street*) from
das **Gehackte** (*adj. decl.*) chopped
meat
geheimnisvoll mysterious

gehen, ging, gegangen (*s*) to go;
to walk; to run (*of clocks*); **es**
sich gut — lassen* to have a
good time; **auf den Garten**
hinaus —, to face on the garden;
zu Grunde —, to perish; **an**
die Hand —, to give a hand, to
assist; **zu Werke —,** to go
about it; **ich gehe ins Wasser**
I'll drown myself; **es geht mir**
gut I am fine *or* I'm doing well
or I'm well off; **es geht hoch**
her spirits are running high; **es**
geht bei mir alles wie me-
chanisch I do everything mechanically (*or* like clockwork);
meine Uhr geht genau my
watch keeps good time; **die Uhr**
geht wohl falsch the watch is
probably wrong; **wie geht's?**
how are you? **geh doch ein-**
mal! do go!
gehören (*dat.*) to belong to; **dazu**
gehört viel that requires much
gehorsam obedient
der **Gehsteig, -e** sidewalk; **am**
—, at the curb
geistig intelligent; intellectual
gekleidet dressed
das **Geld, -er** money
das **Geldstück, -e** coin
die **Gelegenheit, -en** opportunity
der **Gelegenheitskauf, ⸚e** bargain
gelegentlich occasionally; on oc-
casion
gelingen, a, u (*s*) to succeed; **es**
gelingt mir I succeed
gelten, a, o (i) to apply, to be
valid; **es gilt** it is a matter of;
es gilt mir it is meant for me
gemeinsam together
der **Gemüsehändler, —** vegetable
dealer
die **Gemüsesuppe, -n** vegetable
soup
gemütlich genial
genau exactly, precise; **— so** just
as
der **General, ⸚e** general
die **Generalin, -nen** general's
wife
genießen, genoß, genossen to
enjoy

genug enough
genügen to suffice; to be sufficient
die **Geographie** geography
das **Gepäck, -e** baggage, bag
gerade even; straight; exactly; just; on the point of; **nicht —** not quite; **— recht** just in time
geradeaus straight ahead
geraten* (s) in (acc.) to get into; **in Erregung —,** to get excited
das **Gericht, -e** court
das **Geringste** (adj. decl.) slightest thing
gern(e) gladly; **— haben*** to like; **— mögen*** to like (to); **— tun*** to like to do
geröstet fried
das **Geschäft, -e** business; store; **das — geht glänzend** business is booming
geschäftig busy
der **Geschäftsmann, -leute** businessman
die **Geschäftsreise, -n** business trip
der **Geschäftsreisende** (adj. decl.) traveling salesman
das **Geschäftsverhältnis (-sses), -sse** business condition
geschehen, a, e (ie) (s) to happen
die **Geschichte, -n** story
das **Geschirr, -e** (set of) dishes
geschlossen closed
das **Geschrei** shouting
der **Geselle (-n), -n** journeyman; companion
die **Gesellschaft, -en** company
gesenkt low(ered)
das **Gesicht, -er** face
der **Gesichtspunkt, -e** point of view
gespannt tense
die **Gestalt, -en** figure; form
gestehen* to confess
gestern yesterday; **— früh** yesterday morning
gestikulieren to gesticulate
gestohlen stolen
gestreift striped
gesund sound; healthy; **der -e Menschenverstand** common sense
die **Getreideart, -en** type of grain

gewaltig tremendous; powerful; huge
das **Gewebe, —** weave
das **Gewerbe, —** trade
der **Gewinn, -e** profit
gewinnen, a, o to win, to gain
gewiß certain; no doubt
die **Gewohnheit, -en** habit
gewohnheitsmäßig as usual, customarily
gewöhnlich ordinary; usual; customary
gewohnt usual; ordinary
gewöhnt accustomed
gewünscht desired
glänzend splendid; **das Geschäft geht —,** business is booming
das **Glas, -er** glass
glatt smooth
der **Glaube (-ns)** belief
glauben (dat.) to believe; **— an** (acc.) to believe in
gleich straight; equal; alike; same; right (away); **— zu** right at; **— sein*** (s) to (be) equal (to)
gleichzeitig simultaneously
gleiten, glitt, geglitten (s) to slide; **trübe —,** to cast a dull light
das **Glück** luck, fortune; **— haben*** to be lucky
glücklich happy
glücklicherweise luckily; fortunately
gnädig gracious; **-e Frau** madame
goldbraun goldenbrown
gotisch Gothic
der **Gott, -er** god; **um Gottes willen** for God's sake; **mein —!** good God!
der **Grad, -e** degree
gratulieren to congratulate; **sich —,** to congratulate oneself
grau grey
grauenhaft gruesome
grausam cruel
greifen, griff, gegriffen to reach; **— nach** (dat.) to reach for
grinsen to sneer, to grin
das **Grinsen** grinning
die **Grippe, -n** grippe
grollen to growl; to grumble
groß large, big, tall; **sich — an-**

226

blicken to look at each other in amazement; **im —en ganzen** by and large, generally speaking; **größer** larger
die **Größe, -n** size
die **Großstadtstraße, -n** big city street
grün green
der **Grund** basis; ground; soil; **zu — gehen*** (*s*) to perish
der **Grund, ⸗e** reason
gründlich thorough
grüßen to salute; to greet; to tip one's hat
gültig valid
der **Gummiabsatz, ⸗e** rubber heel
der **Gummischuh, -e** rubber
günstig favorable
das **Gut, ⸗er** estate, goods
gut good; well; **nun —,** very well; **—e Reise!** bon voyage! (have a) good trip!
gut-gehen* (*s*) to go well; **es geht mir gut** I am doing well
gütig kindly; **—st** (most) kindly
gut-machen to make up (for)
gutmütig genial; kind; good-natured
gut-tun* to help, to do some good

H

das **Haar, -e** hair; **sich** (*dat.*) das **— kämmen** to comb one's hair
das **Haarschneiden** haircut(ting)
haben, hatte, gehabt (hat) to have; **lieber —,** to prefer; **am liebsten —,** to like best
der **Hafen, ⸗** harbor
der **Haifisch, -e** shark
der **Haifischrachen, —** jaws of the shark
der **Haken, —** hook
halb half
halblang medium long
der **Hals, ⸗e** neck; throat
die **Halsentzündung, -en** inflammation of the throat
halt halt
halten, ie, a (ä) to stop; to hold; **— von** (*dat.*) to think of; **das Wort —,** to keep one's word

die **Haltestelle, -n** streetcar stop
halt-machen to stop
die **Haltung, -en** posture; **— an-nehmen*** to straighten (*or* brace) up
hämmern to hammer
die **Hand, ⸗e** hand; **die — geben*** (*or* **reichen**) to shake hands; **an die — gehen*** (*s*) to give a hand; **es in der — haben*** to be up to (*a person*); **die Sache in die — nehmen*** to take personal charge of a matter; **zur — nehmen*** to pick up; **alle Hände voll zu tun haben** to have all one can do to take care of it
die **Handelsschule, -n** business school; **die höhere —,** business (course in high) school
das **Handtuch, ⸗er** towel
hängen, i, a to hang
die **Harmonie, -n** harmony
hart hard; severe; harsh
häßlich ugly
hastig hasty, quick
das **Haupt, ⸗er** head; **hocherhobenen —es** head held high
die **Hauptsache, -n** main thing
hauptsächlich primarily
das **Hauptzugstück, -e** main attraction
das **Haus, ⸗er** house; **ins — schicken** to (have) deliver(ed); **nach -e** home; **von — zu — grüßen** to convey regards to one's family; **zu -e** at home
die **Hausarbeit, -en** home (*or* house) work
der **Hausflur, -e** hallway
die **Hausnummer, -n** house number
die **Hebebühne, -n** (*hydraulic*) grease rack
heben, o, o to lift; to heighten; to raise
heftig violent
hegen to entertain; **den Gedanken —,** to entertain the thought
die **Heide, -n** heath(er)
das **Heidenröslein, —** heather rose
der **Heilige** (*adj. decl.*) saint

die **Heimat, –en** home town; native land
heimatlos homeless
heimlich secretly
der **Heimweg, -e** way home
heiraten to marry
heiser hoarse
heiß hot
heißen, ie, ei to be called
heiter gay
heizen to heat
die **Heizplatte, –n** hot plate, griddle
der **Held (-en), -en** hero
heldenmütig heroical
helfen, a, o (i) (*dat.*) to help; **sich —,** to help oneself; **in die Höhe —,** to help (get) up; **es hilft mir kein Weinen** no amount of crying is of avail (to me); **es hilft mir nichts** it avails me nothing
hell bright, light; **am -en Tag** in broad daylight; **ein Glas Helles** one (glass of) light (beer)
hellbraun light brown
her hither, here
herab down
herab-blicken to look down; **ich blicke an mir herab** I look down at myself
herab-drücken to drive (*or* get) down
heran up to
heran-rasen (*s*) to race toward; to approach at top speed
heran-sausen (*s*) to race toward; to approach at top speed
heran-sein* (*s*) to be (*or* come) up to
heran-treten* (*s*) **an** (*acc.*) to step up to
heraus out
heraus-bringen* to find out
heraus-geben* to edit; **— auf** (*acc.*) to change
heraus-nehmen* to take out
heraus-senden* to send out
sich heraus-stellen to turn out to be
herbei-stürzen (*s*) to rush over
herbei-winken to signal (*or* motion) someone to come over

herein in
herein-kommen* (*s*) to come in; to enter
herein-regnen to rain in
herein-treten* (*s*) to enter; to step in
her-geben* to hand over; **gib's her!** let's have it!
her-gehen* (*s*) to walk along; to go on; **es ging hoch her** spirits ran high
her-kommen* (*s*) to come here
die **Herkunft** origin; descent; **deutscher —,** of German descent
der **Herr (-n), -en** gentleman, man, mister; Mr.; Lord; **der —, Sir; — im Himmel** God in Heaven
der **Herrgott** Lord
herrisch insistent, commanding
herrlich splendid; magnificent
her-stellen to produce; **eine (telefonische) Verbindung — mit** (*dat.*) to reach (telephonically)
herum-gehen* (*s*) **um** (*acc.*) to walk around
herum-gestikulieren to gesticulate about
herum-liegen* to lie about
herum-schreien* to shout about; **mit einem —,** to bark at
herum-wirbeln to whirl about
herunter down off; **— müssen*** to have to get off
herunter-fallen* (*s*) to fall down
hervor-stoßen* to blurt out
das **Herz (-ens), -en** heart; **das — bleibt mir stehen** my heart stops beating; **die Angst kriecht ihr zu —en** fear creeps up her spine
das **Herzklopfen** pounding of the heart
herzlich cordial; **— lieb haben*** to love dearly
hetzen to hound; to race
heute today; nowadays; **— früh** *or* **morgen** early today, this morning; **— abend** this evening
heutzutage nowadays
hier here; (*on the phone*) this is . . .

hierher hither; **bis —,** up to this point
hie und da now and then
die **Hilfe** help, aid; **ich komme ihm zu —,** I come to his aid; **um — an-rufen*** to appeal to . . . for help
hilflos helpless
hilfsbereit eager (or ready) to help
der **Himmel, —** sky, heaven; **lieber —!** good heavens!
der **Himmelskörper, —** celestial body
hin thither; there; **— und wieder** now and then (or again); **kann ich mit dem Wagen —?** can I get there by car?
hinauf-stürzen (s) to rush up
hinaus-gehen* (s) to walk out, to go out; **— auf** (acc.) to face on
das **Hinausgehen** walking out
hinaus-schicken to send out
hinaus-streuen to scatter about
hinaus-stürzen (s) to rush out
das **Hindernis** (-sses), -sse obstacle
hinein in(to)
hinein-beißen* to bite into
hinein-rufen* to call in
hin-kommen* (s) to be able to get there
sich hin-lümmeln to lounge
hin-murmeln to mumble away; **vor sich —,** to mumble to oneself
sich hin-setzen to sit down
hin-singen* to sing away; **vor sich —,** to sing to oneself
hinten behind; in back
hinter behind; **— einem her sein*** (s) to be after a person
das **Hinterbein, -e** hind leg
hinunter-gehen* (s) to go down
hinweg-fegen to sweep away
hin-weisen* auf (acc.) to point to; to refer to
hinzu-fügen to add
hinzu-treten* (s) to step up; to join
die **Hitze, -n** heat
hoch high; **höchst** highest; **höchstens** at most
hocherhoben held high

hochgeschlagen turned up (of collars)
hoch-halten* to hold up
der **Hochofen, ⁼** blast furnace
hoch-steigen* (s) to rise (or climb) up
höchstens highly; at most; at best
der **Hof, ⁼e** yard
hoffen to hope
das **Hoffen** hope(s)
hoffentlich let us hope
höflich courteous
die **Höhe, -n** height; **in die —,** up
höher higher; **-e Schule** secondary school
höhnisch mocking
holen to fetch; **— lassen*** to send for; **sich** (dat.) **—,** to fetch (for oneself)
hören to hear
der **Hörer, —** receiver; **den — auf das Telefon legen** to put down the receiver
das **Hörrohr, -e** stethoscope
die **Hose, -n** trouser(s)
das **Hotel, -s** hotel
der **Hotelbeamte** (adj. decl.) hotel clerk
hübsch pretty
hüllen to wrap
die **Hunderttausende** (pl.) hundreds of thousands
hungern to go hungry
hungrig hungry
die **Hupe, -n** horn
hupen to blow (or sound) the horn
das **Hupen** sounding of the horn
hüpfen (s) to hop
der **Hut, ⁼e** hat
hüten to guard; **das Bett —,** to stay in bed; **sich — vor** (dat.) to guard against
das **Hutgeschäft, -e** hat shop
die **Hutkrempe, -n** brim of a hat

I

im = in dem; — Durchschnitt on the average; **— Telefon** over the telephone; **— voraus** in advance

immer always; — **noch** still; **noch** — **nicht** still not; — **wieder** again and again

in in; — **der Regel** as a rule; — **die Schule** to school

indessen meanwhile

der Ingenieur (g *as in "garage" and* eu *as* ö), –e engineer

der Inhaber, — owner

der Inhalt content

innen inside; **nach** — **hinein** inwardly

innerhalb inside of, within

inoffiziell unofficial

ins = **in das;** — **Büro** to the office

die Insel, –n island

insgeheim secretly

die Instanz, –en instance; **in letzter** —, in the highest court

das Interesse, –n interest; **es ist mir von** —, it is of interest to me

der Invalide (–n), –n invalid

inwiefern to what extent

inzwischen meanwhile

irgend some; — **etwas** something

irgendwie somehow

sich irren to err, to be mistaken

der Irrtum, ⸗er error

J

ja yes; so; really; to be sure to; but

die Jacke, –n jacket

das Jackenkleid, –er (women's) suit

das Jahr, –e year; **lange** —e for many years

die Jahreszahl, –en date

das Jahrhundert, –e century

jammern to wail, to moan

jawohl yes, indeed

je ever; — ... —, the ... the; — ... **desto** the ... the

jeder every(body), each (one)

jedoch however

jemand someone

jener that (one)

jenseits on the other side of

jetzt now

die Jugend youth

das Jugendland, ⸗er land of youth

jugendlich youthful

jung young

der Junge (–n), –n boy

der Jüngere (*adj. decl.*) younger (person)

der Jüngste (*adj. decl.*) youngest (person)

der Junggesselle (–n), –n bachelor

K

der Kaffee coffee

die Kaffeemaschine, –n coffee machine

der Kaktus (–), –teen cactus

der Kalbsbraten, — roast veal

kalt cold

die Kälte cold(ness)

der Kamerad (–en), –en comrade

sich kämmen to comb (one's hair)

das Kämpfen struggle

kämpfen to fight; — **mit** (*dat.*) to struggle against; **mit Tränen** —, to fight back the tears

die Kapelle, –n band

der Kapitän, –e captain

die Kappe, –n cap

kariert cheque(re)d

der Karlsplatz Charles Square

die Karte, –n card; map; ticket; **nach der** — **speisen** to order (*i.e.* eat) à la carte

die Kartoffel, –n potato

der Karton, –e *or* –s carton, box

der Käsekuchen, — cheese cake

die Kasse, –n cashier's window; box office

der Kasten, ⸗ box, crate

der Kastenbau, –ten crate construction

die Katze, –n cat

kaufen to buy; **sich** (*dat.*) —, to buy (for) oneself

der Kaufmann, –leute merchant

kaum scarcely; — **mehr** scarcely

kegeln to bowl; to roll

kehrt-machen to make an about face; to turn about
kein no (one); not a; not any
keiner nobody
der **Kellner,** — waiter
kennen, kannte, gekannt to know; **sich** —, to know one another
kennen-lernen to meet; to come to know; to make the acquaintance of
der **Kenner,** — expert; connoisseur
die **Kenntnis, -sse** knowledge
der **Kerl, -e** fellow; cad; rascal
das **Kilo, -s** kilo (= *2.2 pounds*)
das (*or* der) **Kilometer** kilometer (= $\frac{5}{8}$ *mile*)
das **Kind, -er** child
der **Kinderchor,** ⸚e children's choir
die **Kindheit** childhood
das **Kino, -s** movies
die **Kirche, -n** church
klagen über (*acc.*) to complain about
der **Klang,** ⸚e (musical) sound; **unter den Klängen der Musik** to the sound of the music
klappern to clatter, to rattle
klar clear
die **Klasse, -n** class
klatschen to clap; to applaud
sich kleiden to dress
klein small
der **Klient (-en), -en** client
das **Klima, -s** climate
klingeln to ring (*a bell*)
klingen, a, u to ring (*a bell*); to sound
die **Klinik, -en** clinic
die **Klinke, -n** doorknob; **die —n fremder Leute putzen** to depend on the whim of other people; to ring doorbells
klirren to rattle
klopfen to knock; to pound
klug clever
der **Knabe (-n), -n** boy
knapp close
das **Kniegelenk, -e** knee joint
der **Knoblauch, -e** garlic
knusperig crisp
kochen to cook

das **Kochen** cooking
der **Koffer,** — trunk; suitcase; bag; case
der **Kollege (-n), -n** colleague
(das) **Köln** Cologne; **Kölner** (*pertaining to*) Cologne
das **Kölnische Wasser** Eau de Cologne
komisch comical
kommen, kam, gekommen (*s*) to come; to get; **in Bewegung** —, to start moving; **zu spät** —, to be (too) late
der **Komplex, -e** complex
das **Konfektionsgeschäft** (*–tsjon*), -e (men's) clothing store
der **König, -e** king
können, konnte, gekonnt (**kann**) to be able (can)
der **Kopf,** ⸚e head; **den — in den Nacken werfen*** to throw one's head back
die **Kopfschmerzen** (*pl.*) headache
das **Kopftuch,** ⸚er kerchief
kopfüber head over heels
der **Korb,** ⸚e basket; **einen — geben*** to turn (a suitor) down
das **Korn,** ⸚er corn, grain
der **Körper,** — body
kostbar expensive; precious
die **Kosten** (*pl.*) cost(s)
kosten to cost
köstlich delicious
der **Krach, -e** crash; **es gibt einen** —, there will be fireworks
die **Kraft,** ⸚e strength, power, force; energy
der **Kragen,** — collar
sich krampfen to clench
krank sick
der **Kranke** (*adj. decl.*) sick (*male*) person; patient
die **Kranke** (*adj. decl.*) sick (*female*) person
das **Krankenhaus,** ⸚er hospital
das **Krankenzimmer,** — sickroom
die **Krankheit, -en** sickness, disease
kraß rank, sheer
der **Kredit, -e** credit; **— geben*** to extend credit

231

der **Kreis, -e** circle; **aus dem —e** from (amongst)
die **Krempe, -n** brim
kreuzen to cross
die **Kreuzung, -en** crossing
kriechen, o, o (*s*) to creep; **die Angst kriecht ihr zu Herzen** fear creeps up her spine
der **Krieg, -e** war; **— führen** to wage war
das **Kriegserlebnis (-sses), -sse** war experience
krumm crooked; bent; **—e Beine haben*** to be bow-legged
die **Küche, -n** kitchen
der **Kuchen, —** cake
die **Kugel, -n** bullet
die **Kuh, ⸗e** cow
kühl cool
der **Kühler, —** radiator
die **Kultur, -en** culture
sich kümmern to be concerned; **— um** (*acc.*) to be concerned about; to pay attention to
der **Kunde (-n), -n** customer
künftig future
die **Kunst, ⸗e** art
der **Kurs, -e** exchange rate
kurz short; brief
kürzen to shorten
die **Kusine, -n** girl cousin

L

lächeln to smile
lachen to laugh; **— über** (*acc.*) to laugh about; **—d** laughing
der **Laden, ⸗** shop, store
laden, u, a (lädt) to load
der **Ladeninhaber, —** storekeeper
die **Lage, -n** situation
die **Lampe, -n** lamp
das **Land, ⸗er** land; country; **auf dem —e** in the country
das **Landbezirksamt, ⸗er** county hall
landen (*s*) to land
die **Landmaschine, -n** farm machine(ry)
die **Landschaft, -en** landscape; countryside
der **Landwirt, -e** farmer

lang(e) long; **drei Tage —,** for three days; **schon —e** for some time
der **Lange** (*adj. decl.*) tall person
die **Länge, -n** length; **in die — ziehen*** to draw out
länger longer; for some time
langsam slow
längst long ago
langweilig boring
lassen, ließ, gelassen (läßt) to let; **holen —,** to send for; **es sich nicht sagen —,** not wait to be told; **auf sich warten —,** to keep one waiting; **erscheinen —,** to make appear; **ich lasse Ihre Koffer auf Ihr Zimmer bringen** I'll have your bags taken to your room; **kein Auge wurde von ihr gelassen** they didn't take their eyes off her
das **Lastauto, -s** truck, van
der **Lastwagen, —** truck, van
lauern auf (*acc.*) to lie in wait for
laufen, ie, au (äu) (*s*) to run; **einem in den Weg —,** to run into one's path; **über den Weg —,** to cross the street; **—d** running
der **Laufsteg, -e** gangplank
laut loud
lauten to sound; to be; **es lautet wie folgt** it sounds (*or* reads) as follows
läuten to ring
das **Lazarett, -e** field hospital
der **Lebemann, ⸗er** man of the world
leben to live
das **Leben, —** life
lebendig alive; living
lebenslänglich life-long
das **Lebensmittelgeschäft, -e** grocery store
die **Leber, -n** liver
das **Leder, —** leather
ledig single
leer empty; **— aus-gehen*** (*s*) to go empty-handed
legen to lay; to put
lehnen to lean; **sich — gegen** (*acc.*) to lean against
lehren (*acc.*) to teach

der **Lehrer,** — teacher
die **Lehrerin,** **-nen** (*female*)
teacher
die **Lehrfreiheit** freedom to teach
leicht light, easy; — **dämmern**
to get dark slowly
das **Leid** suffering, sorrow
leid: es tut mir —, I am sorry
leiden, litt, gelitten to bear, to
endure; — **an** (*acc.*) to suffer
from
die **Leidenschaft,** -en passion
leider unfortunately
leihen, ie, ie to lend; **sich** (*dat.*)
—, to borrow
leise soft
leisten to accomplish; **einen Eid**
—, to take an oath
die **Leiter,** -n ladder
die **Leitung,** -en line; wire
lenken to guide, to steer
lernen to learn
lesen, a, e (**ie**) to read; — **über**
(*acc.*) to read about; **zu Ende**
—, to finish reading
letzt- last; —**en Endes** in the last
analysis; —**er Glaube** ultimate
belief; **in** —**er Zeit** of late
das **Letzte** (*adj. decl.*) last thing
leuchten to gleam; to glow
die **Leute** (*pl.*) people
das **Licht,** -er light
licht light
lieb dear; **es ist mir** —, I value it
die **Liebe,** -n love
lieben to love, to like
Lieber: mein —, my dear man
(*or* fellow)
lieber preferably; — **haben*** to
prefer; — **backen*** to prefer to
bake
das **Liebesschicksal,** -e love experience
die **Liebhaberei,** -en hobby
der **Liebling,** -e darling
liebst- dearest; **am** —**en haben***
to like best
das **Lied,** -er song
liegen, a, e to lie; to be situated;
to be (ill) in bed; **daran liegt
mir** I am concerned; **wie lange
liegt er?** how long has he been
in bed?

die **Linie,** -n line
links to the left, on the left
das **Liter,** — liter
die **Litfaßsäule,** -n billpost
das **Loch,** -er hole
die **Locke,** -n lock
logisch logical
los loose; —! go *or* get going! **was
ist** —? what is the matter?
los sein* (*s*) (*acc.*) to be rid of
die **Lotterie,** -n lottery
die **Ludwigstraße** Ludwig Street
die **Luft** air; **nach** — **schnappen**
to gasp for air
die **Luftpumpe,** -n air pump
die **Lüge,** -n lie
lügen, o, o to lie
lullen to lull
die **Lunge,** -n lung
die **Lupe,** -n magnifying glass;
unter die — **nehmen*** to give
a careful going over
der **Lustgarten,** - park
lustig gay
der **Lustmörder,** — sex killer
lutschen to suck (on)

M

m = Meter
machen to do, to make; to pass *or*
take (*of exams*); **aufmerksam**
— **auf** (*acc.*) to call attention to;
frisch —, to refreshen; **ihn zum
. . .** —, to make him a . . .; **sich
ein Bild** —, to get a picture; **sich
Luft** —, to give vent to one's . . .;
das läßt sich —, that can be
done; **sich oben frei** —, to
unbutton *or* open one's shirt,
etc.; **sich Sorgen** —, to worry;
wieviel macht das how much
is it (*or* that)
mächtig mighty; powerful
das **Mädchen,** — girl
mähen to mow; to reap
mahnen to admonish
das **Mal,** -e time; instance; **zum
ersten** —, for the first time
mal = einmal (*often not translated*); **sag** —, say; **lassen Sie**
— **sehen** let's see

malen to paint
der **Maler,** — painter
die **Mama, -s** mama
manch– many a; **-e** (*pl.*) some;
so —er many a person; **so —es**
many a thing
manchmal sometimes
mangeln (*intrans. impers.*) **an**
dat.) to (be) lack(ing); **es mangelt hier an vielem** much is
lacking here; **ihm mangelt es
an Geld** he lacks money
der **Mann, ⁻er** man; husband
die **Männerstimme, -n** male voice
der **Mantel, ⁻** coat
das **Märchen,** — fairy tale
das **Märchenbuch, ⁻er** book of
fairy tales
die **Mark** mark
die **Marke, -n** brand
der **Markt, ⁻e** market; die **Markt-
frau, -en** market woman
die **Marmelade, -n** marmalade
der **Marmeladeneimer,** — tin of
marmalade
die **Maschine, -n** machine
das **Maß, ⁻e** measure; **nach —,**
made to order
mäßig moderate; fitting
die **Maßnahme, -n** measure
das **Material, -ien** material
materialistisch materialistic
der **Matrose (-n), -n** sailor
der **Mechaniker,** — mechanic
mechanisch mechanical; **wie —,**
mechanically; like clockwork
med. = *medicinae*, of medicine
die **Medizin, -en** medicine
das **Meer, -e** sea, ocean
der **Meeresgrund, ⁻e** bottom of
the sea
mehr more
die **Mehrzahl** majority
meinen to think; to mean; to
opine; to be of the opinion
meinetwegen so far as I am concerned; on my account
meist most
die **meisten** most
meistens mostly
melden to report; **sich —,** to
report, to announce oneself, to
answer (*the telephone*)

der **Mensch (-en), -en** human being, man
menschenleer deserted
der **Menschenverstand** common
sense
die **Menschheit** humanity; man-
kind
merken to notice; to mark; —
an (*dat.*) to (be able to) tell by;
es einem an-— to note in a
person; **sich —,** to note
merkwürdig strange
messen, maß, gemessen (mißt)
to measure
der **Messias (—)** Messiah
das **Metall, -e** metal
das **Metallstück, -e** piece of metal
das *or* der **Meter,** — meter
die **Miete, -n** rent
sich mieten to rent
die **Milch** milk
mild mild; gentle; generous; le-
nient
mildernd ameliorating, extenuating
die **Minute, -n** minute; — **auf —,**
minute after minute
das **Mißverständnis (-sses), -sse**
misunderstanding
mit with; about; — **der Straßenbahn** by streetcar
miteinander with one another
mit-fahren* (*s*) to drive along
with
mit-gehen* (*s*) to go along
mit-kommen* (*s*) to come along
mit-machen to take part in; to
participate; to come along; to
go along with; to do (together)
with
mit-nehmen* to take along
mit-reden to have something to
say
der **Mittag, -e** noon
mittags at noon
die **Mittagszeit, -en** lunchtime
mittel medium
das **Mittel,** — drug; means; **ein
— gegen** (*acc.*) a cure for
der **Mittelplatz, ⁻e** seat in the
center
mittelschwer medium heavy
die **Mitternacht, ⁻e** midnight

234

mit-wirken to participate
die **Mode, –n** style, fashion
modern modern
mögen, mochte, gemocht (mag) to like (to); to be possible; to be permitted (may)
die **Möglichkeit, –en** possibility
der **Monat, –e** month
moralisch moral
der **Mörder, —** murderer
der **Morgen, —** morning
morgen tomorrow; **— früh** tomorrow morning
die **Morgenluft, ‑e** morning air
morgens in the morning
morgenschön beautiful as the morrow
die **Morgenzeitung, –en** morning paper
die **Mosel** Moselle (*river*)
der **Motor, –toren** motor; **was ist am — in Unordnung?** what's wrong with the motor?
müde tired
die **Mühe, –n** effort; **sich — geben*** to take the trouble, to make an effort
(das) **München** Munich
der **Mund, ‑e(r)** mouth
die **Mündung, –en** mouth, estuary; **— eines Revolvers** barrel of a gun
munter gay, cheerful
die **Münze, –n** coin
murmeln to mumble; to mutter
die **Musik** music
müssen, mußte, gemußt (muß) to have to (must)
das **Muster, —** pattern
der **Mut** courage; **— bekommen*** to take courage
die **Mutter, ‑** mother
das **Mütterchen, —** little mother
mütterlich motherly, as a mother would

N

na well
nach to(ward); according to; **— Hause** home; **— der Karte speisen** to order (*i.e.* eat) à la carte; **— Tisch** after dinner;

— innen hinein lachen to laugh to oneself
der **Nachbar, –n** neighbor
die **Nachbarschaft, –en** neighborhood
nach-blicken (*dat.*) to stare at; to follow with one's eyes
nachdem after (having)
nachdenklich pensively
nach-fragen to inquire
nachgeahmt imitated, counterfeit
nach-geben* to give in
nach-gehen* (*s*) to follow; to pursue; **Liebhabereien —,** to indulge in hobbies; **die Uhr geht nach** the watch is slow
nachher afterwards
nach-laufen* (*s*) to run after; to pursue
nach-machen to imitate
der **Nachmittag, –e** afternoon
nachmittags afternoon(s)
nach-prüfen to test
die **Nachricht, –en** news, information
nach-rufen* to call after
nach-schreien* to shout after
nach-sehen* (*dat.*) to check; to look to see; to look in; to turn to watch (*or* look)
die **Nachspeise, –n** dessert
nächst next; nearest
nächstens in the near future
die **Nacht, ‑e** night
nachts at night
der **Nachttisch, –e** night stand
nach-zählen to (verify the) count
der **Nacken, —** (nape of the) neck; **den Kopf in den — werfen** to throw one's head back
nageln to nail
nah near
die **Nähe** vicinity; proximity; nearness; **in der — von** in the vicinity of
nähen to sew
sich nähern (*dat.*) to approach
die **Nahrung** food, nutrition
der **Name (–ns), –n** name
nämlich namely (*often omitted in translation*)

närrisch foolish
naß wet
die Nässe wetness; dampness
die Nation (-*tsjon*), -en nation
die Natur, -en nature
natürlich naturally
der Nebel, — mist; fog
nebenan next door
der Nebenmann, ⸗er man next to
a person
nee = nein
der Neffe (-n), -n nephew
nehmen, nahm, genommen
(nimmt) to take; allein in die
Hand —, to take the matter
in one's own hands; zur Hand
—, to pick up; Platz —, to be
seated
die Neigung, -en bent
nein no
nennen, nannte, genannt (*acc.*)
to call; to name; den Namen
—, to give one's name
nett nice; — sein* (*s*) zu (*dat.*)
to be nice to
neu new
die Neuanstellung, -en new appointment
das Neue (*adj. decl.*) (the) new
neuestens recently
nicht not; gar —, not at all;
— doch but don't; mit —en
by no means
die Nichte, -n niece
nichts nothing
nichtsdestoweniger nonetheless
nicken to nod
nie never; — wieder never again
nieder down
niedrig low
niemals never
niemand nobody
nirgends nowhere
nit = nicht
noch still; extra; else; — bevor
even before; — ein another, one
more; — einmal once more;
— nicht not yet; — nie never
before; — so however
nochmals once more
die Nordsee North Sea
die Normaluhr, -en official clock;
standard time

die Not distress; in höchster —,
in utter distress
der Notfall, ⸗e emergency; im
—, in an emergency
(sich) notieren to note down
notwendig necessary
nüchtern sober
die Nummer, -n number
nun well; now; — gut very well
nur only; merely; just; possibly;
— so just; sich — so durch-
hungern (to) barely eke out an
existence
der Nutzen, — use; benefit; —
ziehen* to derive benefits, to
profit from

O

ob if, whether
oben above; top
der Oberarmbruch, ⸗e fracture
of the upper arm
oberhalb on top of, above
Oberkirchner (*pertaining to*) Ober-
kirchen (*town in Northern Germany*)
obgleich although
objektiv objective
obwohl although
obzwar although
der Ochse (-n), -n ox
der Odeonsplatz Odeon Square
oder or
der Ofen, — oven
offenbar obvious
der Offizier, -e officer
öffnen to open; sich —, to open
oft often
öftern: des —, frequently
ohne without
ohnmächtig unconscious
das Ohr, -en ear; ganz —, all
ears
das Öl, -e oil
der Ölstand, ⸗e oil (level)
der Omnibus (-sses), -sse bus
der Onkel, — uncle
die Operation (-*tsjon*), -en operation
operieren to operate on
das Opernglas, ⸗er opera glasses

der **Orden,** — decoration
ordentlich orderly, decent; properly
die **Ordnung,** -en order; **für die**
— **sorgen** to maintain order; **in**
— **bringen*** to straighten out
der **Ort,** -e *or* ⸚er place
(das) **Österreich** Austria
die **Ostsee** Baltic Sea

P

das **Paar,** -e pair
paar: ein —, a few
sich pachten to lease
packen to pack
der **Pakt,** -e compact
die **Panne,** -n car trouble; **eine**
— **reparieren** to make (minor)
car repairs
der **Papa,** -s papa
das **Papier,** -e paper
das **Papierene** (*adj. decl.*) paper
(thing)
der **Paragraph** (-en), -en section;
paragraph
parken to park
das **Parkett,** -s orchestra (*of
theater seats*)
parteiisch partial
der **Passagier** (g *as in "garage"*), -e
passenger
passen to suit; to fit; — **zu** (*dat.*)
to go well with
passieren (*s*) to happen
das **Passionsspiel,** -e Passion play
der **Patient** (*-tsjent*), (-en), -en
(*male*) patient
die **Patientin** (*-tsjentin*), -nen
(*fem.*) patient
die **Person,** -en person
das **Personal** personnel
die **Pfanne,** -n (frying) pan
die **Pfeife,** -n pipe
pfeifen, pfiff, gepfiffen to whistle
der **Pfennig,** -e penny
Pfizerisch (*pertaining to*) Pfizer
das **Pflaster,** — pavement
die **Pflicht,** -en duty
der **Pförtner,** — guard (*at the gate*)
das **Pfund,** -e pound
phantastisch fantastic

der **Philosoph** (-en), -en philosopher
der **Physiker,** — physicist
der **Physiklehrer,** — physics
teacher
der **Plan,** ⸚e plan; map
der **Platz,** ⸚e place; square; seat;
room; — **nehmen*** to be seated
platzen (*s*) to burst; to blow out
plaudern to chat
plötzlich suddenly
plump stocky
die **Polizei** police
der **Polizist** (-en), -en policeman
die **Pomade,** -n hair cream
das **Portal,** -e portal, main entrance
die **Portion** (*-tsjon*), -en portion
positiv positive
die **Post** mail; post office
das **Postamt,** ⸚er post office
der **Posten,** — post, job
der **Postinspektor,** -oren postal
inspector
prächtig splendid
die **Präzisionsuhr,** -en precision
watch
der **Preis,** -e price
preisen, ie, ie to praise
sich pressen to press; to crowd
pro per
probieren to try
die **Produktion** (*-tsjon*) production
der **Professor,** -oren professor
der **Prolog,** -e prologue
die **Prothese,** -n artificial leg
das **Prozent,** -e percent
der **Prozeß** (*-sses*), -sse trial
prüfen to check; to test; to try;
— **auf** (*acc.*) to test for
die **Prüfung,** -en test
der **Psychologe** (-n), -n psychologist
der **Puls,** -e pulse
punkt exactly; promptly; punctual; — **eins** one o'clock sharp
pünktlich punctual, prompt
die **Pünktlichkeit** punctuality
das **Puppenspiel,** -e marionette
theater
putzen to clean; to polish; **sich**
(*dat.*) —, to clean (one's) . . .

Q

die **Quelle, -n** source
die **Querstraße, -n** cross street; intersection

R

der **Rachen,** — jaws
das **Rad, ̈er** wheel; bicycle
radeln (*s*) to ride a bicycle
das **Radio, -s** radio; **im** —, on the radio
der **Radler,** — bicyclist
der **Rand, ̈er** edge; rim
der **Rang, ̈e** rank; **erster** —, first balcony
rasch fast; quick
rasen (*s*) to race
der **Rasierapparat, -e** razor
das **Rasieren** shaving
sich rasieren to shave
die **Rasierklinge, -n** razor blade
der **Rasierpinsel,** — shaving brush
die **Rasierseife, -n** shaving soap
der **Rat** council; advice
raten, ie, a (ä) (*dat.*) to advise
ratsam advisable
rauben to rob
der **Rauch** smoke
rauchen to smoke
'rauf-schicken to send up
'rauf-senden* to send up
rechnen to figure
die **Rechnung, -en** bill; check
recht right; **ist es Ihnen so —?** is that the way you like it? does that suit you? — **haben*** to be right; — **dünn** rather thin; — **früh** quite early; — **gut** rather (*or* quite) well; — **viele** a good many
die **Rechte** (*adj. decl.*) right hand
rechts to the right
der **Rechtsanwalt, ̈e** attorney at law
rechtzeitig in time
die **Rede, -n** speech; **die — sein*** **von** (*dat.*) to be a question of, to make mention of; **bei mir ist die — von** I talk about

reden to speak; — **über** (*acc.*) to speak about
die **Rederei, -en** empty talk
die **Redeweise, -n** idiom
redlich decent, sincere
der **Redner,** — speaker
die **Regel, -n** rule; **in der** —, as a rule
der **Regen,** — rain
der **Regenmantel, ̈** raincoat
die **Registrierkasse, -n** cash register
regnen to rain
das **Reich, -e** realm
reichen to reach; to hand (to); to last; to go far (*or* a long way); **Feuer** —, to offer (a) light; **die Hand** —, to shake hands
der **Reifen,** — tire
die **Reihe, -n** row; **an der — sein*** (*s*) to be one's turn, to be next
rein clean; veritable (*as in Chapter 24*)
'rein-gehen* (*s*) to go in; to take
reinigen to clean
die **Reise, -n** trip; journey; **gute — bon voyage,** (have a) good trip
das **Reisebüro, -s** travel bureau
reisen (*s*) to travel
der **Reisescheck, -s** traveler's check
das **Reißbrett, -er** drawing-board
reißen, riß, gerissen to tear; **aus dem Munde** —, to take out of one's mouth
reiten, ritt, geritten (*s*) to ride (on horseback)
der **Reiz, -e** charm
reizlos unattractive
der **Rektor, -oren** rector, chancellor
rennen, rannte, gerannt (*s*) to run
die **Reparatur, -en** repair
die **Reparaturwerkstatt, ̈en** repair shop
reparieren to repair
resigniert resigned
der **Rest, -e** rest
retten to save
der **Rettich, -e** radish

die **Rettung, –en** rescue; salvation
der **Revolver, —** revolver
das **Rezept, –e** prescription
der **Rhein** Rhine (*river*)
der **Rhythmus (—), –men** rhythm
sich richten nach (*dat.*) to be guided by
der **Richter, —** judge
der **Richtertisch, –e** judge's bench
richtig right, correct; **— stellen** to (re)set
richtig-stellen to correct
die **Richtung, –en** direction
riechen, o, o to smell; **— nach** (*dat.*) to smell of
riesig tremendous
der **Rinderbraten, —** roast beef
ringen, a, u to struggle; **— nach** (*dat.*) to struggle for
die **Ringstraße** Ring Street
der **Ritter, —** knight
rollen (*s*) to roll; **— über** (*acc.*) to roll across
die **Rose, –n** rose
das **Röslein, —** little rose
rösten to roast, to fry
rot red
rothaarig red-haired
die **Rötung, –en** reddening; **eine — im Hals haben*** to have an inflamed throat
die **Rubrik, –en** column
der **Rücken, —** back
die **Rückkehr** return
rückwärts backward
das **Rückwärts** (a) going back-(ward)
der **Ruf** reputation; **in schlechtem — stehen*** to have a bad reputation
rufen, ie, u to call; to shout
die **Ruhe** calm; rest; quiet; **in —,** calmly
der **Ruhetag, –e** day of rest
ruhig calm; quiet
sich rühmen to boast
rund round; **— um die Welt** around the world
der **Rundfunk** radio; **im —,** on the radio
die **Rundreisekarte, –n** roundtrip ticket

(das) **Rußland** Russia
rüstig vigorous
rutschen (*s*) to slide

S

's = es; das
die **Sache, –n** thing, matter
säen to sow
die **Sage, –n** legend
sagen to say, to tell; **— über** (*acc.*) to say about; **sich —,** to say to oneself; **es sich nicht zweimal — lassen** not to wait to be told twice
die **Salzkartoffel, –n** boiled potato
sanitär sanitary
die **Sanitätswache, –n** first aid station
satt having enough (of)
der **Sattel, ⸗** saddle
sattelfest firm in the saddle
satteln to saddle
der **Sattler, —** saddle maker
der **Satz, ⸗e** sentence
der **Schädel, —** skull; head
schaden (*dat.*) to harm
schaffen to do; to manage
der **Schaffner, —** conductor
schalten to switch; **— auf** (*acc.*) to switch to
der **Schalter, —** switch; (ticket) window
sich schämen to be ashamed
die **Schande, –n** disgrace
die **Schar, –en** flock
der **Schatten, —** shadow
das **Schaufenster, —** display window
das **Schaukelpferd, –e** rocking horse
das **Scheckkonto, –tos** *or* **–ten** checking account
die **Scheibe, –n** window (pane); slice
scheiden, ie, ie (*s*) to part, to leave
die **Scheidung, –en** separation
der **Schein** appearance
der **Schein, –e** bill
scheinen, ie, ie to shine; to seem; to appear; to look
der **Scheinwerfer, —** head light

239

schelten, a, o (i) (*acc.*) to reproach; to chide; to call (names)
scheu shy
schicken to send; **ins Haus — lassen*** to (have) deliver(ed); — **nach** (*dat.*) to send for
das **Schicksal, -e** fate
schießen, schoß, geschossen to shoot
das **Schiff, -e** ship
schildern to describe
schimpfen to scold; to curse; to complain
der **Schirm, -e** umbrella
der **Schlaf** sleep
der **Schlafanzug, ⸗e** pajama
schlafen, ie, a (ä) to sleep
schlaflos sleepless
schlagen, u, a (ä) to strike, to pound; to roll (*of drums*); **in Fesseln —**, to cast in fetters; **er schlug mit der Faust auf den Tisch** he struck his fist on the table; **das Herz schlug ihr zum Halse** her heart was in her mouth; **wieviel es geschlagen hat** what the score is
die **Schlagzeile, -n** headline
die **Schlange, -n** snake; **— stehen*** to stand in line
schlank slender
schlecht bad
schleichen, i, i (*s*) to creep stealthily
der **Schlepper, —** tractor
schließen, schloß, geschlossen to conclude; to close
schließlich after all
der **Schlips, -e** bow tie
das **Schloß (-sses), ⸗sser** lock; **ins — werfen*** to throw (*or* slam) shut
der **Schlosser, —** locksmith
schluchzen to sob
der **Schluß (-sses)** end; **es ist —,** that is enough
der **Schlüssel, —** key
das **Schlüsselein, —** small key
schmal narrow
schmecken to taste; to enjoy
schmeißen, schmiß, geschmissen to throw; to slam
der **Schmerz (-ens), -en** pain

schnappen to snap; **nach Luft —,** to gasp for air
schnarren to snap
schneiden, schnitt, geschnitten to cut
der **Schneider, —** tailor
schnell fast; quick
der **Schnellzug, ⸗e** fast train; express
der **Schnurrbart, ⸗e** mustache
der **Schöffe (-n), -n** juror
der **Schokoladenpudding, -s** chocolate pudding
schon already; in itself; all right; yet; — **am nächsten Tag** the very next day; — **einmal** ever; — **gut** very well; — **lange** for some time; **das —,** grant that
schön nice; pretty
das **Schönste** (*adj. decl.*) (the) most beautiful thing
schrecklich terrible
der **Schrei, -e** scream
schreiben, ie, ie to write
das **Schreiben, —** letter
der **Schreibtisch, -e** desk
schreien, ie, ie to shout; to scream; — **auf** (*acc.*) to shout at; **—d** screaming
das **Schreien** shouting
der **Schritt, -e** step; **in gleichem — und Tritt** in the same step; keeping in step with
schüchtern timid
schuften to work hard; to slave
der **Schuh, -e** shoe
der **Schuhkrem, -en** *or* **-s** shoe polish
der **Schuhladen, ⸗** shoe store
die **Schuhwerkstatt, ⸗en** shoe repair (*or* cobbler) shop
die **Schuld, -en** debt
schulden to owe
schuldig guilty (of)
die **Schule, -n** school; **die höhere —,** secondary school; **in der —,** at school
der **Schüler, —** pupil
der **Schuppen, —** shed
der **Schuster, —** shoemaker
die **Schusterwerkstatt, ⸗en** shoe (repair) (*or* cobbler) shop
der **Schüttelfrost** shivers; chills

der **Schutzmann,** –leute policeman
der **Schwamm,** ⸚e sponge
schwanken to sway
schwarz black
schwarzgekleidet dressed in black
schwarzhaarig black-haired
schweigen, ie, ie to be silent
der **Schweinebraten,** — roast pork
die **Schweiz** Switzerland
der **Schweizerkäse,** — Swiss cheese
die **Schwelle,** –n threshold
schwer hard; serious; heavy
schwerhörig hard of hearing
die **Schwester,** –n sister
die **Schwiegermutter,** ⸚ mother-in-law
der **Schwiegersohn,** ⸚e son-in-law
schwierig difficult
schwimmen, a, o (s) to swim; —d swimming
schwirren (s) to whir; **einem durch den Kopf** —, to run through one's mind
schwören, u, o to swear
die **See,** –n sea; **an die** — **fahren*** (s) to go to the seashore
die **Seele,** –n soul
der **Seelendoktor,** –ǫren mind doctor
seelisch emotional, spiritual
die **Seereise,** –n sea voyage
der **Seetang** seaweed
das **Segel,** — sail
der **Segen,** — blessing
sehen, a, e (ie) to see; to look; **in den Spiegel** —, to look in the mirror; — **auf** (acc.) to look at; — **nach** (dat.) to look at
das **Sehnen** longing
sehr very
sei see **sein**
die **Seife,** –n soap
sein, war, gewesen (ist) (s) to be; **es ist mir, als ob** I feel as if
seit since
die **Seite,** –n side; page; **auf die andere** — **drehen** to turn over on the other side; **von unberufener** —, by some unauthorized (or "helpful") person
die **Seitenstraße,** –n side street

der **Sekretär,** –e secretary
selbst even; — **ich** even I; **ich** —, I myself; **du** —, you yourself; *etc.*
selbstverständlich obvious; of course
die **Selbstverwaltung,** –en administrative autonomy
selten seldom; rare
die **Seltenheit,** –en rarity
seltsam strange
das **Semester,** — semester
die **Serviette** (*servjęte*), –n napkin
der **Sessel,** — armchair
setzen to set; **an den Mund** —, to put to one's lips; — **über** (acc.) to put in charge of
sich setzen to sit down; to be seated; **sich in Bewegung setzen** to start to move; **sich um** (acc.) **. . . setzen** to be seated by (or around)
seufzen to sigh
der **Seufzer,** — sigh
sicher sure; — (*gen.*) sure of
sicherlich undoubtedly
der **Siebziger** (*adj. decl.*) man in his seventies; **in den** —n in the seventies
siehe da lo and behold
das **Silber** change; silver
das **Silbergeld,** –er silver money; change
singen, a, u to sing; —d singing
sinken, a, u (s) to sink
der **Sinn,** –e sense; **es will mir nicht aus dem** —, I can't get it out of my mind
die **Sitte,** –n custom
der **Sitz,** –e seat
sitzen, saß, gesessen to sit; to fit
die **Sitzung,** –en meeting; session
so so; there; thus; like that; that is the way; —**bald als** as soon as; —**gar** even; — **gegen** around; — **viel** as much
sofort immediately; at once; — **wenn** as soon as
die **Sohle,** –n sole
solch– such
der **Soldat** (–en), –en soldier
das **Soll** debit (*as opposed to* das **Haben** credit)

sollen, sollte, gesollt (soll) to be supposed to (shall)
der **Sommer,** — summer
der **Sommeranzug,** ⁀e summer suit
sonderbar strange
der **Sonderbote** (-n), -n special (delivery) messenger
sondern but; on the contrary
die **Sonne,** -n sun
sonnig sunny
sonst else; or (else); otherwise; usually; — **alles** everything else; — **(noch) etwas** anything else; — **noch jemand** anybody else; — **was?** what else? **wie** —, as usual
die **Sorge,** -n worry, care; —**n haben* um** (*acc.*) to worry about; **sich** —**n machen um** (*acc.*) to worry about
sorgen für (*acc.*) to worry about; to care for; **für die Ordung** — to maintain order
soviel that (*or* as *or* so) much
sozusagen so to say
sparen to save
der **Spargel,** — asparagus
spärlich scarcely; sparse; — **bemessen** a tight fit
der **Sparpfennig,** -e saving(s)
der **Spaß,** ⁀e jest; **es hat mir viel** — **gemacht** I enjoyed it very much
spät late; —**er** later
spazieren (*s*) to walk; to go for a walk
die **Speisekarte,** -n menu
speisen to dine, to eat
der **Sperling,** -e sparrow
der **Spiegel,** — mirror
das **Spiegelei,** -er fried egg
das **Spiel,** -e game; play
spielen to play
der **Spieler,** — gambler
der **Spinat,** -e spinach
das **Spital,** ⁀er hospital
die **Sprache,** -n language
sprechen, a, o (i) to speak; — **über** (*acc.*) to talk about; **man kam auf alte Zeiten zu** —, the conversation turned to the old days; they got to talking about

the old days; (*telephone operator*) **Sprechen Sie!** Go ahead!
die **Sprechstunde,** -n office hour
springen, a, u (i) (*s*) to jump; to leap; to run
die **Sprosse,** -n rung
der **Sprudel** (club) soda
der **Sprung,** ⁀e jump; (a) stone's throw
die **Spur,** -en trace; **keine** —, not at all
der **Staat,** -en state
staatlich (*pertaining to*) state
der **Staatsanwalt,** ⁀e district attorney
der **Staatsbeamte** (-n), -n state civil servant
der **Staatsmann,** ⁀er statesman
die **Stadt,** ⁀e city
das **Städtchen,** — town
der **Stadtkoffer,** — attaché case
der **Stadtrand,** ⁀er outskirts of town
der **Stamm,** ⁀e (tree) trunk, stem
stammen aus (*dat.*) to stem from; to come from
der **Stand,** ⁀e class, estate
ständig constant; steady; permanent
die **Stange,** -n rod; **fertig von der** —, ready-made
stark strong; severe
statt instead
stechen, a, o (i) to prick
stecken to put; to stick
stehen, stand, gestanden to be; to stand; **in schlechtem Ruf** —, to have a bad reputation; **Schlange** —, to stand in line; **vor der Tür** —, to be just around the corner; **es steht in der Zeitung** the paper says; **es steht mir frei** I am at liberty; **wie steht der Dollar heute?** what is the rate of the dollar today? **wie steht es mit der Kunst?** what is the state of art? **wie stehen Sie zu Goethes 'Faust'?** what are your views on Goethe's 'Faust'?
stehen-bleiben* (*s*) to stop; **das Herz bleibt mir stehen** my heart stops beating

242

das **Stehenbleiben** stop(ping)
stehen-lassen* to leave standing
stehlen, a, o (ie) to steal; **er ist mir gestohlen worden** it was stolen from me
steigen, ie, ie (*s*) to climb; to rise; to mount; to increase; — **aus** (*dat.*) to climb out of, to get off
das **Stelldichein** rendezvous, date; **zum — gehen*** (*s*) to go on a date
die **Stelle, -n** place; spot
stellen to put; to set (*of clocks*); — **bei** (*dat.*) to set by; **sich —**, to pretend; to place oneself; **sich unter die Brause —**, to step into the shower; **wie stellt er sich dazu?** what is his attitude concerning it?
die **Stellung, -en** position; job
stempeln to stamp; — **gehen*** (*s*) to collect unemployment insurance
sterben, a, o (i) (*s*) to die
sterblich mortal
das **Steuer, —** (steering) wheel
still quiet; silent
still-stehen* to stand still
die **Stimme, -n** voice
stimmen to check; to be correct
die **Stirn, -en** forehead
der **Stock, ⸚e** cane; stick; floor; **im ersten —**, on the second floor
stockheiser completely hoarse
der **Stoff, -e** material; cloth
stöhnen to groan
stolpern (*s*) to stumble
stoppen to stop
das **Stopplicht, -er** stop light
stören to disturb, to distress
stoßen, ie, o (ö) to kick; to push; — **auf** (*acc.*) to come (suddenly) upon
die **Strafe, -n** punishment; penalty; sentence
das **Strafgesetzbuch, ⸚er** penal code
der **Strahl, -en** beam; ray; jet
die **Straße, -n** street; (street) block; **auf der —**, in the street
die **Straßenbahn, -en** streetcar; **mit der —**, by streetcar

der **Straßenbahnwagen, —** streetcar
die **Straßenbeleuchtung, -en** street lights
die **Straßenecke, -n** street corner
der **Straßengraben, ⸚** ditch
die **Straßenseite, -n** side of the street
streben to strive
der **Streich, -e** blow; trick
der **Streit, -e** quarrel; battle; **die Trommel schlug zum —e** the battle drums were rolling
streiten, stritt, gestritten to quarrel; **sich — über** (*acc.*) to argue over
streng severe
streuen to strew
stricken to knit
das **Strickzeug, -e** knitting; knitting bag
das **Stroh** straw
der **Strohhut, ⸚e** straw hat
der **Strom, ⸚e** river; **ein — von Gedanken** a flood of thoughts
strömen (*s*) to stream
der **Strumpf, ⸚e** stocking
das **Stück, -e** piece; **ein — (des Weges)** a bit (of the way)
der **Student (-en), -en** student
der **Studienrat, ⸚e** high school teacher
studieren to study
das **Studium, -dien** study
der **Stuhl, ⸚e** chair
stumm silent; mute
die **Stunde, -n** hour
stündlich every hour
stürzen (*s*) to crash; to dash
stutzen to trim
stützen to support; to hold up
subjektiv subjective
suchen to seek
sündig sinful; mortal
surren to spin; to buzz

T

die **Tablette, -n** tablet, pill
der **Tag, -e** day; **am hellen —**, in broad daylight; **schönen guten —**, (*I bid you*) a pleasant

243

good day; **von — zu —**, from
day to day; **eines -es** one day;
drei -e lang for three days
der **Tagesbeginn** daybreak
das **Tagesgericht, -e** special
(*meal*) of the day
täglich a day, daily
taktlos tactless
der **Taler, —** (*an old silver coin
from which derives the term*) dollar
der **Tank, -s** tank
die **Tankstelle, -n** gasoline station
der **Tankwart, -e** gasoline station
attendant
die **Tante, -n** aunt
der **Tanz, ⁼e** dance
tanzen to dance
tapfer brave
die **Tasche, -n** pocket
die **Taschenlampe, -n** flashlight
die **Taschenuhr, -en** pocket
watch
die **Tasse, -n** cup
die **Tat, -en** deed; action; **in
der —**, in fact
tätig active; **im Finanzamt —
sein*** (*s*) to work in the Office of
the Treasury
tatsächlich actually
die **Tauglichkeit** suitability
tausenderlei a thousand kinds of
der **Tee, -s** tea
der **Teil, -e** part
der **Teilhaber, —** partner
das **Telefon, -e** telephone
die **Telefonistin, -nen** telephone
operator
das **Telegramm, -e** telegram
das **Telegrammformular, -e**
telegram blank
der **Teller, —** plate; **die — waschen*** to do dishes
das **Tellerwaschen** washing of
dishes
das **Tempo** tempo; speed
der **Test, -e** test
teuer expensive
der **Teufel, —** devil
teuflisch devilish
das **Theater, —** theater
die **Theaterkasse, -n** theater
ticket office
die **Theke, -n** counter

die **Theorie, -n** theory
das **Thermometer, —** thermometer
tief deep
die **Tiefe, -n** depth
das **Tier, -e** animal
die **Tierzucht** animal husbandry
der **Tisch, -e** table; **zu —**, at
table (*or* dinner)
der **Titel, —** title
die **Tochter, ⁼** daughter
die **Todesursache, -n** cause of
death
die **Tomate, -n** tomato
der **Ton, ⁼e** tone; sound
tot dead
töten to kill
der **Totenschein, -e** death certificate
tragen, u, a (ä) to carry; to
wear; to bear; **sich . . . tragen**
to wear
die **Träne, -n** tear
träumen to dream
träumerisch dreamily
traurig sad
die **Traurigkeit** sadness
treffen, traf, getroffen (trifft)
to hit (the mark); **Maßnahmen —**, to take measures; **sich
— mit** (*dat.*) to meet with
der **Treibstoff, -e** fuel
die **Treppe, -n** stair(s)
treten, a, e (tritt) (*s*) to step;
— an (*acc.*) to step up to; **— zu**
(*dat.*) to step up to, to join
treu (*dat.*) true (to)
trinken, a, u to drink
der **Tritt, -e** step
das **Trittbrett, -er** running board;
platform (step)
sich trocknen to dry
die **Trommel, -n** drum
trotz in spite of
trotzdem in spite of the fact
trotzig obstinate
der **Trotzkopf, ⁼e** pighead
trübe dull
trübsinnig melancholy
die **Tugend, -en** virtue
sich tummeln to romp
tun, tat, getan (tut) to do; **—
auf** (*acc.*) to put on; **es tut mir**

244

leid I am sorry; **es ist um ihn getan** he is done for
die **Tür, -en** door; **vor der — stehen*** to be just around the corner; **zur — herein-treten*** (s) to walk in the door
die **Türkei** Turkey
der **Turm, ⁼e** tower
die **Turmuhr, -en** tower clock

U

übel evil; ill; **einem — werden*** (s) to feel sick
über over; about; across; **heute — acht Tage** a week from today
überall everywhere
überdurchschnittlich above average
überfallen* to attack
überhaupt altogether; **— erst** actually only; **— nicht** not at all
überholen to overtake
die **Überlandsfahrt, -en** ride in the country; cross-country trip
überleben to survive
überlegen to reflect
übermorgen day after tomorrow
überqueren to cross
überraschen to surprise
überreichen to hand to
überstehen* to get over
überwinden, a, u to overcome; to defeat
überzeugt convinced
übrigens by the way
die **Uhr, -en** watch; clock; o'clock; **fünf —,** five o'clock; **geht die — genau?** does the watch keep time? is your watch accurate? **wieviel — ist es?** what time is it?
um in order to; around; for; **— alles in der Welt** by all that is dear to you; **— sieben Uhr** at seven o'clock
sich um-blicken to look back
um-drehen to turn round; **sich — nach** (dat.) to turn (one's head) to look at, to follow with one's eyes
um-fahren* to run over
umfahren* to skirt

die **Umgebung** surroundings, environs
umher-wandern (s) to wander about
umkehrbar retrievable
um-lernen to relearn
der **Umriß (-sses), -sse** outline
um-satteln to change one's trade, etc.
die **Umschweife** (pl.) fuss; talk
sich um-sehen* to look back; to turn around; **— nach** (dat.) to look around for
umso all the (more)
umsonst in vain; for nothing
der **Umstand, ⁼e** circumstance; **unter Zubilligung mildernder Umstände** in view of extenuating circumstances
um-steigen* (s) to change (trains, etc.)
die **Umwelt** world (about)
um-wenden* to turn around; **sich — nach** (dat.) to turn (one's head) to look at
um . . . willen for the sake of
unauffällig unobtrusive
unbarmherzig merciless
unbekannt unfamiliar, strange
unberufen unauthorized; **von -er Seite** by some unauthorized (or "helpful") person
und and
undeutlich indistinct
unendlich infinite
unerbittlich relentless
unergründlich unfathomable; obscure
unerhört outrageous, unheard of
unerwartet unexpected
ungeduldig impatient
ungefähr approximately
ungemütlich uncomfortable, unpleasant; **einem — zu Mute sein*** (s) to be uncomfortable, to be uneasy
das **Ungetüm, -e** monster
ungewöhnlich unusual
das **Unglück** misfortune
unglücklich unlucky, unhappy, misfortunate
unglücklicherweise unfortunately

unheimlich uncanny; uncomfortable

die Universität, –en university; die Universitätsstadt university town

unmittelbar direct

unmöglich impossible

unordentlich disorderly

die Unordnung disorder

unparteiisch impartial

unregelmäßig irregular

unruhig restless

unschuldig innocent

unsichtbar invisible

der Unsinn nonsense

unsterblich immortal

das Unsterbliche (adj. decl.) immortal part

untätig inactive; idle

unten below; downstairs; down; bottom

unter among; under; amidst; ganz — uns just between us

unterbrechen* to interrupt

untereinander among one another

der Untergebene (adj. decl.) subordinate

unterhalten* to entertain; to chat; sich —, to entertain one another; to amuse oneself

das Unternehmen, — enterprise

unterrichten to instruct

der Unterschied, –e difference

unterschreiben* to sign

untersuchen to examine

unumkehrbar irretrievable

unvoreingenommen unprejudiced

unwiderstehlich irresistable

unwillkürlich involuntarily; accidentally

die Urgroßeltern (pl.) great-grandparents

der Urgroßvater, ⸚ great-grandfather

der Urlaub, –e leave; in —, on leave (or vacation); in — gehen* (s) to go on vacation

die Ursache, –n cause

das Urteil, –e verdict; judgment

usw = und so weiter and so forth

V

der Vater, ⸚ father

väterlicherseits on the father's side

die Vaterstadt, ⸚e home town

der Ventilator, –oren ventilator

die Verabredung, –en date; appointment

sich verabschieden to bid adieu; to say good-bye

veranstalten to arrange (for)

die Verantwortung, –en responsibility

der Verband, ⸚e bandage

verbessern to improve; to correct

verbinden* to connect

die Verbindung, –en connection

der Verbrauch consumption

verbrauchen to use; to consume

verbringen* to spend

verdächtig (dat.) suspicious to

verdammt cursed

verdienen to deserve

verdient deserved

verdrießlich annoying; annoyed; vexing

vereint united

verfahren* (s) (intrans.) to proceed; — (h) (trans.) to drive into a rut

das Verfahren, — trial; proceedings

verfolgen to pursue; sich verfolgt fühlen to feel that one is being followed

der Vergaser, — distributor

vergebens in vain

vergeblich in vain

das Vergehen, — crime; transgression

vergehen* (s) to pass

vergessen, vergaß, vergessen (vergißt) to forget

das Vergnügen, — pleasure

vergnügt elated; in good humor

vergüten to compensate

das Verhältnis (–sses), –sse condition

verheiratet married

verkaufen to sell

der Verkäufer, — salesman, (sales) clerk

die **Verkäuferin, -nen** salesgirl
verkünden to proclaim; to announce
verlangen to demand
verlängern to lengthen
die **Verlängerung, -en** extension
verlassen* to leave; **sich — auf** (*acc.*) to rely on
verlegen embarrassed
verleihen* to award
verlernen to forget
verlieren, o, o to lose
vermehren to increase
vermerken to note down
vermieten to let, to rent
das **Vermögen** ability; wealth
verneinen to deny
die **Veröffentlichung, -en** publication
verraten* to betray; to say; to indicate
verrinnen, a, o (*s*) to pass; to slip away; to tick away
versagen to deny; to fail
versäumen to miss
verschicken to send away
verschieden different; **Verschiedenes** different thing(s)
verschlingen, a, u to swallow up; to wolf
verschreiben* to prescribe
verschwenden to waste
verschwinden, a, u (*s*) to disappear
versichern (*dat.*) to assure; **sich —**, to assure oneself
versorgen to provide (for)
sich verspäten to be late
die **Verspätung, -en** lateness; **— haben*** to be late (*of trains*)
versprechen* to promise
verstehen* to understand; **— von** (*dat.*) to understand about
verstellen to turn back; **sich —**, to pretend
verstohlen furtive
verstopft stopped up; plugged
verstummt silent
der **Versuch, -e** attempt
versuchen to try
der **Vertrag, ⸚e** contract
verurteilen to convict

vervielfältigen to duplicate; to multiply
der **Verwandte** (*adj. decl.*) relative
verweilen to tarry
verwenden* to employ, to use
die **Verwendung** use
verwirrt confused
verwunden to injure; to wound
verwundert surprised
verzeihen, ie, ie to pardon (*a person*)
die **Verzierung, -en** decoration; adornment
verzweifelt desperate
die **Verzweiflung** desperation; **voller —**, in desperation
viel much; **—e** many
vielfach often
der **Vielfraß, -e** glutton
vielleicht perhaps
vielmals many (times); frequently
viermal four times
das **Viertel, —** quarter
die **Viertelstunde, -n** quarter hour
vierundzwanzigjährig twenty-four years of age
die **Villa, Villen** villa
der **Vogel, ⸚** bird
das **Volk, ⸚er** people; nation
das **Volksbuch, ⸚er** chapbook
voll full; **—er Verzweiflung** in desperation
völlig complete(ly)
die **Vollstreckung, -en** execution
von of; from; by; about
vor ahead; before; in front of; **— drei Jahren** three years ago; **— der Tür stehen*** to be just around the corner
voran ahead; **die Kapelle —**, preceded by the band
voran-kommen* (*s*) to advance
voraus: im —, in advance
voraus-bestellen to reserve; to make (*or* have) a reservation
voraus-setzen to presuppose
voraussichtlich so far as one can tell
vorbei gone; past
vorbei-gehen* (*s*) **an** (*dat.*) to walk past

247

vorbei-greifen* to reach past; to miss

vorbei-kommen* (*s*) **an** (*dat.*) to come by

vor-bereiten to prepare

das **Vorderbein, -e** front leg

voreingenommen gegen (*acc.*) prejudiced against

der **Vorfahr** (**-en**), **-en** ancestor

vor-fahren* (*s*) to drive up; to drive ahead

der **Vorfall,** ⸗**e** accident; occurrence

die **Vorgartentür, -en** front gate

vor-gehen* (*s*) to walk ahead; to be fast (*of clocks*)

der **Vorgesetzte** (*adj. decl.*) superior; boss

vorgestern the day before yesterday

vor-haben* to intend to do

vorhin previously; **von —,** from before

vorig- last

vor-kommen* (*s*) to occur; **es kommt mir vor** it seems to me

das **Vorleben** past

vor-lesen* to read to

die **Vorlesung, -en** lecture (*or* course)

die **Vorliebe, -n** preference

der **Vormittag, -e** morning, forenoon

vorn in front

der **Vorname** (**-ns**), **-n** first name

vornehm distinguished

vor-nehmen* to make (*of repairs*)

vor-schlagen* to propose

die **Vorsicht** caution

vorsichtig careful

die **Vorstadt,** ⸗**e** suburb

vor-stellen to introduce, to present; to set ahead; **sich —,** to introduce oneself

die **Vorstellung, -en** performance

der **Vorteil, -e** advantage

vorüber-gehen* (*s*) **an** (*dat.*) to walk past

vorvorgestern three days ago

vorwärts forward

das **Vorwärts** going forward

vor-zeigen to show; to present (*for inspection*)

vor-ziehen* to prefer

das **Vorzimmer, —** anteroom; hall(way)

der **Vorzug,** ⸗**e** preference; advantage

der **Vulkan, -e** volcano

W

wach awake

wachsen, u, a (ä) (*s*) to grow

die **Wachstuchtasche, -n** (*wax cloth*) waterproof bag

der **Wachtmeister, —** (police) sergeant; (police) officer

wackeln to wobble

der **Wagen, —** cart; car; wagon; carriage

wählen to dial; to elect

wahr true

während during; while; **— der Fahrt** en route

wahrscheinlich probable

der **Wald,** ⸗**er** forest; woods

die **Wand,** ⸗**e** wall

wandern (*s*) to wander; to hike

wann when

warm warm

die **Wärme** warmth

warnen to warn; **— vor** (*dat.*) *or* **gegen** (*acc.*) to warn against

warten to wait; **— auf** (*acc.*) to wait for; **auf sich — lassen*** to keep one waiting

das **Wartezimmer, —** waiting room

warum why

was what; which; that which; whatever; **— machst du** how are you; **— für** what sort of; **— sonst** what else

die **Waschanlage, -n** car wash

(sich) waschen, u, a, (ä) to wash

das **Wasser, —** water; **ins — gehen*** (*s*) to jump in the lake (*etc.*), to drown oneself

das **Wasserfest, -e** water festival

der **Wasserstrahl, -en** jet of water

wechseln to change

wecken to wake; to awaken

der **Wecker, —** alarm clock

der **Weg, -e** way; road

weg away

wegen on account of; — **Diebstahls bestraft** convicted of theft

weg-nehmen* to take away

weg-reißen* to tear (or whisk) away

das **Weh** woe; — **und Ach** groaning and moaning

sich **wehren** to defend oneself; to resist

sich **weh tun*** to hurt oneself

weich soft

weichen, i, i (s) to yield

weichgekocht soft boiled

sich **weigern** to hesitate

weil because

der **Wein, -e** wine; die **Weinlese, -n** vintage, gathering the grapes

weinen to cry; to weep

das **Weinen** weeping, crying

weinerlich weeping; tearful

die **Weise, -n** manner; **auf welche** —, in what way

weise wise

weisen, ie, ie (auf) (acc.) to point (to)

weiß white

weit wide; far; **so** —, well along; — **über** (acc.) way past; — **und breit** far and wide; **bei** —em by far; **wie in** —er **Ferne** as from far away

weiter farther; further

weiter-fahren* (s) to journey on

weiter-fragen to continue to ask

weiter-gehen* (s) to walk along; **den Weg** —, to continue along the way

weiter-hetzen (s) to hasten on

weiter-klappern (s) to rattle on

weiter-stricken to keep on knitting

weithin far (and away); extensive

weitverbreitet widespread; common; widely known (dispersed or used)

welch which

welcher which; who

die **Welle, -n** wave

die **Welt, -en** world

die **Weltreise, -n** world tour

wem (to) whom

wen whom

wenden, wandte, gewandt to turn; — **nach** (dat.) to turn toward

wenig little

die **Wenigkeit, -en** trifle

wenigstens at least

wenn when(ever); if

wer who; he who; which; whoever

werden, wurde, geworden (wird) (s) to be(come); to grow; — **aus** (dat.) to become of (a person); **wird's bald** will you make it snappy

werfen, a, o (i) to throw; to cast; **die Tür ins Schloß** —, to throw the door shut; **sich** —, to throw oneself; **den Kopf in den Nacken** —, to throw one's head back

der **Werfer, —** thrower

das **Werk, -e** work; deed; **zu** —e **gehen*** (s) to go about (something); die **Werkbank, ⁻e** workbench

werken to labor

die **Werkstätte, -n** (work) shop

der **Werktag, -e** workday

werktätig working

das **Werkzeug, -e** tool

der **Wert, -e** value

wert worth; worthy of

das **Wesen** nature

wesentlich essential; basic

weshalb why; for what reason

wessen whose

die **Wette, -n** wager

das **Wetter, —** weather

der **Wetterbericht, -e** weather report

das **Wettgebrüll** competing clamor

wichtig important

wie as; like; how; — **ist ihre Nummer** (what is) her (their) number; — **gut** how fortunate

wieder again; — **einmal** once more

wieder-haben* to have back

wiederholen to repeat

wieder-kommen* (s) to come back

das **Wiedersehen** reunion; **auf** —, good-bye

(das) **Wien** Vienna
die **Wiese, –n** meadow
wieso how
wieviel how much; how many;
— **macht das?** how much is it
(*or* that)? **um** — **Uhr?** at what
time? — **Uhr ist es?** what time
is it?
der **Wievielte** (*adj. decl.*) how
manieth; **den** —**n haben wir**
what is the date (today)
wild wild
der **Wille** (**–ns**) will
willkommen heißen* to bid wel-
come
der **Winker,** — turn signal
der **Winter,** — winter
der **Wintermantel,** ⁼ winter coat
wirken to effect; to be effective;
to work
wirklich really; actually
wirr confused
der **Wirt, –e** host; innkeeper
die **Wirtin, –nen** (lady) innkeeper;
landlady
wirtschaftlich economic
wissen, wußte, gewußt (**weiß**)
to know; (can); **Bescheid** —,
to know the facts (*or* one's way
around); **du weißt doch noch**
you (still) remember
die **Witwe, –n** widow
der **Witz, –e** joke
wo where; when
die **Woche, –n** week
das **Wochenende, –n** weekend
der **Wochenlohn,** ⁼**e** weekly wage
(*or* pay)
der **Wochentag, –e** weekday
wogegen against what
wohin where(to); whither
wohl (full) well; probably; perhaps; I wonder; I suppose
das **Wohlgefallen** delight; satisfaction; — **an sich selbst** self-
satisfaction
der **Wohlstand** wealth
wohnen to live; to reside; to
dwell
der **Wohnort, –e** residence; address
die **Wohnung, –en** apartment
die **Wolle** wool

wollen, wollte, gewollt (**will**) to
want to; **will gesehen haben**
claims to have seen
womit with what
wonach after what; according to
what
woran by what
worauf whereupon; on what
woraus of what
worin in which
das **Wort, –e** word (*in context*);
das **Wort,** ⁼**er** word (*out of context*); **einem ins** — **fallen***
(*s*) to interrupt a person, to
break into one's conversation
das **Wörtchen,** — little word; **ein**
— **mitzureden haben*** to have
something to say
wortlos without saying a word
worüber about what
worum for which
wovon of (*or* about) which; of
(*or* about) what
wozu (to) what; for what
das **Wunder,** — miracle
wunderhübsch very lovely
wundersam wonderful
wunderschön exquisite
der **Wunsch,** ⁼**e** wish; **einen** —
haben* to (have a) wish
wünschen to wish
die **Wurst,** ⁼**e** sausage
das **Würstchen,** — sausage; wiener; "hot dog"
die **Wut** rage; fury
wütend furious

X

x-beliebig just any, any given

Z

die **Zahl, –en** number
zahlen to pay; **Kellner,** —!
Waiter, check!
zählen to count; **zehn Jahre** —,
to be ten years old
zahlreich numerous
der **Zahn,** ⁼**e** tooth
der **Zahnarzt,** ⁼**e** dentist

die **Zahnbürste, –n** toothbrush
die **Zahnpasta, –en** toothpaste
die **Zapfanlage, –n** (gasoline) pump (installation)
das **Zeichen, —** sign
zeichnen to draw; to sign
zeigen to show; **die Ampel zeigt grünes Licht** the light turns green; **sich —,** to appear; to show oneself to be; **sich hilfsbereit —,** to be ready to help; **es zeigt sich** it turns out
die **Zeit, –en** time; **in letzter —,** lately; **mit der —,** in time; **nimm dir —,** take your time; **zur —,** at present; **man kam auf alte –en zu sprechen** the conversation turned to the old days
der **Zeitabstand, ⁺e** time interval
die **Zeitansage, –n** (*newscaster's announcement of the*) time signal
die **Zeitkrankheit, –en** modern (stylish) disease; disease of the times
die **Zeitschrift, –en** periodical; magazine
die **Zeitung, –en** newspaper
der **Zeitungsmann, ⁺er** newspaper vendor
die **Zentralheizung, –en** central heating
zerbrechen* to break; **sich den Kopf —,** to wrack one's brain
zerfahren* to ruin (*by driving over*)
zerfallen* (*s*) to fall apart
zerknittern to crumple
zerreißen* to break up
zerschneiden* to cut apart
zertreten* to crush; to trample
der **Zettel, —** slip of paper
der **Ziegel, —** brick
ziehen, zog, gezogen to draw; **in die Länge —,** to draw out; **Nutzen — von** (*dat.*) to profit from
die **Zigarette, –n** cigarette
die **Zigarre, –n** cigar
der **Zigarrenladen, ⁺** cigar store
das **Zimmer, —** room
die **Zimmersuche** apartment hunting

zischen to hiss; to fizzle
zitieren to cite; to quote
zittern to tremble; to shudder
zivilisiert civilized
zögern to hesitate
der **Zoll** inch
zolltechnisch pertaining to (*the technical problem of*) tariff
der **Zorn** anger
zu to; too; **— ihrem Kaffee** with her coffee; **— Abend essen*** to eat supper; **— Ehren** in honor of; **— Hause** at home; **— dieser Zeit** at this time, about that time
zu-bereiten to prepare
die **Zubilligung** consent; **unter — mildernder Umstände** in view of extenuating circumstances
die **Zucht** breeding
der **Zucker** sugar
zu-drücken to squeeze shut
zuerst at first
zufällig by chance; accidentally
zu-flüstern (*dat.*) to whisper to
zufrieden satisfied; contented
die **Zufriedenheit** contentment; satisfaction
der **Zug, ⁺e** train
zu-geben* to admit; to concede
zu-gehen* (*s*) to happen; **lustig —,** to be gay; **— auf** (*acc.*) to head for, to approach
zugleich at the same time
zu-hören (*dat.*) to listen to
der **Zuhörer, —** listener; (*pl.*) audience
zu-kommen* (*s*) **auf** (*acc.*) to come up to, to approach
die **Zukunft** future
zukünftig future
zu-lassen* to admit
zuletzt finally, last(ly), in the end
zum = zu dem; — Frühstück for breakfast; **— Landwirt** being a farmer; **— Teufel** (to) the devil
zu-machen to close
zumindest at least
die **Zündkerze, –n** spark plug
der **Zündschlüssel, —** ignition key
die **Zunge, –n** tongue

zu-nicken (*dat.*) to nod to
zur = zu der
zu-reden (*dat.*) to urge
zurück back
zurück-bringen* to bring back
zurück-fahren* (*s*) to return; to journey back
zurück-geben* to give back
zurückgezogen reserved; — leben to lead a sheltered life
zurück-sehnen to wish back
zurück-sein* (*s*) to be back
zurück-stellen to set back
zurück-weisen* to reject; to turn down
zurück-ziehen* to pull back
zu-rufen* to call out to
zu-sagen (*dat.*) to agree with; es sagt mir zu it suits my taste
zusammen together; etwas Geld — haben* to have saved up some money
zusammen-kommen* (*s*) to come (*or* get) together
zusammen-raffen to gather up; to scoop up; to snatch up; sich —, to pull oneself together
sich zusammen-schließen* to unite; to fuse
zusammen-ziehen* to pull (*or* draw) together; to contract
zu-schicken to send to (*or* over)

zu-sehen* to see to it; to look on, to watch; ich werde schön zuschen I'll just watch
zu-stehen* to belong to
zu-stoßen* (*dat.*) to happen to
zu-tun* to close; kein Auge —, not to sleep a wink
zu-werfen* to slam (shut); ihr einen Blick —, to cast a glance at her
zwanzigmal twenty times
der Zwanzigmarkschein, –e twenty mark bill
zwar to be sure
zweierlei two kinds of
das Zweifamilienhaus, ⁻er two-family house
der Zweifel, — doubt
zweifelhaft questionable; dubious
zweifeln to doubt
das Zweifeln doubt(s)
zweimal twice
zweit– second; eins —er one (ticket) second class; —ens secondly
zwingen, a, u to force; sich —, to force oneself
zwinkern to twitch
zwischen between
das Zwischenexamen, — course (*or* qualifying *or* intermediary) exam

English-German

A

a, an ein; — **bit** etwas; — **few**
ein paar
abide aus-stehen*
able: be —, können*
about (*prep.*) über, um (*acc.*); von
(*dat.*); (*adv.*) ungefähr, etwa;
— **to erupt** vor der Eruption
accident der Zufall, ⁀e; **by** —,
zufällig
acquaintance der Bekannte (*adj.
decl.*); **make the** —, kennen-
lernen
across (*the street*) **from** gegenüber
add hinzu-fügen
adornment die Verzierung, –en
after (*prep.*) nach (*dat.*); — (**having**) (*conj.*) nachdem; **be** —
someone hinter einem her-sein*
(*s*)
afternoon der Nachmittag, –e;
this —, heute nachmittag
again wieder; — **and** —, immer
wieder
against gegen (*acc.*); — **it** dagegen
age die Zeit, –en; das Zeitalter, —;
das Alter, —; **at the** — **of** im
Alter von
ago: years —, vor . . . Jahren
agree with zu-sagen (*dat.*)
ahead of vor (*dat. or acc.*)
air die Luft; **to toss one's head
in the** —, den Kopf in den
Nacken werfen*
alarm der Wecker, —
alcohol der Alkohol, –e
all (= *whole*) ganz; — **ears** ganz
Ohr; (= *everybody*) — **of them**
alle; — **one can do to handle it**
alle Hände voll zu tun haben*;
— (*adj.*) all–; **with** — **his might**
aus Leibeskräften; (= *everything*) alles; — **alone** ganz allein,
ohne Familie
allow lassen*; **be** —**ed** dürfen*
almost fast; beinahe
alone allein
already schon
also auch

although obgleich; obzwar
always immer
American (*person*) der Amerikaner
(*adj. decl.*)
amount to something es zu etwas
bringen*
and und
angrily wütend
annoyed ärgerlich
another ander–
answer beantworten; antworten
(*dat.*); — **the phone** sich am
Telefon melden
any irgend; **not** —, kein
anyone jemand; **not** —, niemand
anything etwas; **not** —, nichts;
not — **else** sonst nichts, weiter
nichts
appear (= *seem*) scheinen*; (= *look
like*) aus-sehen*; (= *make an appearance*) erscheinen* (*s*)
applicant der Bewerber, —
arm der Arm, –e
around um, gegen (*acc.*)
arrive an-kommen* (*s*); — **at** an-
kommen* (*s*) in (*acc.*)
as als; wie; (eben)so; —, (*conj.*)
(*causal*) da; (*temp.*) als, indem,
wie; — **far** —, bis; — **a child**
als Kind; — **a rule** in der
Regel; — **suddenly** ebenso
schnell
ashamed: to be —, sich schämen
ask (= *inquire*) fragen; (= *request*)
— (**for**) bitten* (um) (*acc.*); —
oneself sich fragen; — **questions** Fragen stellen*
at an, auf (*dat. or acc.*); bei, in, zu
(*dat.*); um (*acc.*); — **the age of**
im Alter von; — **the door** an
der Tür; — **home** zu Hause;
— **last** endlich; — **least** wenigstens; — **the moment** in dem
Augenblick; — **once** sofort; —
the sight beim Anblick *or* als
sie . . . ansah; — **supper** beim
Abendbrot; — **the same time**
zugleich; — **times** zuweilen
attaché case der Stadtkoffer, —
attention die Aufmerksamkeit,
–en; **to call** — **to the fact**
aufmerksam machen auf (*acc.*)
aunt die Tante, –n

automobile der Wagen, —; das
Auto, -s

B

bachelor der Junggeselle (–n), -n
back zurück; **hand —,** zurück-
geben*
bad schlecht
bag der Koffer, —
band das Band, ⁻er
bank die Bank, -en
barber der Frisör, -e
barely kaum
bargain der Gelegenheitskauf, ⁻e
be sein* (s); (*pass. aux.*) werden*
(s); **to — acquainted with**
kennen*; **to — after someone**
hinter einem her-sein* (s); **to —
just** (*or* **almost**) **around the
corner** schon vor der Tür stehen*; **to — in love with** verliebt sein* (s) in (*acc.*); **to —
lucky** Glück haben*; **to — passing on the way through** auf
der Durchreise sein* (s); **to —
up** auf-sein* (s); **I am to** ich
soll; **there is** (**are**) es ist (sind),
es gibt
beat schlagen*; **her heart stops
beating** das Herz bleibt ihr
stehen
beautiful wunderschön
because (*coord. conj.*) denn;
(*subord. conj.*) weil, da
become werden* (s)
bed das Bett, -en
before ehe, bevor
beg (**for**) bitten* (um) (*acc.*)
beggar der Bettler, —
begin an-fangen*; beginnen*
behind (*adv.*) hinten; (*prep.*) hinter
(*dat. or acc.*)
believe glauben (*dat. of pers.*);
— in glauben an (*acc.*)
bell die Glocke, -n
belong to gehören (*dat.*); zu-
stehen* (*dat.*)
beside neben (*dat. or acc.*)
besides außer(dem); **— all that**
außerdem
best best-; **—,** (*adv.*) am besten

better besser; **she was —,** (= *im-
proving*) es ging ihr besser
between zwischen (*dat. or acc.*)
bicycle das Rad, ⁻er; das Fahrrad,
⁻er
bicyclist der Radler, —
bill der Schein, -e
birthday party die Geburtstagsfeier, -n
black schwarz; **—haired** schwarzhaarig
blow blasen*; **to — the horn**
hupen; **— out** platzen (s)
boat das Boot, -e; **by —,** mit dem
Schiff
both beide
bottom of the sea der Meeresgrund
bow tie der Schlips, -e; die
Schleife, -n
box der Kasten, ⁻
boy der Knabe (–n), -n
breakfast das Frühstück, -e; **to
—,** frühstücken
breath der Atem; **all out of —,**
ganz außer Atem
breathe atmen; **— in** ein-atmen
breathing a sigh of relief aufatmend
bring bringen*; **— down** herab-
drücken
broad breit; **in — daylight** am
hellen Tage
brown braun
brush bürsten; **to — one's teeth**
sich die Zähne putzen
build bauen
burn brennen*
business das Geschäft, -e; **to
take a — course in high
school** die höhere Handelsschule
besuchen; **—man** der Geschäftsmann, -leute; **— was splendid**
das Geschäft ging glänzend
busy geschäftig
but (*conj.*) aber; (= *on the contrary*) sondern; (*adv.*) dennoch,
doch, jedoch; (= *only*) nur
butcher shop der Fleischerladen, ⁻
buy kaufen; **— oneself a hat**
sich (*dat.*) einen Hut kaufen
by an, von, bei, mit (*dat.*); an
(*acc.*); **— accident** zufällig; —

254

means of mit (*dat.*); durch (*acc.*)

C

call (= *summon*) rufen*; (= *name*) nennen*; (= *telephone*) an-rufen*; — **to one's attention the fact** jemanden darauf aufmerksam machen; **to be —ed** heißen*
calm ruhig
can (= *be able*) können*
can (= *container*) die Dose, –n
candidate der Kandidat (–en), –en
cap die Kappe, –n
car der Wagen, —; das Auto, –s
careful vorsichtig; genau
cart der (kleine) Wagen, —
case der Koffer, —
cause die Ursache, –n; — **of death** die Todesursache, –n
central heating die Zentralheizung, –en
certain gewiß; sicher; **—ly** gewiß; **on a — day** an einem gewissen Tage
change wechseln; aus-wechseln; wenden*
chat plaudern
cheap billig
child das Kind, –er
childhood die Kindheit
chilling kalt
chilly kalt
choice die Auswahl, –en
cigar die Zigarre, –n; — **store** der Zigarrenladen, ⸗
cigarette die Zigarette, –n
civilized zivilisiert
clean rein; **to —,** putzen
clerk der Büroangestellte (*adj. decl.*)
clinic die Klinik, –en
coat der Mantel, ⸗
coated belegt
coffee der Kaffee
coin die Münze, –n
collar der Kragen, —
collect unemployment insurance stempeln gehen* (*s*)
column die Rubrik, –en

comb der Kamm, ⸗e; **to —** kämmen; **to — one's hair** sich (das Haar *or* die Haare) kämmen
come kommen* (*s*); — (*or* **chance**) **along** daher-kommen* (*s*); — **along** (= *be a party to*) mitmachen; — **in** herein-kommen* (*s*); — **with** (*a person*) mitkommen* (*s*) (*dat.*); **it comes over me** es fällt mich an
comfortable gemütlich; bequem; behaglich
company die Gesellschaft, –en; die Begleitung, –en
complain klagen; — **of** klagen über (*acc.*)
concert das Konzert, –e
confident zuversichtlich, mit Zuversicht
confused verwirrt
congratulate gratulieren; — **oneself** sich (*dat.*) gratulieren
consist of bestehen* aus (*dat.*)
content (= *satisfied*) zufrieden
content(s) der Inhalt
continue fort-fahren*; — **to improve** immer wieder verbessern, ständig (= *constantly*) verbessern; — **on one's way** seinen Weg fort-setzen, seines Weges (weiter-)gehen* (*s*)
contract der Vertrag, ⸗e
convinced überzeugt
cook kochen
cordially freundlich
corner die Ecke, –n
correct richtig
cost der Preis, –e
count zählen
country das Land, ⸗er; **in the —,** auf dem Lande; **cross-— trip** die Überlandsfahrt, –en; — **house** die Villa, Villen
county office das Landbezirksamt, ⸗er
courage der Mut
course: take a business —, die höhere Handelsschule besuchen
court das Gericht, –e
courteous höflich
credit der Kredit, –e
cringe sich ducken
cross überqueren

cross-country trip die Überlandsfahrt, –en
crumpled zerknittert
cry schreien*
culture die Kultur, –en
cup die Tasse, –n
curb der Randstein, –e; **at the —,**
am Gehsteig
curl die Locke, –n
cursed verdammt
customary gewöhnlich
customer der Kunde, –n

D

dark dunkel
dark-rimmed mit dunklem Rand
dash up herauf-stürzen (s)
daughter die Tochter, ⸚
dawn das Morgengrauen, die Dämmerung
day der Tag, –e; **every —,** jeden
Tag, von Tag zu Tag; **one —,**
eines Tages; **the old —s** die
alten Zeiten
dear teuer; lieb
death der Tod; **it will be the —**
of me das überlebe ich nicht;
cause of —, die Todesursache,
–n; **— certificate** der Totenschein, –e
decent anständig
decide sich entscheiden*
decision der Entschluß (–sses),
⸚sse; **make (or come to) a —,**
den Entschluß fassen
declare erklären
decoration der Orden, —; die
Verzierung, –en
deed die Tat, –en
deep tief; **the —,** die Tiefe, –n
defiant trotzig
delivered: to have —, ins Haus
schicken lassen*
desperation die Verzweiflung; **in**
—, voller Verzweiflung
die sterben* (s)
different verschieden; **— in their**
silence verschieden in ihrer
Sprache schweigen
diligent fleißig
direction die Richtung, –en

director der Direktor, –oren
disappear verschwinden* (s)
discharge entlassen*
dishwashing das Tellerwaschen
ditch der Straßengraben, ⸚
do machen, tun*; an-fangen*
doctor der Doktor, –oren; der
Arzt, ⸚e
don't we (or you, etc.) nicht
wahr
door die Tür, –en; **—bell** die
Glocke, –n
doubt der Zweifel; **there is no —,**
es besteht kein Zweifel
drag out in die Länge ziehen*
dress (oneself) (sich) kleiden; **to —,**
sich an-ziehen*; **–ed** gekleidet;
dressed in black schwarzgekleidet
dress (= apparel) das Kleid, –er;
(= lady's dress suit) das Jackenkleid, –er; das Kostüm, –e
drive (intrans.) fahren* (s); (trans.)
fahren*
driver's test die Fahrprüfung, –en
drown oneself sich ertränken; ins
Wasser gehen* (s)
drugstore die Drogerie, –n
during während (gen.)
dusk die Abenddämmerung

E

each jeder
ear das Ohr, –en; **all —s** ganz
Ohr
eat essen*; (of animals) fressen*;
— supper zu Abend essen*; **—**
up verschlingen*
edge of town der Stadtrand, ⸚er
egg das Ei, –er
electric elektrisch
else: anything —, sonst etwas;
not anything —, sonst nichts
embarrassed verlegen
employ ein-stellen, an-stellen
employed angestellt; beschäftigt
employee der Angestellte (adj.
decl.)
empty leer; **go —-handed** leer
aus-gehen* (s)
enjoy genießen*; sich schmecken

lassen*; **I (am) enjoy(ing)
my breakfast** das Frühstück
schmeckt mir gut, ich lasse mir
das Frühstück gut schmecken
enough genug
enter herein-kommen* (s)
enthusiastic begeistert
entrance der Eingang, ⸗e
equip with versehen* mit (dat.)
Europe (das) Europa
even eben; sogar; — **before** noch
bevor; — **more heavily** noch
tiefer
ever immer; je; **hardly** —, fast
nie; **not** —, nicht einmal
every jeder; —**one** (or —**body**)
jeder, alle(s); — **four hours** alle
vier Stunden; — **hour** stündlich; —**thing** alles
examine untersuchen
excitement die Aufregung, –en
existence das Dasein, das Leben
expensive teuer
explain erklären
extend credit Kredit geben*
extreme äußerst
eye das Auge, –n

F

face das Gesicht, –er
faint in Ohnmacht fallen* (s); —
into ohnmächtig fallen* (s) in
fall: — **silent** verstummen (s), still
werden* (s)
far weit; — **into the night** bis
spät in die Nacht hinein
fashion die Mode, –n
fast schnell
feel fühlen; **to — about** sich
stellen zu (dat.), stehen* zu (dat.);
**I — that someone is following
me** ich fühle mich verfolgt
fellow der Kerl, –e
fever das Fieber
few wenig; **a —**, einige, ein paar
field das Feld, –er; — **hospital**
das Lazarett, –e
fiery red feuerrot
fill füllen; **(gasoline)** (Benzin)
ein-füllen
finally endlich

find finden*; (= figure out) heraus-
bringen*; — **fault with** aus-
setzen an (dat.); — **oneself
without a roof over one's head**
auf der Straße stehen* (as in
Chapter 17); — **out** ausfindig
machen, heraus-finden*
fine dünn; famos
finger der Finger, —
finished fertig; **to have —**, fertig
sein* (s)
firm die Firma, Firmen
first (zu)erst; **on — sight** auf
den ersten Blick; —**ly** erstens
fish der Fisch, -e; **little —**, das
Fischlein, —
flat tire die Reifenpanne, –n
flock die Schar, –en
flower die Blume, –n
follow folgen (s) (dat.)
food die Nahrung
for (conj.) denn; (prep.) für (acc.);
the train leaves — Hamburg
der Zug fährt nach Hamburg;
— **new jobs** bei Neuanstellungen
force die Kraft, ⸗e
forget vergessen*
free frei; **to speak —ly** frei von
der Leber weg reden
French französisch
fresh frisch
friend der Freund, –e
from von, aus (dat.); — **dawn to
dusk** von früh bis spät
front: in — vorn; vor (dat. or
acc.); — **leg** das Vorderbein, –e
full voll
furious wütend, wütig
future (noun) die Zukunft; (adj.)
zukünftig

G

garden der Garten, ⸗
gas(oline) das Benzin
gas station die Tankstelle, –n;
— **attendant** der Tankwart, –e
gasp for breath nach Luft schnappen, nach Atem ringen*
gather up auf-sammeln
gentleman der Herr (n), –en

German deutsch; — (*person*) der Deutsche (*adj. decl.*)
Germany (das) Deutschland
gesticulate gestikulieren
get (= *become*) werden* (*s*); (= *receive*) bekommen*; (= *come* or *go*) — **to** heran-sein* (*s*); herankommen* (*s*); — **along** auskommen* (*s*); — **along on** auskommen* (*s*) mit; — **to bed** zu Bett gehen* (*s*); — **hungry** Hunger bekommen*, hungrig werden* (*s*); — **on** ein-steigen* (*s*); — **out of** aus-steigen* (*s*); — **thirsty** Durst bekommen*, durstig werden* (*s*); — **up** aufstehen* (*s*); — **to work** sich an die Arbeit machen
girl das Mädchen, —; (**sales**) —, die Verkäuferin, –nen
give geben*; — **courage** Mut machen (*dat.*); **to** — **kind regards** schön grüßen lassen*
glad froh; — **of it** (dessen) froh
glance der Blick, –e
glass das Glas, ̈er
glasses die Brille, –n
gleaming leuchtend
go gehen* (*s*); — **along with** mitmachen; — **empty-handed** leer aus-gehen* (*s*); — **out** aus-gehen* (*s*); — **well with** passen zu (*dat.*)
God der Gott
gold coin die Goldmünze, –n
gone fort
good gut
good-by auf Wiedersehen
grasp fassen
gratefully dankend
gray grau
great groß; **a** — **deal** viel, sehr
green grün
greet grüßen
grippe die Grippe
groan ächzen, jammern, stöhnen
grow (= *wax*) wachsen* (*s*); (= *become*) werden* (*s*); — **pale** erbleichen* (*s*); — **white** weiß werden* (*s*)
guide richten; **to be** —**d by** sich richten nach (*dat.*)

H

hair das Haar, –e
half halb; — **past six** halb sieben
hand die Hand, ̈e; — **back** zurück-geben*; — **over** überliefern; — **it over!** gib es her!
happen geschehen* (*s*)
happy froh; glücklich
hard: — **of hearing** schwerhörig; —**ly** kaum; —**ly ever** kaum, fast nie
hat der Hut, ̈e; — **shop** das Hutgeschäft, –e; **straw** —, der Strohhut, ̈e
have haben*; — **to** müssen*; — **all one can do to handle it** alle Hände voll zu tun haben*; — **on** auf-haben*; — **delivered** ins Haus schicken lassen*; — **a reputation** im Rufe stehen*
head der Kopf, ̈e; der Schädel, —; — **first** kopfüber; —**ache** die Kopfschmerzen (*pl.*); —**light** der Scheinwerfer, —
hear hören
heart das Herz (–ens), –en; **her** — **was in her mouth** die Angst kroch ihr zu Halse; **her** — **stops beating** das Herz bleibt ihr stehen
heave a sigh of relief auf-atmen
heavy-set dick; — **person** der Dicke (*adj. decl.*)
help helfen* (*dat.*); gut-tun* (*dat.*); — **up** in die Höhe helfen*; —**less** hilflos
here hier; da
hero der Held (–en), –en
high hoch; — **school** die höhere Schule
hind leg das Hinterbein, –e
hit on the idea auf den Gedanken kommen* (*s*)
hobby die Liebhaberei, –en
hold halten*; (= *contain*) fassen; — **back one's tears** seinen Tränen Einhalt tun*
home das Haus, ̈er; **at** — zu Hause; —**-fried** gebraten; —(**ward**) nach Hause
horn die Hupe, –n
hot heiß

hour die Stunde, –n
house das Haus, ̈er
how wie; —ever aber
human (being) der Mensch (–en), –en
hurry eilen (s)
husband der Mann, ̈er

I

I ich; — am sorry es tut mir leid
idle untätig
if wenn
impatient ungeduldig
improve verbessern; to continue to —, immer wieder verbessern; ständig (= constantly) verbessern
in auf; in (dat. or acc.); — broad daylight am hellen Tage; — the country auf dem Lande; — front of vor (dat. or acc.); — June im Juni; — short kurz; — vain vergeblich; —to ins, in (acc.)
indeed gewiß, sicher, bestimmt, wirklich, jawohl
indicate zeigen
inexpensive billig
inflamed entzündet; — throat eine Rötung im Hals
information die Auskunft, ̈e; — bureau das Auskunftsbüro, –s
inquire about nach-fragen nach (dat.)
inquiry die Nachfrage, –n; die Erkundigung, –en; to make inquiries about Erkundigungen einziehen* über (acc.)
instead statt dessen
insurance die Versicherung, –en; to collect unemployment —, stempeln gehen* (s)
intend vor-haben*
intersection die Kreuzung, –en
introduce vor-stellen
invention die Erfindung, –en
invite ein-laden*; — over for tea zum Tee bitten*
irretrievable nicht umkehrbar
it: — suits my taste es sagt mir zu; — takes dazu gehört; — takes . . . to be a zum . . . ge-

hört; — will be the death of me das überlebe ich nicht

J

jacket die Jacke, –n; der Rock, ̈e
jaws der Rachen, —
job die Stellung, –en; die Stelle, –n; die Anstellung, –en; new —, die Neuanstellung, –en
juice der Saft, ̈e
jump springen* (s)
just nur; eben; gerade; be — around the corner vor der Tür stehen*; he — arrived er kam eben (or gerade) an; — one nur einer; — speak your mind freely reden Sie nur frei von der Leber weg

K

keep on knitting weiter-stricken
killed in the war gefallen
kind nett, herzlich
knee das Knie, —
knit stricken; keep on knitting weiter-stricken
know (a thing or a fact) wissen*; (a person or a thing) kennen*; — one another sich kennen*; — one's way around sich aus-kennen*; — the score wissen*, wieviel es geschlagen hat

L

lady die Dame, –n
land landen (s)
large groß
last letzt–; —ly zuletzt
late spät; —ly letztens; kürzlich; —r später; —st style die neueste Mode
latter dieser; the former . . . the —, jener . . . dieser
lay legen; — off ab-legen; be-(come) laid off arbeitslos werden* (s)

259

lead a sheltered life zurückgezogen leben

lean sich lehnen; — **against** sich dagegen lehnen; — **out the window** sich aus dem Fenster lehnen

learn lernen

leave (= *depart*) ab-fahren* (*s*); ab-reisen* (*s*); (= *let, forget*) lassen*; (= *forsake*) verlassen*; (= *leave behind*) zurück-lassen*

leg das Bein, –e

lend leihen*

leniency die Milde; das milde Urteil

let lassen*; — **in** ein-lassen*

lie liegen*

life das Leben, —; **to lead a sheltered —,** zurückgezogen leben

light das Licht, –er; (**traffic**) —, die Ampel, –n; **the — is green** die Ampel zeigt grün

like (= *as*) wie; (= *alike*) gleich

like (= *to love*) lieben; mögen; **I — it** es gefällt mir; **I would —,** ich möchte; **I — to read** ich lese gern; **to — oneself very much** sein Leben herzlich lieb haben*

little klein

live (= *exist*) leben; (= *dwell*) wohnen

long lang; — **distance moving van** der Fernlastwagen, —

look (= *see*) sehen*; (= *appear*) aus-sehen*; — **at** an-sehen*; **I'll — at it** ich werde es mir an-sehen; — **back** sich um-blicken; — **for** sich um-sehen* nach (*dat.*); — **in on** nach-sehen* nach (*dat.*); — **over** unter die Lupe nehmen*; — **up** auf-sehen*

loom up sich auf-türmen

Lord der Herrgott

lottery die Lotterie, –n

love (*noun*) die Liebe, –n; **in — with** verliebt in (*acc.*); (*verb*) lieben

lovely hübsch, herrlich

luck das Glück

lucky glücklich; **to be —,** Glück haben*

M

m = **meter** das *or* der Meter, —

machine die Maschine, –n

mail die Post

main office die Direktion (*–tsjon*), –en

make machen; — **a contract** einen Vertrag ab-schließen*; — **a decision** den Entschluß fassen; — **a desperate effort** verzweifelte Versuche machen; — **inquiries about** Erkundigungen ein-ziehen* über (*acc.*); — **minor repairs** kleine Reparaturen vor-nehmen*; — **nothing of it** sich nichts daraus machen; sich über etwas nicht den Kopf zerbrechen*; — **someone a section head** jemand zum Abteilungsleiter machen; — **use of** benutzen; — **the best of it!** mach das Beste daraus!

man der Mann, ⸚er; der Mensch (–en), –en; — **next to a person** der Nebenmann, ⸚er

manager der Direktor, –oren

many viele; — **a** manch–

map die Karte, –n

mark die Mark, —

market der Markt, ⸚e

married verheiratet

marry heiraten

match passen

material das Material, –ien

matter die Sache, –n; **to take —s in one's own hands** die Sache allein in die Hand nehmen*

may darf, dürfen

meager ärmlich

meanwhile inzwischen; indessen

meat ball die Bulette, –n

medicine die Medizin, –en

meet (= *make the acquaintance of*) kennen-lernen

merely nur

merrily lustig

midnight die Mitternacht, ⸚e

might die Macht; **with all his —,** aus Leibeskräften

milk die Milch

minute die Minute, –n

modest bescheiden

260

moment der Augenblick, –e
money das Geld
month der Monat, –e
more mehr; —**over** außerdem
morning der Morgen, —; **in the**
—, am Morgen; —**s** morgens; —
air die Morgenluft; — **paper** die
Morgenzeitung, –en
mother die Mutter, ⸚
motion die Bewegung, –en; **to** —
impatiently eine ungeduldige
Bewegung machen
mouth der Mund, ⸚er
movies das Kino, –s
Mr. der Herr (–n), –en
Mrs. die Frau, –en
much viel
mumble murmeln; — **to oneself**
vor sich hin-murmeln
Munich (das) München
must müssen*
mustache der Schnurrbart, ⸚e

N

name der Name (–ns), –n; **my** —
is ich heiße
narrow schmal
near nah; in der Nähe von (*dat.*);
—**by** nah(e) an (*dat.*); —**est**
nächst
need brauchen
neighbor der Nachbar, –n; —**ing**
benachbart
neighborhood die Nachbarschaft
nephew der Neffe (–n), –n
never nie; —**theless** doch
new neu; — **job** die Neuanstellung, –en
newspaper die Zeitung, –en
next nächst–; **the** — **morning**
am nächsten Morgen
nice nett
night die Nacht, ⸚e; **far into the**
—, bis spät in die Nacht hin-
ein
no nein; (= *not any*) kein; —
longer nicht mehr; — **longer**
any . . . keine . . . mehr; — **one**
(—**body**) keiner, niemand
nod nicken; — **to** zu-nicken (*dat.*)
not nicht; —**a** kein; — **anything**

else sonst nichts, weiter nichts;
— **even** nicht einmal; sogar . . .
nicht
notice bemerken
now nun, jetzt; — **and then** hin
und wieder
nowadays heutzutage
number die Zahl, –en; **a** — **of**
eine Anzahl von

O

obstacle das Hindernis (–sses),
–sse
o'clock Uhr
odd seltsam
of von, aus (*dat.*); (*often rendered
by the gen. case*); — **it** daraus
off ab; — **and on** hin und wieder
offer an-bieten*
office das Büro, –s; — **hour** die
Sprechstunde, –n
old alt
on in, an, auf (*dat. or acc.*); — **first
sight** auf den ersten Blick; — **it**
darauf; — **Monday** am Mon-
tag; — **the radio** im Radio;
— **the way home** auf dem Weg
nach Hause
once einmal
one (*indef. art.*) ein; (*numeral*)
eins; (*pron.*) einer; (*indef. pron.*)
man; — **day** eines Tages; —
another einander
only nur
open offen; **to** —, öffnen
operation die Operation (*-tsjon*),
–en
or oder
orange juice der Apfelsinensaft, ⸚e
order bestellen
ordinary gewöhnlich
other ander–
ought sollen*
out (**of**) aus (*dat.*); — **of breath**
außer Atem; **to go** —, aus-
gehen* (*s*); —**side** draußen
over über (*dat. or acc.*); vorüber;
zu Ende
own eigen
ox der Ochse (–n), –n

P

pack packen
painting das Bild, –er
pair das Paar, –e
paper das Papier, –e
parents die Eltern (*pl.*)
park (*car*) parken
park (= *public garden*) der Lustgarten, ⸗
pass (= *go away*) vergehen* (*s*); —, (*examination*) bestehen*; **to be —ing through** auf der Durchreise sein* (*s*)
past nach (*dat.*); **half — five** halb sechs; **quarter —,** Viertel nach
patient (= *tolerant*) geduldig
patient (*male patient*) der Patient (*-tsjęnt*) (–en), –en; (*female patient*) die Patientin, –nen
pavement das Pflaster, —
pay attention to sich kümmern um (*acc.*)
pedestrian der Fußgänger, —
permit erlauben (*dat.*); **to be —ted** dürfen*
person der Mensch (–en), –en
phone das Telefon, –e; der Apparat, –e
physician der Arzt, ⸗e
pill die Tablette, –n
place in charge of setzen über (*acc.*)
plate der Teller, —
play spielen
please bitte; **to — someone** jemandem gefallen*
point: — to hin-weisen* auf (*acc.*); **— out** zeigen
police die Polizei
popular beliebt
portray dar-stellen
potato die Kartoffel, –n
pray beten; **—er** das Gebet, –e
prepare vor-bereiten; **—d** bereit
pretty hübsch; nett; schön
price der Preis, –e
probably wohl
produce erzeugen
promotion die Beförderung, –en
prove to be sich erweisen* als
psychologist der Psychologe (–n), –n; der „Seelendoktor,“ —oren

pull ziehen*; **—ed down over one's eyes** ins Gesicht gedrückt
pump pumpen; **— (gasoline)** (Benzin) ein-füllen
pupil der Schüler, —
purchase der Kauf, ⸗e
pursue nach-gehen* (*s*) (*dat.*)
put air into tires Reifen auf-füllen

Q

quarter das Viertel, —
question die Frage, –n
quick schnell
quiet still, leise; (= *quietude*) die Ruhe

R

radio das Radio, –s; **on the —,** im Radio
raging wütend
rain der Regen, —
razor das Rasiermesser, —; (*electric*) — der Rasierapparat, –e; **— blade** die Rasierklinge, –n
reach erreichen
read lesen*; **— to** vor-lesen*
ready bereit; fertig
really wirklich
recently vor kurzem
recognize erkennen*
red rot; **—-headed** rothaarig
refer to sich beziehen* auf (*acc.*)
refresh erfrischen
regard: give kind —s schön grüßen lassen*
regret bereuen
reject zurück-weisen*
relax es behaglich haben*; **I —,** ich mache es mir bequem
remain bleiben* (*s*); **— idle** untätig bleiben* (*s*)
remind (of) erinnern (an) (*acc.*)
rent (*verb*) sich (*dat.*) mieten; (*noun*) die Miete, –n
repair reparieren
reply antworten (*dat.*)
reputation der Ruf; **to have a good —,** im guten Rufe stehen*

resolution der Entschluß (–sses),
    ̈sse; **make a —,** den Entschluß
    fassen
resolve sich entscheiden*; —d ent-
    schlossen
restaurant das Gasthaus, ̈er
revolver der Revolver, —
reward belohnen
rhythm der Rhythmus, —men
ribbon das Band, ̈er
rich reich
ride: (*verb*) — **a bicycle** radeln
    (*s*); (*noun*) — **in the country** die
    Überlandsfahrt, –en
right (= *correct*) richtig; (= *opp.
    of left*) rechts; — **away** sofort,
    gleich; — **back** bald (*or* gleich)
    wieder zurück
ring (*intrans.*) klingeln; —, (*intrans.
    and trans.*) läuten; — (= *sound*)
    like klingen* wie
rise auf-stehen* (*s*); —, (*of celestial
    bodies*) auf-gehen* (*s*)
roam wandern (*s*)
roast braten*
rob rauben; berauben
roll (*verb*) drehen, rollen
roll (= *bun*) das Brötchen, —
romp about sich tummeln
room das Zimmer, —
route der Weg, –e
rumble grollen
run laufen* (*s*); **spirits — high**
    es geht hoch her; — **after** nach-
    laufen* (*s*) (*dat.*)
rush eilen (*s*); — **off** davon-
    rasen (*s*)
Russia (das) Rußland

S

sadness die Traurigkeit
sail segeln; — **by boat** mit dem
    Schiff fahren* (*s*)
salary der Lohn, ̈e; **weekly —,**
    der Wochenlohn, ̈e
salesgirl die Verkäuferin, –nen
salesman der Kaufmann, –leute
same: the —, derselbe, dieselbe,
    dasselbe; **at the — time** zu-
    gleich
satisfied zufrieden

save retten
say sagen; — **to oneself** sich (*dat.*)
    sagen; **they are said to** sie
    sollen
scarcely kaum
scatter zerstreuen, herum-streuen
school die Schule, –n
sea das Meer, -e; —**weed** der
    Seetang
seated: to be —, sich setzen, Platz
    nehmen*
second zweit–
secretary die Sekretärin, –nen
secretly insgeheim, heimlich
see sehen*
seem scheinen*; **it seems to me**
    es kommt mir vor
seize fassen
selection die Auswahl, –en
sell verkaufen
send schicken; — **for** holen las-
    sen*; — **here** hierher-schicken;
    — **over** zu-schicken
serve (= *wait on*) bedienen
set: — out on an-treten*; —
    things straight die Sache in
    Ordnung bringen*
seventy: in the seventies in den
    Siebzigern
severe schwer
shark der Haifisch, -e
shave (oneself) (sich) rasieren
shed der Schuppen, —
sheet das Blatt, ̈er
sheltered zurückgezogen
shine scheinen*
shiny blank
ship das Schiff, -e
shoe polish die Schuhkrem, -e *or* –s
shop der Laden, ̈; das Geschäft,
    -e; **hat —,** das Hutgeschäft, -e;
    tobacco —, der Zigarrenladen, ̈
shopping das Einkaufen; **to do
    some —,** einige Einkäufe ma-
    chen
short(ly) kurz; **in —,** kurz
shout schreien*; rufen*
show zeigen
shower die Brause, –n; **step into
    the —,** unter die Brause treten*
    (*s*)
shy scheu
side street die Seitenstraße, –n

263

sidewalk der Gehsteig, –e
sigh seufzen; — **heavily** tief seufzen; (*noun*) der Seufzer, —; **with a — of relief** aufatmend
silence die Stille; **in their —,** (wie sie) schweigen*
silent still
simply einfach
since (*prep.*) seit (*dat.*); (*conj., causal*) da; — **then** seither, seit dieser Zeit
sit sitzen*; — **down** sich setzen; — **at** (*or* **by**) sich setzen an (*acc.*)
sleepless schlaflos
slight leicht; **a — temperature** etwas Fieber
slip aus-rutschen (*s*)
slow langsam
small klein
smile lächeln; — **at** an-lächeln (*acc.*)
snap open auf-springen* (*s*)
soft-boiled weichgekocht
softly leise
soil die Erde, –n
some (*adj.*) einige, manch–, etwas; **—one** (*or* **—body**) jemand; **—thing** etwas; **after — time** nach einiger Zeit; **—times** manchmal; **—what** etwas; (*adv.*) etwa
son der Sohn, ⸚e; **—-in-law** der Schwiegersohn, ⸚e
sorry: I'm —, es tut mir leid
soul die Seele, –n
sparkplug die Zündkerze, –n
speak sprechen*; reden; **to — one's mind freely** frei von der Leber weg reden; **—er** der Redner, —
specialist der Facharzt, ⸚e
spin surren
spirit: —s run high es geht hoch her
splendid glänzend
spring der Frühling, –e
stairs die Treppe, –n
stand stehen*
starve verhungern; darben
station der Bahnhof, ⸚e
stay bleiben* (*s*); **to — in bed** das Bett hüten

step treten* (*s*)
still (= *yet*) noch
stop stehen-bleiben* (*s*); stoppen; halten*; (*exclamation*) Halt!
store der Laden, ⸚; **cigar —,** Zigarrenladen, ⸚
storekeeper der Ladeninhaber, —
storm stürzen (*s*)
strange fremd; seltsam
street die Straße, –n; **—car** die Straßenbahn, –en; — **corner** die Straßenecke, –n; — **light** die Straßenlampe, –n
study studieren
stumble stolpern (*s*)
style die Mode, –n
subjective subjektiv
suburb der Vorort, –e
sudden plötzlich; **—ly** auf einmal, plötzlich
suit passen; — **my taste** mir zusagen
suit: dress —, das Jackenkleid, –er
sun die Sonne, –n
superior (= *distinguished*) vornehm; (= *boss*) der Vorgesetzte (*adj. decl.*)
supper das Abendbrot, –e; das Abendessen, —; **to eat —,** zu Abend essen*
suppose sollen*
swim schwimmen* (*s*)

T

table der Tisch, –e
tail light das Stopplicht, –er
take nehmen*; — **a business course in high school** die höhere Handelsschule besuchen; — **care of** sorgen für (*acc.*); — **matters in one's (own) hands** die Sache allein in die Hand nehmen*; — **your time!** nimm dir Zeit! **it —s ... to be a** zum ... gehört; **it —s an operation** eine Operation (*–tsjon*) ist notwendig; **taking a deep breath** aufatmend
tall groß
tank der Tank, –s
teacher der Lehrer, —

264

tear die Träne, –n
telephone (*noun*) das Telefon, –e;
(*verb*) an-rufen*
tell (*time*) an-geben*; (= *relate*)
erzählen; (= *say*) sagen; (= *betray*) verraten*; I won't — anybody ich sage (*or* verrate) es
niemandem
temperature die Temperatur, –en;
to have a —, Fieber haben*
test prüfen
thank danken (*dat.*)
that (*demon. and adj.*) der, dieser,
jener; (*rel. pron.*) der, welcher;
(*after* alles, etwas, nichts) was;
(*indef. rel.*) was; (*conj.*) daß
theater das Theater, —
then damals, dann; (*inferential*)
so, darauf, nachher; since —,
seitdem, seither, seit dieser Zeit
there da, dort; — are es gibt;
es sind; — is es gibt; es ist; es
besteht
therefore daher
thereupon darauf
these diese
they sie; — are said to sie sollen;
— say man sagt
thing die Sache, –n; das Ding, –e;
of all —s ausgerechnet; set —s
straight die Sache in Ordnung
bringen*
think denken*; don't you — so,
too? findest du nicht auch? —
nothing of it mach dir nichts
daraus
third dritt–
thirsty durstig; to be —, Durst
haben*
this dieser, der
thought der Gedanke (–ns), –n
threshold die Schwelle, –n
throat der Hals, ⸗e
through durch (*acc.*)
throw werfen*; — one's arms
around someone's neck einem
um den Hals fallen* (*s*); — shut
zu-werfen*, zu-drücken
tie binden*
time die Zeit, –en; after some —,
nach einiger Zeit; at the same
—, zugleich; it is —, es ist an
der Zeit; at —s zuweilen

timid schüchtern
tire der Reifen, —
tired müde
to zu (*dat.*); in (*dat. or acc.*);
— (*of places*) nach (*dat.*), bis
(*acc.*); — the next ins andere;
— him (bei) ihm
tobacco shop der Zigarrenladen, ⸗
today heute
tomorrow morgen
tongue die Zunge, –n
too auch; — expensive zu teuer
tool das Werkzeug, –e
tooth der Zahn, ⸗e
toss werfen*; — her head in the
air den Kopf in den Nacken
werfen*
town das Städtchen, —
trade der Beruf, –e
train der Zug, ⸗e
travel reisen (*s*)
tremble (with excitement) zittern
(vor Aufregung)
trousers die Hose, –n
try versuchen; — on auf-probieren
turn (= *bend*) biegen*; (= *twist*)
drehen; — blue blau werden*
(*s*); — the corner um die Ecke
biegen* (*s*); — off ab-biegen* (*s*);
— to stare at sich um-drehen
nach (*dat.*); it —s out to be
es stellt sich heraus; —ed up
aufgeschlagen
twice zweimal
twist drehen
two-family house das Zweifamilienhaus, ⸗er
two kinds of zweierlei

U

umbrella der Regenschirm, –e
unattractive nicht hübsch
uncle der Onkel, —
unemployment die Arbeitslosigkeit; to collect — insurance
stempeln gehen* (*s*)
unfold entfalten
until bis; — recently bis vor
kurzem
unusual ungewöhnlich
up auf (*dat. or acc.*); — to bis

(*prep. acc.*); **be** —, hoch sein*
(*s*); auf den Beinen stehen*
use gebrauchen
usual(ly) gewöhnlich
utter sprechen*

V

vain: in —, vergeblich
value der Wert, –e; **I** — **life** ich
habe mein Leben lieb
very sehr
Vienna (das) Wien
violent heftig
visit besuchen
voice die Stimme, –n
volcano der Vulkan, –e

W

wage führen
wail jammern
wait (for) warten (auf) (*acc.*);
—**ing room** das Wartezimmer, —
walk gehen* (*s*); — **down** hinab-
gehen* (*s*); — **someone home**
jemanden nach Hause be-
gleiten; — **in** treten* (*s*) in
(*acc.*); — **out of the door** zur
Tür hinaus-gehen* (*s*); — **with**
mit-gehen* (*s*)
want wollen*
war der Krieg, –e
warm warm
waste verschwenden
watch die Uhr, –en
water das Wasser
way der Weg, –e; — **home** der
Heimweg; **on the** —, auf dem
Wege; — **past** weit über (*acc.*);
a —**s** ein Stück (des Weges)
wear tragen*, auf-haben*, an-
haben*
week die Woche, –n; —**end** das
Wochenende, –n; –**ly salary** der
Wochenlohn, ⸚e
well wohl; —**-liked** beliebt
well up auf-steigen* (*s*); frei-
werden* (*s*)
what was
wheel das Rad, ⸚er; **(steering)** —,
das Steuer, —
when (*interrog. adj.*) wann; (*conj.*,
at a time when) als; (= *if*) wenn

whether ob
which (*rel. pron.*) welcher, der;
(*indef.*) was; — **(one)** (*interrog.
pron.*) welcher
while während
whisper flüstern; — **to** zu-
flüstern (*dat.*)
white weiß
who (*interrog. pron.*) wer; (*rel.
pron.*) der, welcher; (*indef.*) wer;
he —, wer
whose (*interrog. pron.*) wessen;
(*rel. pron.*) dessen, deren
why warum
wide breit
widow die Witwe, –n
wiener das Würstchen, —
wife die Frau, –en
wildly wild
window das Fenster, —
window pane die Scheibe, –n
wish back zurück-sehnen; **they
cannot be** —**ed back** sie lassen
sich nicht zurück-sehnen
with mit; bei; von (*dat.*); — **all
his might** aus Leibeskräften;
— **a sigh of relief** aufatmend
without ohne (*acc.*); — **a roof
over one's head** auf der Straße
woman die Frau, –en
(women's) suit das Jackenkleid,
–er
wonderful wunderbar
woods der Wald, ⸚er
word (*in context*) das Wort, –e;
(*out of context*) das Wort, ⸚er
work die Arbeit, –en; (*verb*) —,
arbeiten; –**ing method** das
Arbeitsverfahren, —
world: — **about him** seine Umwelt; — **of dreams** die Traum-
welt, –en
worry sorgen; **not** —, sich keine
Sorgen machen
wound verwunden
write schreiben*

Y

year das Jahr, –e
yes ja
young jung
youthful jugendlich

266

INDEX

The numbers refer to the grammar portions of the lesson, as 9.2 (chapter 9, section 2), parts of the Appendix, or the introduction to the end Vocabulary.